A History of the

NATURE
CONSERVANCY
of CANADA

A History of the

NATURE CONSERVANCY

of CANADA

BILL FREEDMAN

OXFORD
UNIVERSITY PRESS

OXFORD
UNIVERSITY PRESS

Oxford University Press is a department of the University of Oxford.
It furthers the University's objective of excellence in research, scholarship,
and education by publishing worldwide. Oxford is a registered trade mark of
Oxford University Press in the UK and in certain other countries.

Published in Canada by
Oxford University Press
8 Sampson Mews, Suite 204,
Don Mills, Ontario M3C 0H5 Canada

www.oupcanada.com

Library and Archives Canada Cataloguing in Publication

Freedman, Bill
A history of the Nature Conservancy of Canada / Bill Freedman.

Includes bibliographical references and index.
ISBN 978-0-19-900416-4

1. Nature Conservancy of Canada—History. 2. Nature
conservation—Canada—History. I. Title.

QH77.C3F74 2013   333.7206'071   C2012-907244-3

Cover photo: A view looking towards the Grassy Place, located at the headwaters of
the Robinson's River in a remote valley of the Long Range Mountains of southwestern
Newfoundland. This 1,574-hectare (3,890-acre) property is well known as a productive oasis
of wetlands and lowland forest, and it had long been a target for conservation. It was acquired
by the Nature Conservancy of Canada in 2011. Photo courtesy of NCC.

Author photo: Bill Freedman and gannets at Cape St. Mary's, Newfoundland, 2008.
Credit: Sheldon Bowles

Oxford University Press is committed to our environment.
Wherever possible, our books are printed on paper which comes from
responsible sources.

Printed and bound in the United States of America

1 2 3 4 — 16 15 14 13

Contents

Preface

I am a bit of a worrier. In my personal life most of my fretting is about family, especially for the long-term prospects of my kids. Will they find happiness in their relationships and livelihoods? As for me, my concern is whether I am living a worthwhile life: Am I a sufficiently supportive person, a decently skilled naturalist, and a reasonably competitive squash player, and has my career as an ecologist been meaningful? Although listed last, that latter bit is quite important to me, as I have had a privileged opportunity in Canadian society through my tenured job as a professor at Dalhousie University. I have worked there for more than three decades, doing research in ecology and environmental science and teaching classes in those fields to wide-eyed undergraduates. But I worry about whether I have used that professional opportunity and responsibility in a helpful way.

The principal context for my professional angst is apprehension I feel about the long-term prospects for the natural world—our heritage of biodiversity. I mourn the loss of extinct species and am worried about the survival of many others that are now endangered, and even of entire natural ecosystems that are being increasingly battered by a burgeoning human economy. I have had these anxious feelings for at least five decades, ever since as a young teenager who loved nature I began to learn of the crisis of the natural world. Looking back, using hindsight, my career path was largely founded on dread for the prospects of biodiversity on the only planet in the universe where life and ecosystems are known to exist. That is not quite all. I also worry about the sustainability of the human enterprise: about future catastrophes that may befall my own species and that are likely to be caused by our irresponsible economic growth.

Within those personal and professional contexts, one of the best and most useful things that I have done was to become engaged in volunteer work with the Nature Conservancy of Canada (NCC). This non-profit organization exists to conserve the natural world by creating protected areas in places that are carefully selected to make an important difference to the survival of native species and natural ecosystems. NCC works mostly in the south of Canada, where those natural values are most at risk and there are also extensive private lands that can potentially be conserved by this kind of organization. Because that kind of direct-action conservation strums a visceral chord in my soul, my engagement in support of that mission has been intensely rewarding. It has provided a certain usefulness to my life that might otherwise have gone missing. Moreover, I believe that all supporters of the organization and its conservation mission can and should experience a comparable feel-good satisfaction.

But enough about me and my manifesto, this book is about the Nature Conservancy of Canada. It was written with the encouragement of several long-standing directors and employees of the organization. They felt that, with NCC approaching its fiftieth birthday, a substantive chronicle was needed that would explain the context of the work of NCC and some details of its accomplishments, while also helping to build enthusiasm for achieving even greater results in the future. Those ongoing achievements are most necessary, because the biodiversity of Canada, and of the world more generally, is getting hammered, and one of the ways of stopping that awful harm and repairing some of the damages already caused is to create more and larger protected areas.

This book is dedicated to helpful and hopeful conservationists everywhere, and to the natural world and its biodiversity that they are seeking to forever maintain.

Acknowledgements

The idea for this book was sparked and fostered by a number of senior employees and long-standing directors of the Nature Conservancy of Canada (NCC), who assembled into an ad hoc committee. Listed alphabetically, they are Bob Alexander, Shelley Ambrose, Bob Carswell, Jim Coutts, Bruce Falls, Robin Fraser, Bill Freedman, Jane Gilbert, John Lounds, Adele Poynter, and Michael Rea. We realized that with NCC approaching its fiftieth birthday, a tome was needed that would describe the origin and history of the organization, catalogue some of its important achievements, and proclaim the necessity of doing additional conservation of this sort in Canada. While Bill Freedman wrote the document, many people offered vital information and reviewed parts of the text.

Essentially, this effort to document the raison d'être and history of the Nature Conservancy of Canada was undertaken by a like-minded commune of environment-minded people who are passionate about the natural world and have dedicated part of their lives to its sustainable conservation. In fact, this is how the Conservancy works more generally to achieve its direct conservation action of creating and stewarding protected areas across Canada: through the collaborative actions of an assembly of generous people, foundations, companies, environmental non-governmental organizations (ENGOs), and governmental agencies that are dedicated to sustaining the natural heritage of Canada.

Many people provided vital information and commented on draft material for this book. Employees of NCC that helped in this way were Bob Alexander, Colin Anderson, Christina Appleby, Katie Blake, Michael Bradstreet, Wendy Cridland, Bob Demulder, James Duncan, Tim Ennis, John Foley, Gene Fortney, Larry K. Gabruch, Jane Gilbert, Lynn Gran, John Grant, Louise Gratton, Randal Greene, Diane Griffin, Renny Grilz, Samantha Hines-Clark, Jordan Ignatiuk, Carmen Leibel, John Lounds, Rob Mortin, Dan Myers, Paula Noel, Kendra Pauley, Kimberly Pearson, Barbara Pryce, Kamal Rajani, Karen Ray, John Riley, Denise Robertson, Marie-Michèle Rousseau-Clair, Denise Roy, Bob Santo, Nicole Senyi, Larry Simpson, Craig Smith, Mark Stabb, Linda Stephenson, Kara Tersen, Erica Thompson, Rob Wilson, Julie Wood, and Nathalie Zinger. Several past and present directors were also helpful: Bob Carswell, Paul Catling, Jim Coutts, Bruce Falls, Robin Fraser, Michael Rea, and Wayne Wright. The efforts of Alexander, Carswell, Falls, Fraser, Gilbert, Lounds, and Rea are especially appreciated, as they read and provided comments on most or all of the manuscript. Advice was also received from people working with other organizations: Mark Carabetta of Ontario Nature, Jan Garnett of EcoLegacy International, Dennis Garratt of the Nova Scotia Nature Trust, Randi Mulder of Yukon Environment, Ben Sawa of the Saskatchewan Ministry of Environment, and John Williams of the Otonabee Region Conservation Authority. Two anonymous reviewers for Oxford University Press Canada also provided helpful comments.

1

Introduction

We are quickly losing our natural heritage of species and distinctive eco-systems. This terrible kind of environmental damage is sufficient in extent and intensity to be labelled a catastrophe—a crisis of biodiversity that is playing out on a global scale, not just in Canada. The crisis is witnessed by well-documented extinctions and endangerment of many native species. We will never again see a great auk or a passenger pigeon, and the biosphere is worsened by the loss of the important roles they played within their eco-systems. These and other damages sustained by the natural world will be examined in more depth later in this book.

For now, it is important to recognize two things: (1) the native biodivers-ities of the world and Canada have already been severely damaged and there are threats of many further losses, and (2) effective measures can be taken to repair some damages that have already occurred and to prevent others that have not yet happened. Those solutions involve all sectors of our soci-ety: individual Canadians, our various levels of government, businesses of all scales, and environmental non-governmental organizations (ENGOs).

In this book we will concentrate on the mission and importance of the work of land trusts, not-for-profit organizations that secure private property and set it aside as protected areas to conserve our natural herit-age. Within that context our focus will be on a particular organization: the Nature Conservancy of Canada (NCC, also referred to in this book as "the Conservancy"). This organization works throughout our country and has achieved remarkable progress in its mission of directly conserving our indigenous biodiversity.

Any sustainable conservation of biodiversity requires that a well-managed network of protected areas be implemented, and that is a respon-sibility of both governments and the private sector. It is also vital that areas that are "working" more directly to serve the human economy are hospitable to reasonable abundances of native species and natural habitats. This means that conservation measures must also be undertaken in areas that are primarily used for urbanization, agriculture, forestry, and other human purposes. Biodiversity cannot be conserved *only* in protected areas.

Within this framework, land trusts such as NCC have a vital mission: to work within the private sector to establish protected areas for the benefit of native biodiversity. These protected areas are good for people and their economy. But the land trusts' primary inspiration is to support the conservation of natural values.

This activity is known as direct-action conservation. It involves acquiring properties that are in good ecological condition, and then protecting them from intensive economic use in order to sustain their native biodiversity. Direct action is different from conservation work that achieves indirect results through education, advocacy, or lobbying. In a sense, indirect action is talking the talk, while direct efforts are walking the talk to produce tangible results. Both strategies are important, but the direct protection of natural habitats produces immediate conservation results.

NCC was the first land trust to adopt a mission of acquiring and conserving natural habitats on private lands throughout Canada. It began to do this in 1962, as a tiny volunteer organization. However, the few prescient individuals who founded NCC had big aspirations. Initially, they had little money to invest in their conservation mission, but within five decades the organization has grown enormously in scope and size. It now receives enthusiastic support across society to establish nature reserves throughout Canada. That support is coming from tens of thousands of individuals, private companies and foundations, and governments.

The Conservancy has also made remarkable progress in its application of conservation science, which is now routinely used to identify the ecoregions and specific locations where limited private resources should be strategically focused to make the most difference in conserving the biodiversity of Canada. Scientific knowledge is also used to advise NCC's stewardship actions toward maintaining or enhancing its portfolio of properties.

This book celebrates the first half-century of the Nature Conservancy of Canada. By any measure NCC, in these initial five decades of work, has achieved remarkable progress. It has worked in partnerships across the length and breadth of Canada. It has engaged the support of Canadians from all walks of life, as well as private foundations, corporations of diverse sizes, and governments at all levels, from federal to provincial, territorial, Aboriginal, and municipal. This is a "good news" story in the environmental realm, and useful lessons can be learned from it.

A societal-level agenda such as conserving biodiversity can be realized only if all the interested players are diligent in accomplishing their sector of the work. The participants include multiple levels of government, various non-governmental conservation organizations (including land trusts such as NCC), private corporations and foundations, and individual Canadians. As with any endeavour that is based on diffuse teamwork, success requires a comprehensive effort of the entire group. If only one or a few of the players are successful, the overall effort may fail.

This book explores the context of the mission of land trusts, the ways that the work of NCC has progressed over time, and the lessons to be learned from that organizational journey. The story is one of great hope, while recognizing that much work remains to be done.

2

The Nature Conservancy of Canada

Before we begin to examine the history of the Nature Conservancy of Canada, let us consider its self-identified vision, mission, and values. Although these have changed somewhat over time, their vital essence has not.

A clear vision underlies the raison d'être of the organization: "The Nature Conservancy of Canada protects areas of natural diversity for their intrinsic value and for the benefit of our children and those after them."[1] In other words, NCC creates and manages nature reserves to conserve the inherent value of the native biodiversity of Canada, and also because those natural values benefit the present and future generations of Canadians.

The mission of NCC explains the ways by which it aspires to achieve its goals: "The Nature Conservancy of Canada will lead, innovate and use creativity in the conservation of Canada's natural heritage. We will secure important natural areas through their purchase, donation or other mechanisms, and then manage these properties for the long term."[2] NCC intends to follow a responsible yet nimble corporate model to achieve conservation results. The focus is on the use of conservation science to identify private properties that support important natural values, to acquire those tracts, and to then steward them as protected areas in ways that maintain or improve their ecological condition.

During the past five decades the Conservancy has built a brand that evokes "a natural legacy through partnership." This tells us that NCC works in a collaborative manner to help ensure that the natural heritage of Canada will be conserved.

This attitude is reflected in the stated values of the Conservancy, which are the reasons for its existence and the ethics that guide its work:

> The Earth's biological diversity is being lost at a rate that impoverishes our quality of life and threatens our future. NCC's work is guided by the belief that our society will be judged by what it creates

in the present and what it conserves for the future. Wherever we work across Canada, we share and apply values that reflect this philosophy:

- We are guided by the best available conservation science.
- We work in a non-confrontational manner.
- We manage lands and waters for their intrinsic, natural values.
- We respect and promote nature's own processes of growth, succession and interaction.
- We recognize the need to create avenues for people to sustain themselves and live productively while conserving biological diversity.[3]

In other words, NCC undertakes its conservation work to prevent further losses of the biodiversity of Canada, a kind of damage that poses risks to the ecological sustainability of the human economy. This statement reminds us that future generations of Canadians will judge the present ones on the effectiveness of their conservation actions. The values of NCC are the foundation of a corporate culture that is informed by scientific knowledge, primarily in the realms of biology, ecology, conservation, and environmental science.

The conservation actions of NCC are designed to accommodate natural ecological dynamics and other environmental influences in the management of properties so as to maintain or enhance the properties' ecological integrity.[4] Moreover, NCC recognizes that people and their economic needs are meaningful considerations in the implementation of viable conservation actions. This fact is recognized in stewardship plans, most of which allow for limited land use for nature study, outdoor recreation, regulated hunting, and sometimes even grazing by livestock, as long as these uses do not compromise the natural values that are being conserved on the property.

Unlike most other ENGOs, NCC does not engage in public advocacy related to environmental issues. This non-advocacy position is a longstanding aspect of NCC corporate policy. It means that the organization does not express public opinions on such controversial matters as the environmental effects of logging, mining, hunting, pollution, climate change, or urban or industrial development, whether on or near its own properties or more generally in the economy. Many other environmental organizations engage in public advocacy in an important and effective way, and NCC prefers to leave that role to those other ENGOs.

Instead, NCC encourages industrial, commercial, and governmental interests to co-operate in projects to protect natural areas that are important to conserving biodiversity. This does not mean that such collaborations are an indication that NCC endorses all that a partner may do in the course of its entire business. Rather it means that NCC wants all sectors of society to assist in conserving natural areas and to share some of their assets for that purpose. As such, NCC's energies are resolutely focused on conservation planning, land securement, and stewardship of properties; it takes direct action to create natural protected areas—to achieve results we can walk on.

This is not to say, however, that the Conservancy does not have some policy-related interactions with governments. Like other corporate citizens, NCC has from time to time made its views quietly known to politicians and bureaucrats in government on matters of public policy related to the mission of conservation. Almost always, however, these efforts have been confined to such matters as the tax treatment of donations and to legislation and funding related to the protection of natural areas.

NCC policy with respect to public advocacy is long-standing, yet there is ongoing discussion by volunteers and staff of some of the implications. A downside of the policy is that NCC does not position itself on the front lines of public controversies, which results in the organization not being as well known as it might be. Instead, the organization works diligently to achieve direct conservation results and expects those worthwhile achievements will be sufficient to attract dedicated conservationists to its mission.

Interestingly, for most of its history, the mission statement of NCC indicated that in addition to securing ecologically important natural areas, a criterion for its work was to conserve "places of special beauty." Although all NCC projects do conserve areas of great "special" or natural beauty, since 2001 this aesthetic criterion has no longer been specifically mentioned in the mission or values statements of the organization. Instead, the focus has been one of science-driven conservation planning to identify strategic areas where private-sector securement and stewardship will create protected natural areas that are vital to conserving the biodiversity of Canada.

In the next chapter we examine the qualities of the natural world, including its living components of biodiversity and ecosystems. This discussion is followed by an explanation of the causes and consequences of the global biodiversity crisis that is characterized by rapid losses of species and natural habitats, occurring in Canada and throughout the world. We then examine how conservation actions can help to fix this problem of biodiversity loss, in the sense of preventing further depletion and repairing some of the damage that has already been caused. The necessary actions include the work of land trusts, such as the Conservancy, which help to mitigate the damage by securing and stewarding natural areas. Once we have established this context for the work of the Conservancy, we will examine the history of the organization in some depth. Its most spectacular conservation projects will be highlighted, as will be the special contributions made by a too-brief selection of key volunteers, employees, and supporters of the organization. Finally we examine the present state of affairs of NCC and the prospects for future successes in its mission of conservation.

3

The Natural World

We *do* love the natural world.

But sometimes we hurt the one we love. That simple declaration captures a big part of the complex and tension-filled relationship between human society and nature.

The damage being caused is largely about the endangerment of wild species and the destruction of irreplaceable ecological communities, two important components of what is known as biodiversity.

The worst injuries occur when natural habitats are destroyed through conversion for agriculture, urban areas, forestry, or other human-focused purposes. In addition, the release of alien species and diseases to new regions where they affect native species and ecosystems can cause critical ecological damage. Many species are also at risk from excessive commercial harvesting. And then, on a global scale, climate change is a longer-term threat to much of the biological richness of Earth, and likely also to the human economy.

In the aggregate, terrible damage has already been done to the biodiversity of Earth, and the situation is worsening. Moreover, the damage is almost entirely anthropogenic, meaning it is a result of human activities. Having caused such harm to nature, we are ethically bound to assist in its healing.

That remedial work is known as conservation, an enterprise that advances along several fronts, all of which are necessary if comprehensive success is to be achieved. For one thing, research is needed to identify and prioritize the species and natural ecosystems that are declining most rapidly and to understand the causes and consequences of those damages. Of course, direct conservation actions must be undertaken if those at-risk biodiversity values are to survive and recover. This means that depleted species must be protected from unsustainable harvesting and systems of protected areas (or nature reserves) must be established in which the priority is to conserve natural values rather than to serve the human economy. Those direct conservation actions must be guided by science-based planning to ensure that protected areas are in the right places, are large enough, are sufficiently connected, and receive the right stewardship to do the vital job that is expected of them.

In most countries, governments own much of the natural habitat. Because these are already public lands, it may be relatively straightforward for governmental agencies to create protected areas, such as those managed by Parks Canada or by provincial authorities. Such actions are not necessarily easy, however, because there may be intense competition for the use of public lands. Powerful interests may want to use them for agriculture, forestry, mining, or other purposes. In regions where this is the case, governments may find it difficult to make the hard decisions that are required to conserve natural habitats on public lands for biodiversity. Despite such tensions related to potentially conflicting uses, governments throughout Canada are engaged in the designation of protected areas within their jurisdictions.

In addition, enormous areas of prime natural habitat exist on privately owned lands. This is particularly the case of regions of southern Canada where the human population is largest and economic activities are most intensive and extensive. Governments often do not have sufficient resources or political will to acquire privately held natural properties in those regions. Non-governmental organizations have therefore been organized to undertake conservation actions in the private sector. These are collectively known as land trusts.

The Natural World

At its grandest scale, the natural world is all of existence: all the space, mass, energy, and dynamics of the universe, including the complex interactions occurring among its components. The universe is immense beyond imagination. By one estimate it contains some 3×10^{23} stars, or 300 sextillion, or 300-thousand-billion-billion of them.[1]

One of those stars, an ordinary one known to us as the Sun, is orbited by eight planets and many smaller bodies. Although practically all the natural world is inanimate, the minutest fraction is biotic and alive. As far as we know, that life occurs only on the third most-distant planet from the Sun, Earth, which has a habitable enveloping film called a biosphere. The existence of life and ecosystems on Earth is an extraordinary and singular phenomenon.

The extent of the biosphere is determined by the limits of where organisms can be found. Therefore, it extends from a few kilometres into the crust to several tens of kilometres into the atmosphere.[2] Those limits are, however, the extreme bounds of the occurrence of life. In fact, almost all organisms and ecological processes occur in a much more restricted veneer close to the surfaces of the oceans and continents, where environmental conditions are relatively moderate. This is the part of the natural world that most biologists and ecologists study. Because organisms and ecosystems are prevalent in this region, it is also the focus of most of the worry of conservationists.

We Love the Natural World

People have always pondered over the natural world and their place in it: not just about themselves as individuals, but in terms of the entire human collective.

In fact, we appear to have an inherent love of living things, a feeling known as biophilia. This is an innate fondness of organisms and ecosystems, which is felt subconsciously and sometimes more overtly. The word *biophilia* was coined by the philosopher Erich Fromm in 1964 and then popularized by the biologist Edward Wilson in a 1984 book by that title.[3,4]

The love of nature is mostly directed toward living things, but not exclusively so. An ecosystem includes organisms but also the non-living components of their environment—water, rocks, atmospheric conditions, and so on. In this larger sense, biophilia might be extended beyond organismic limits to an ecophilia that includes affection for all natural existence. As such, ecophilia may be expressed locally as well as at the levels of landscape or seascape, and perhaps even a skyscape of twinkling stars. In fact, the domain of ecology includes skyscapes because almost all ecological energetics are driven by starlight. Especially important, of course, is that miniscule fraction of the Sun's emission of electromagnetic radiation that, after a distant but quick passage through space, reaches the surface of Earth where some of it drives photosynthesis.

A love of the natural world may be a hard-wired, or inherent, attribute of our species, meaning it is ingrained in our genome—the information encoded in the nucleic acid sequences of the DNA (deoxyribonucleic acid) that ultimately defines the essence of humanness. Nevertheless, actual expressions of biophilia and ecophilia are somewhat variable, being influenced by social factors and individual experience. Geneticists define a phenotype as the actual expression of the genetic potential of an organism, but in a manner that is highly variable depending on environmental conditions that an individual may have encountered during its life (this environment-dependent variability is referred to as phenotypic plasticity).

In any event, the diverse ways that biophilia may be expressed can include the love of a pet, or of plants cultivated in a home or garden. Although these companion organisms are non-human, they may be regarded fondly and even as part of the family. Biophilia might also be reflected as admiration felt for wild animals that are encountered during an excursion into a natural habitat. At a higher level, however, biophilia (and ecophilia) may be expressed as a love of all life on Earth and as a deeply felt concern for its prospects.

Biodiversity

Biodiversity, or biological diversity, refers to the richness of the living world.[5] It is a layered concept that ranges from the varied genetic information encoded within the DNA of populations, or of entire species, to the numbers of species occurring in a particular area, to the diversity of habitat types present on a landscape.

Of these various strata of biodiversity, the one to which most people can easily relate is species richness, or the number of species present, including all the plants, animals, and micro-organisms. This term can refer to species occurring in a particular ecological community, in a political region such as a park or country, and ultimately in the entire biosphere.

Biologists specializing in taxonomy, or the naming of organisms, have identified about 1.8 million species.[6] Each species is named with a scientific binomial, such as our own *Homo sapiens,* which translates from Latin as "wise man." The groups of organisms that have been most comprehensively named by taxonomists are the relatively large or abundant ones, particularly vertebrate animals, of which not many "new" species are being "discovered" anymore. In contrast, there appear to be millions of as-yet unnamed species of smaller organisms that inhabit poorly documented ecosystems, especially in the humid tropics and abyssal oceans. Some estimates of the ultimate species richness of the biosphere are as high as thirty to fifty million.

Of the species to which a name *has* been assigned, about one-third occur in tropical habitats and two-thirds in boreal and temperate climes.[7] In stark contrast, about 90 percent of the unnamed biodiversity of the world is thought to exist in the tropics. The denizens of tropical rainforests are especially poorly known, particularly the smaller invertebrates and micro-organisms. Most of this "hidden biodiversity" of unnamed species is thought to be tiny insects, particularly beetles. Although more than 350,000 species of beetles have been named, equivalent to 37 percent of the insects and 20 percent of all named species, there may yet be millions of additional beetles that biologists have not yet described.

Another important aspect of biodiversity is that conservationists value its indigenous elements, also known as natural heritage, much more highly than alien ones. In other words, native species are more cherished than foreign ones that have been introduced from faraway places. Naturally occurring, self-organized ecological communities are also vital components of natural heritage, and they too are more highly valued than anthropogenic habitats, such as those occurring in farmland, forestry plantations, and horticultural parks.

In fact, when alien species penetrate and dominate wild habitats they are deemed to be a kind of biological pollution that degrades ecological integrity.[8] As such, they may be assigned a pejorative label such as invasive alien. For this reason the abundant but non-native dandelion (*Taraxacum officinale*) is referred to as a weed and the alien starling (*Sturnus vulgaris*) as a pest. In reality, both are lovely organisms, but as elements of biodiversity they are highly valued only when occurring in their native habitats, which do not exist in Canada.

Biodiversity Is Important

To conservationists, the principal reason to cherish biodiversity is its intrinsic (or inherent) value. This worth applies to anything that has unique and irreplaceable qualities. It exists and has value "for its own sake." Entities with intrinsic value have moral standing and a right to exist, regardless of whether they also carry any particular importance to people. In a comparable sense, the inherent value of art and other forms of cultural expression is the primary reason to cherish those human artifacts, notwithstanding any perceived economic importance they might have. The same is true of native species and natural communities, and of the expansive values of untamed tracts of wilderness.

Because of the intrinsic value of Canada's biodiversity, we have a responsibility to ensure that it will continue to survive at viable levels of abundance. This must happen even in the southern reaches of our country, where people are most vigorously pursuing their economic interests by using the land for agricultural, industrial, and urbanized purposes.

However, biodiversity is also of vital economic importance. Some elements of biodiversity are valuable as commodities, and so they are harvested and manufactured into products that people can use. Those goods are sold in domestic and international marketplaces, generating employment and value-added during the harvesting and regenerating of the natural resource, in the manufacturing and distributing of the products, and when they are eventually disused, in their recycling or discarding.

There are many familiar examples of these sorts of bioresources. Trees, which are still mostly harvested from wild forests, are used to manufacture lumber, paper, and diverse wooden products, or they are burnt as a renewable source of energy. Waterfowl, deer, and other wild animals are hunted as food, and some mammals are killed for their fur. We collect the fruits and other tissues of many wild plants as food, and sometimes as medicinal products. There are even a few cases of native species that have been brought into cultivation, such as the plains bison (*Bison bison bison*) and lowbush blueberry (*Vaccinium angustifolium*). Collectively, these uses of native biodiversity contribute billions of dollars to the national economy of Canada (between 2007 and 2011, forestry alone contributed \$21–\$28 billion per year to the annual gross domestic product[9]—the actual contribution is even larger, because these figures are only the direct economic benefits and do not include many indirect ones, such as money spent on machinery and the construction of roads).[10]

In addition to the known commercial benefits of products of biodiversity, there are undoubtedly many others whose uses we have not yet discovered or that we have not yet learned to exploit. These also are good reasons to conserve all elements of biodiversity, as is suggested by a famous quotation of the ecologist Aldo Leopold: "To keep every cog and wheel is the first precaution of intelligent tinkering."[11]

There are many cases in which elements of biodiversity once thought to not be "useful" were discovered to have important values for people.[12] Several involve native Canadian plants, such as the Pacific yew tree (*Taxus brevifolia*), which in 1967 was found to contain a biochemical in its bark that is effective at treating various kinds of cancers. For a while, this discovery led to excessive harvesting of yews to produce the medicine, known as Taxol. However, effective analogues have now been synthesized, which has taken the pressure off wild plants. In other examples, native plants with delicious fruits have been brought into cultivation and now provide abundant food and support impressive economies, such as the large cranberry (*Vaccinium macrocarpon*) and the Saskatoon (*Amelanchier alnifolia*; additional folk names of this fruit in various places in Canada include chuckley-pear, Juneberry, pigeonberry, serviceberry, and shadbush; the city of Saskatoon is named after this plant).

Biodiversity is also economically important because many people will pay money to experience its pleasures and intrigues in non-consumptive ways, such as naturalists seeking to observe birds or wildflowers in a natural setting. Serious birders, for example, will spend considerable leisure time in pursuit of their outdoor sport, and they may disburse a lot of cash on the necessary travel and equipment, such as good binoculars, cameras, and a cool hat.

There are also vital ecological reasons why biodiversity is important. Its diverse elements, such as species, interact in myriad ways. Some of the interactions are exceedingly intimate and necessary for the survival of the symbionts, while others are looser but still of biological and ecological significance. Moreover, as a collective those interactions are important to the existence of ecological functions such as productivity, nutrient cycling, carbon storage, flows of clean water, pollination, and others that are essential to the very existence of life and ecosystems. As such, healthy biodiversity provides vital environmental services that sustain both people and the natural world. Being an ecologist, Aldo Leopold would also have considered all the "cogs and wheels" as being vital for these reasons.

In any event, many Canadians are willing to spend considerable time and treasure to help ensure that our natural heritage is properly conserved. No one likes paying taxes, but there is not much criticism of governments when they spend monies to establish and run parks and other protected areas, or to fund the recovery of endangered species. For that matter, many Canadians readily pay a kind of volunteer taxation by giving generously to environmental charities whose mission is to advance the conservation of biodiversity.

4

Threats to the Natural World

Species and ecosystems have always reacted to changes in environmental conditions. In fact, over the extraordinarily long history of life on Earth, environmental disasters and other stressors have caused most of the species that have ever lived to become extinct.

Today, however, the exceedingly high rate of extinction is being driven by the actions of people. This modern crisis of biodiversity is ruthless. It is primarily caused by the destruction of natural ecosystems in order to develop agricultural and urban land uses to serve the human economy. Ecological damage caused by alien species and introduced diseases are also important, as is the excessive harvesting of certain species of economic importance. Moreover, this biodiversity crisis will become much worse in the near future if effective conservation actions are not taken.

Essentially, two integrated clusters of actions can address this issue: (1) improved management practices on "working lands" (meaning those used for agriculture, forestry, urbanization, and other economic uses) that have less harmful ecological effects, and (2) the designation of comprehensive systems of protected areas. Those nature reserves are needed to sustain the critical habitats of biodiversity-at-risk, as well as wilderness-scale tracts of representative ecosystems.

The modern threats to global biodiversity, as well as those in Canada, provide an overarching context for conservation and, more specifically, for the work of land trusts. We briefly examine those threats in the rest of this chapter.

Natural Extinctions

Life and biodiversity has existed on Earth for about 3.5 billion years, ever since its natural genesis and subsequent evolution and proliferation. Extinction, or the irretrievable loss of species or larger taxonomic units (such as families and even up to orders and phyla), has always been a context for the diversity of life. In fact, almost all species that have ever existed are now extinct. The only survivors are the ones presently extant (still occurring).

Natural extinctions have almost always occurred at slow and pervasive rates, as particular species disappeared because they were unable to cope with changes in environmental conditions. Almost all of the history of life has been characterized by such relatively steady rates of extinction, with the losses being more-or-less compensated by the evolution of new species that were better suited to the prevailing environmental milieu. However, those seeming placid circumstances have been punctuated by a number of exceedingly rare cataclysms that affected the biodiversity of ancient times and caused the extinction of many of the species then existing.

The fossil traces of those mass-extinction events are used to mark the passage from one geological era to another. The first event that we know of occurred about 2.5 billion years ago with the evolution of the first photosynthetic organisms, likely cyanobacteria (blue-green algae). Because oxygen is a by-product of photosynthesis, this biogenic gas accumulated in the atmosphere and oceans, poisoning those environments for most of the existing species, which were adapted to anoxic conditions.

Other natural causes of mass extinction have included immense accidents of extraordinary infrequency, such as Earth being whacked by a meteorite and massive events of volcanism. These rare catastrophes resulted in ecological damage of epic proportions, including the extinction of large fractions of the species existing at the time. About ten of these sorts of mass extinctions have taken place, some of which are well known because they involved many organisms that left reliable fossil traces. Five of the biotic crises are particularly famous because such large proportions of the existing biota were lost.[1] The most intensive of these great dyings occurred about 245 million years ago at the end of the Permian period. It resulted in the loss of 96 percent of the existing species of animals, 84 percent of the genera, and 54 percent of the families. Another famous one occurred about 65 million years ago, at the end of the Cretaceous. It was likely caused by a meteorite impacting the planet in the region of Yucatan and causing the loss of 76 percent of species, including the last of the dinosaurs, pterosaurs, and marine ammonites.

Because so many species were lost in those natural mass extinctions, the reassembling ecosystems had many unoccupied niches. As a result, each of the catastrophes was followed by an evolutionary radiation of new species that took advantage of the vacated ecological opportunities. The first such proliferation to be well documented occurred about 570 million years ago at the beginning of the Cambrian period, when there was a radiation of many of the first larger-bodied animals. Much of our understanding of this phenomenon is derived from studying an outstanding bed of fossils known as the Burgess Shale in Yoho National Park that is dated to 505 million years ago (the Middle Cambrian). These rocks have yielded fossils of up to twenty phyla of now-extinct invertebrate animals, including soft-bodied forms such as sponges that rarely preserve well, as well as many kinds of arthropods with hard armours of chitin.

The Modern Biodiversity Crisis

Another mass extinction is taking place today, but this one is not a natural event. Instead, it is entirely caused by human influences. A variety of anthropogenic stressors may directly affect biodiversity, such as when species are overharvested as a natural resource. Biodiversity may also be indirectly damaged, which usually happens when natural habitats are degraded or destroyed.

Typically, these kinds of stressors result in continuous populations becoming rapidly smaller and fragmented. When this happens the remaining population is more vulnerable to the deleterious effects of disturbances and other stressors that might previously have been tolerated. Native species affected in this way may eventually become endangered, and then locally extirpated, or even globally extinct. A comparable damage can be suffered by natural communities, such as old-growth forest and native grassland, if their extent is caused to decline beyond the limits of sustainability.

The modern biodiversity crisis is already severe and is rapidly becoming worse. It began about ten thousand to twelve thousand years ago, when prehistoric people overhunted vulnerable species of large-animal prey and caused them to become extinct. This was the time when camels, giant bison, horses, mammoths, mastodons, and many other kinds of large animals became extinct in the Americas.[2] Since then, the modern biodiversity crisis has rapidly intensified and even accelerated. This amplification is not so much because of continued overharvesting of species, although that remains important, but because natural habitats are being extensively destroyed. These ecological damages have been proceeding especially quickly during the past several centuries. In fact, some of the worst damages of the modern biodiversity crisis are being caused by the actions of people who are presently alive.

The biodiversity crisis of today is a global phenomenon. It involves a high rate of endangerment and extinction of species and even of entire natural communities. By far the most important cause of this damage is the destruction of natural habitats and their conversion into uses for agriculture, industry, and urbanization. This damage is happening most rapidly in low-latitude countries, especially where tropical forest is being cleared. Tropical forest supports higher levels of biodiversity than any other kind of ecosystem. This biodiversity includes a profusion of endemic species that have only local distributions and occur nowhere else, so they are extremely vulnerable to extinction when their limited habitat is destroyed. Extensive damage is also being caused to low-latitude coral reefs, which support the highest levels of biodiversity in the marine realm.

Beyond the outright destruction of natural habitats, the second most important cause of damage to biodiversity today is the ecological effects of alien species and pathogens. When introduced species become abundant in natural habitats, they displace native ones and may cause their abundance to precipitously decline. Examples of some of the worst introduced pathogens include diseases such as the chestnut blight that has almost wiped out the American chestnut (*Castanea dentata*) and the Dutch elm disease that is a similar catastrophe for white elm (*Ulmus americana*). Additional examples are alien insects such as the emerald ash borer (*Agrilus planipennis*) that is killing native ashes of various species and the Asian long-horned beetle (*Anoplophora glabripennis*) that attacks a wide range of native trees.

Other introduced species are plants and animals that become invasive of natural habitats, where they displace native species with which their niches overlap. Some of the nastiest of these alien scourges are such invasive weeds as the garlic mustard (*Alliaria petiolata*) of the bottomland forests in Southern Ontario and Quebec, leafy spurge (*Euphorbia esula*) of the prairie grasslands, and gorse (*Ulex europaeus*) of southwestern British Columbia. These are among a great variety of alien ecopathogens that have been accidentally or deliberately introduced to Canada through the horticultural trade and other vectors. They pose grave threats to the survival of many of our native species.

Another well-known cause of the biodiversity crisis is excessive harvesting of species that have commercial value. This rapacious use of potentially renewable resources is comparable to the unsustainable mining of non-renewable resources such as fossil fuels. We examine some Canadian examples of overharvested species in a later part of this chapter.

Often, however, species are affected by a complex of damaging stressors that are acting simultaneously. This was the case of the first well-documented extinction during historical times—that of the dodo (*Raphus cucullatus*).[3] This flightless, turkey-sized relative of pigeons lived on Mauritius in the Indian Ocean. That island was discovered by the Portuguese in 1507 and colonized by the Dutch in 1598. The unfortunate dodo was extinct by 1662, mostly because of excessive hunting as food by sailors and colonists, made worse by the clearing of its habitat for agriculture and intense predation by introduced cats, monkeys, and pigs.

Although extinctions have always taken place as the result of natural forces, the losses of today are anthropogenic: the modern biodiversity crisis is being driven by habitat destruction, alien introductions, and other stressors caused by humans. Because people are causing this ecological damage, we have an ethical responsibility to do what is necessary to fix the problem. We need to understand the causes and consequences of damages that are being caused to biodiversity and to then design and implement conservation solutions. This fix must involve effective measures in all countries, so that a global solution becomes possible.

Biodiversity-at-Risk in Canada

The modern biodiversity crisis is largely playing itself out in low-latitude countries because they support tropical forests, coral reefs, and other natural habitats with extraordinarily rich and often endemic biodiversity. Nevertheless, important damage is also being caused to the native species and natural ecosystems of Canada. This is especially the case of southern reaches of our country, where most Canadians live and much of the economic activity occurs. In fact, as is the case of all countries, much of the indigenous biodiversity of Canada is already at risk of being lost from our national domain, and even from the planet.

At the national level, species-at-risk are studied and designated by an organization known as the Committee on the Status of Endangered Wildlife in Canada (COSEWIC). This organization is funded by the Government of Canada, but it operates at arm's length. COSEWIC does its work through a number of committees whose membership consists of volunteer biodiversity specialists and other representatives from governments, universities, non-governmental organizations, and the Aboriginal community. COSEWIC has specialist committees for major groups of biota, such as birds or mammals, which deliberate about the conservation status of species native to Canada. COSEWIC then makes recommendations about at-risk designations to the federal minister of the environment for official listing under the Species at Risk Act.

COSEWIC recognizes several categories of risk, which relate to the intensity of imminent threats to the survival of a species (or a subspecies or other distinct population; collectively these are called taxa). Of course, extinction is the worst possible outcome for a species, because it no longer survives anywhere on the planet. Fourteen species that once lived in Canada have become extinct. The story of each of these extinct species represents an irretrievable loss of natural heritage at a global scale. Here, in brief, are unhappy tales of some of the organisms that were rendered extinct globally during the past two centuries:[4]

- The great auk (*Pinguinus impennis*), a large flightless seabird, once ranged throughout the North Atlantic Ocean, but it became extinct because of excessive harvesting, mostly for its feathers, which were used to stuff bedding.
- The passenger pigeon (*Ectopistes migratorius*) occurred from southeastern Canada through most of the eastern US. Although it was the most abundant landbird in the world, it was rendered extinct by insatiable commercial hunting because it was a seasonal food for urban people.
- The Labrador duck (*Camptorhynchus labradorius*) was an uncommon denizen of the Western Atlantic that was lost because of hunting at its coastal wintering habitats.
- The sea mink (*Mustela macrodon*) of the Bay of Fundy was a rare small carnivore of the lower Bay of Fundy that was excessively trapped for its fur.
- The deepwater cisco (*Coregonus johannae*) occurred only in Lakes Huron and Michigan, where it was initially abundant but became extinct because of commercial fishing.
- The eelgrass limpet (*Lottia alveus*) was a mollusc that lived in estuarine habitats of the Atlantic Coast, but it suffered a population crash during a decline of eelgrass (*Zostera marina*), its key food and habitat, which was possibly caused by an introduced pathogen.
- Macoun's shining moss (*Neomacounia nitida*) was an epiphyte that grew on the bark of elm and cedar trees in swampy forest at only three known locations near Belleville, Ontario. It disappeared between 1864 and

1892 when its habitat was clear-cut. (It is the only extinct plant endemic to Canada.)

- The blue pike (*Stizostedion vitreum glaucum*) was an abundant sub-species of the walleye (*S. v. vitreum*) that occurred only in Lake Erie. It was rendered extinct by overfishing and pollution of its habitat.
- The Queen Charlottes Islands caribou (*Rangifer tarandus dawsoni*) was a subspecies of woodland caribou that occurred only on Haida Gwaii. It was wiped out by excessive hunting.

The COSEWIC designation of *extirpated* refers to a species that once occurred in Canada but now survives only elsewhere, usually to the south in the United States. Some of the twenty-three species extirpated from Canada are actually abundant in the US: their Canadian range represented a northern extension of a more extensive biogeography to the south. Nevertheless, they are now lost components of the natural heritage of Canada. Two examples are the Atlantic grey whale (*Eschrichtius robustus*), which is extirpated from the Atlantic Ocean but abundant on the Pacific side of the continent, and the blue-eyed Mary (*Collinsia verna*), a spring wildflower that once inhabited floodplain woodlands of southwestern Ontario and is still abundant in parts of the US. These cases are regrettable losses of the native biodiversity of Canada, but at least the species as a whole are secure. However, many of the species that are extirpated from Canada are also globally endangered, such as the black-footed ferret (*Mustela nigripes*) and the greater prairie chicken (*Tympanuchus cupido*) of the southern prairies.

A species that is listed as *endangered* is at risk of imminent extirpation from Canada, or even global extinction, unless factors affecting its peril are not reversed. In 2012, there were 287 taxa listed as endangered in Canada, compared with only 153 in 2003.[5] In this case the large increase of endangered taxa does not indicate the speed with which conditions for biodiversity are worsening; rather it reflects the fact that COSEWIC is doing its job of reviewing the status of native species, with the aim of eventually developing a comprehensive list. As is the case with species extirpated from Canada, many of the endangered ones are abundant in the nearby US. In other cases, however, the listed species are endangered throughout their global range. Examples of the latter include the Vancouver Island marmot (*Marmota vancouverensis*), whooping crane (*Grus americana*), piping plover (*Charadrius melodius*), and thread-leaved sundew (*Drosera filiformis*).

Species that are listed as *threatened* are likely to become endangered if their prospects do not improve. As of 2012, there were 161 threatened species in Canada. Those listed under *special concern* are at risk of becoming threatened; there were 179 of these in 2012.

However, it is not just species that are at risk in Canada. Some once-extensive natural communities now exist only as small remnants because most of their original area was converted for agricultural or other economic land uses. In such cases the threat to natural heritage is the loss of entire natural communities, in addition to a suite of dependent species-at-risk that lose their only habitats in Canada. The most endangered natural communities of Canada include the following:[6]

- The tall-grass prairie of southeastern Manitoba and southwestern Ontario is a native grassland that supports herbaceous plants of impressive stature, ranging from one to two metres tall. But almost all of its original extent has been converted into annually cropped and pastoral agriculture, so that now less than 1 percent survives.
- The mixed-grass and short-grass prairies of southern Manitoba, Saskatchewan, Alberta, and British Columbia have also been greatly depleted through conversion into agricultural land uses involving non-native crops, a process that is ongoing.
- The Carolinian forest region of Southern Ontario extends from about Grand Bend on Lake Huron to the vicinity of Toronto, but less than 2 percent survives as mature forest, the rest having been lost to agricultural and urbanized land uses.
- Dry open forest dominated by Garry oak (*Quercus garryana*) occurs only on southern Vancouver Island, and only about 2 percent persists as mature stands because of extensive conversion into urbanized and agricultural uses.
- Dry coastal forest dominated by Douglas-fir (*Pseudotsuga menziesii*) is present only in restricted areas of the southern coastal mainland and on southern Vancouver Island of BC, and less than 2 percent has survived its extensive loss to urban development and logging.
- Semi-desert occurs only in a small area of south-central BC in the vicinity of Penticton and Osoyoos, but agricultural and residential development have diminished this community to less than 5 percent of its original extent.

- Various kinds of old-growth forest communities exist in Canada. While their type depends on ecoregion and local site conditions, all of them are greatly depleted, most grievously so in eastern Canada. For instance, less than 0.5 percent of the forest estate in Nova Scotia is now older than 100 years. Even in coastal British Columbia, where the humid climate is particularly favourable to the development of old-growth forest because stand-replacing disturbances such as wildfire are uncommon, these communities are rapidly becoming depleted, mostly by timber harvesting that converts the primary ecosystem into a younger, second-growth forest, that itself is harvested before the old-growth condition is reattained.
- Natural communities of fish have also been widely decimated in Canada, most notably mixed-species communities in the Great Lakes, salmonids (salmon and trout) in western Canada, and groundfish off the Atlantic provinces.

Because of the huge reductions of these distinctive ecological communities in Canada, it is vital that remaining tracts in good ecological condition are identified and then set aside as protected areas, such as nature reserves and parks. This sort of conservation action is a core aspect of the ecologically sustainable development of the regional and national economies of Canada. It requires action by governments to set aside critical habitats on land they already own, while also encouraging the private sector to act similarly on its own real estate. Private land trusts, such as the Nature Conservancy of Canada, also have a key role to play in identifying the last great places on private land to set aside as protected areas, and to then acquire them if possible. In fact, this reason is why land trusts exist.

5

Conservation

The word *conservation* was first used in the late nineteenth century in relation to the judicious use of renewable resources, such as hunted animals and timber.[1] This early philosophy of the "wise use" of natural resources is captured by a famous quotation by Gifford Pinchot (1865–1946): "Conservation means the greatest good to the greatest number for the longest time."[2] Other early American proponents of this prudent attitude about natural resources were George Perkins Marsh (1801–82) and Theodore Roosevelt (1858–1919), and in Canada, Wilfrid Laurier (1841–1919), Clifford Sifton (1861–1929), and James Harkin (1875–1955).

These early conservationists were also advocates of protected areas, or nature reserves, initially in the form of national parks. These parks were intended to protect areas of natural beauty, while also fostering outdoor recreation and its benefits to health and the economy. The setting aside of tracts of land from intensive economic use, while encouraging public recreation, was a novel and important step forward in the rapidly developing conservation movement. There had been protected areas prior to that time, but they had been created to benefit royalty or other wealthy sectors, rather than the general public. The new idea was much more egalitarian and populist in its conception. Wallace Stegner (1909–93), a novelist and historian, pronounced the new public national parks of America to be "the best idea we ever had."[3]

Yellowstone National Park, established in 1872, was the first in the world. The second, and first in Canada, was Rocky Mountain National Park, designated in 1885. Initially, this park had an area of only 26 square kilometres,[4] centred on the Banff Hot Springs.[5] Then in 1887 the park was greatly expanded to 672 square kilometres, and further in 1902 to 11,400 square kilometres. However, the extent of the park was then reduced several times in response to lobbying by ranching and logging interests, and in 1932 it reached its present area of 6,641 square kilometres, and the area was renamed as Banff National Park.

Such areal dynamics are typical of the kinds of policy-related and environ-mental stressors that all protected areas face. There are now forty-four national parks in Canada, and they comprise by far the largest system of protected areas in the country. However, as impressive as the national park system is, it does not come close to meeting the need for a comprehensive system of protected areas in Canada. There is also an important role for other kinds of protected areas, which may be established on lands owned by provincial, territorial, Aboriginal, and municipal governments, and also on private lands secured by non-governmental organizations, such as the Nature Conservancy of Canada.

Obviously, in the context of land trusts, the conservation being referred to is not primarily the *wise use* of natural resources to benefit people. Rather, the sense is that of *biological conservation*, which refers to the stewardship of native species and other natural values in ways that allow them to be sustained—we hope forever. Often, the focus of this kind of conservation is on natural values whose survival is at risk because of inherent rarity or a precipitous decline caused by anthropogenic stressors. The primary motiva-tion for biological conservation is to preserve the intrinsic value of native species, ecological communities, and wilderness settings. The conservation of nature to benefit people and their economy is also an extremely important consideration, but it is secondary to the inherent values.

The Impetus for Biological Conservation

The conservation of biodiversity is an important societal goal. This is reflected in the fact that many Canadians are concerned about the loss of natural val-ues, both in Canada and globally. They are demanding that effective actions be taken to prevent further damage and repair some of the losses that have already been caused. Governments are increasingly engaged in conservation actions, as are private companies and many citizens. In addition, many non-governmental conservation organizations have been formed, and they too are dealing with issues related to biodiversity. Overall, there is broad-based sup-port for the vision of conserving biological diversity and not much oppos-ition to that goal.

At the international level, the objective of biodiversity conservation is subject to its own treaty, the Convention on Biological Diversity (CBD) under the United Nations Environment Programme (1993). The objectives of the CBD are to ensure that biological diversity is conserved and its products are used sustainably, with an equitable sharing of benefits among countries and peoples of the world. Canada is signatory to that treaty and is thereby obligated to undertake certain actions to conserve biodiversity within its jurisdictions. These measures include the development and implementation of a national action plan[6] and periodic reporting on its implementation.[7] Key elements of Canada's strategy are to (1) conserve our indigenous biodiversity, (2) use bioresources in a sustainable manner, (3) improve scientific knowledge in support of those goals, (4) broaden the understanding of citizens about the importance of biodiversity, (5) implement legislative and governmental frameworks, and (6) work collaboratively with other countries.

It was partly in response to the CBD that Canada enacted its federal Species at Risk Act (2003). This legislation empowered COSEWIC to provide arm's-length advice for designating species-at-risk, while also encouraging provincial and territorial governments to enable comparable legislation within their own domains. A consequence of all this has been large investments in conservation science, education, and the establishment of protected areas in Canada. Although a great deal remains to be done, these actions represent helpful progress toward a sustainable conservation of biodiversity in our country.

Of course, much of this work has been undertaken by governmental agencies, using funds provided by the taxation system. This is appropriate, because governments have the mandate to implement broad societal goals. Consequently, governments at all levels employ conservation scientists to undertake researching, monitoring, and planning for actions necessary to conserve biodiversity. Moreover, the largest parks and other protected areas are owned and managed by governments, which have set aside expanses of Crown land for that purpose. Again, much remains to be done in all these respects, but helpful progress is being made.

It is important to recognize, however, that governments are not able to do all that is necessary to sustainably conserve the biodiversity of Canada. Other sectors of society also have vital roles in this endeavour. Private companies, for example, can run their business in ways that engender fewer risks to biodiversity (and to other aspects of environmental quality). Moreover, some corporations are large landowners, and they can choose to set aside critical habitats on their real estate as protected areas. Individual citizens also have an important role to play, for instance, by managing their property in ways that provide habitat for native species. Finally, all sectors of society can also support non-governmental organizations whose actions involve the conservation of biodiversity. This can include NGOs whose focus is on advocacy and research to advance the conservation agenda, as well as land trusts that undertake direct actions to create and steward protected areas.

The Means of Biological Conservation

We noted above that two broad clusters of actions must be undertaken if biodiversity is to be effectively conserved. Both are necessary if a sustainable resolution is to be achieved.

The first is to do what is possible to conserve natural habitat on lands that are "working" to serve the economy by providing natural resources and opportunities for employment. In the realm of forestry, for example, timber-harvested areas that are allowed to regenerate their trees naturally will generally support much higher levels of biodiversity than will clear-cut tracts that have had a plantation established by planting seedlings of only one or a few conifer species. In general, less-intensive forestry results in improved conditions for a greater richness of species, while also providing other environmental benefits. Similarly, in the fishing industry, less reliance might be put on bottom dragging and other harvesting practices that damage critical habitats such as cool-water coral reefs and sponge beds. Some agricultural practices are also relatively sympathetic to biodiversity, such as maintaining native grassland for grazing rather than converting it into cultivated pasture, and leaving buffers of riparian habitat around streams, ponds, and other wetlands. Even individual homeowners can make choices that are beneficial to native biodiversity, particularly if they use native plants in horticulture instead of the surfeit of alien species that have become so fashionable and readily available in commercial horticulture.

Actions of these sorts are extremely effective at conserving natural values, and they represent an ecologically *wise use* of working lands. If undertaken widely, these less-intensive management practices will benefit many native species, and they are a crucial aspect of biological conservation.

The second fundamental tactic for conserving biodiversity is to create protected areas. The principal goal of these designated tracts is to sustain natural values rather than economic activities. However, this does not mean that protected areas are inconsequential to the economy. In some cases they may support a great deal of economic activity through outdoor recreation and eco-tourism. The key is that those human uses should not unacceptably threaten the natural values that are the primary reason for designating areas as protected.

Protected areas include parks, wilderness areas, ecological reserves, and comparable tracts. Essentially, these areas are intended to sustain natural values that are incompatible with the economic activities that occur on working landscapes and seascapes. For example, the special values of old-growth forest and many of its dependent species are not reconcilable with ecological changes that occur when timber is harvested. Similarly, certain wide-ranging animals—such as bears, wolves, woodland caribou, and orcas—may not be compatible with many kinds of economic activities in their large-scale habitats. If a well-designed network of protected areas is established to accommodate the special needs of vulnerable species and natural ecosystems, it is more likely that they will survive at viable levels of abundance.

Protected areas deliver a number of important goods and services that contribute to sustainable development. These benefits add up to convincing arguments in support of the creation of comprehensive networks of protected areas:[8]

- Protected areas conserve critical habitats for those elements of natural heritage, such as certain species and ecological communities, that would otherwise be at risk of being lost from a jurisdictional area such as a province or country, or from an ecological one such as an ecozone.
- By helping to sustain at-risk elements of biodiversity, protected areas conserve their intrinsic value, their potential economic value, and the ecological functions that they perform.
- Large areas that are maintained in a natural condition deliver important environmental services, such as carbon storage in biomass and the provision of clean water.
- Some protected areas are engines of the local and even regional economies because they sustain outdoor recreation, ecotourism, and other activities that engender large expenditures in rural areas and employ many people.
- Some protected areas host dedicated facilities for research in ecology and environmental science, which provide understanding of the natural world and are vital to determining the causes and consequences of damage that the human economy may be causing to it.
- Protected areas are crucial to national and regional programs of environmental monitoring, because they provide reference habitat against which changes in conditions in "working" ecosystems can be assessed.
- Many educational programs in outdoor education, natural history, and environmental studies are conducted in protected areas.

- Protected areas are places where people can spend time in the natural world, an aesthetic experience that is central to being human, that fosters intellectual development and expression, that is calming and reassuring, and that is vital to building a popular empathy for nature, which is a core aspect of ecologically sustainable development.
- Without protected areas, important aspects of natural heritage could not be passed on to future generations for their wonderment and sustainable use.

Because protected areas involve defined tracts of landscape or seascape, they are in some respects static entities in terms of their area. Yet a complex milieu of environmental stressors affect protected areas, which causes their natural values to change over time. To prevent those changes from causing an unacceptable degradation of ecological integrity, protected areas must be stewarded in appropriate ways.[9] The necessary adaptive management includes monitoring of key ecological attributes, and if necessary the application of corrective measures and other mitigations to repair damages that may be occurring. It may also be necessary to align management practices in the surrounding areas so as to ensure that natural values are being sustained in the "greater protected area" (this comprises both protected and working habitats). It is important to recognize that the designation of a protected area is not a simple matter of erecting a fence and prohibiting certain economic activities. Rather, protected areas must be adaptively stewarded in a coordinated action with what goes on in their surrounding matrix.

We saw above that the largest networks of protected areas have been established by governments. This has typically been accomplished by setting aside large blocks of public land, especially in relatively remote regions, where there is less competition with the potential use of natural resources for economic purposes. In the southern regions of Canada, however, much of the land is privately owned, and so it is often necessary to purchase ecologically important properties in order to set them aside as protected areas. However, governments are often reluctant to spend their funds for this purpose, or to otherwise interfere with many of the activities of private landowners. Within this societal context, there is an opportunity and need for private conservation organizations to acquire ecologically important properties and to steward them in favour of their natural values. This is the role of land trusts, such as the Nature Conservancy of Canada.

6

Land Trusts and Conservation

A land trust, also known as a land or nature conservancy, is an environmental charity whose mission is to acquire and steward private property for the purpose of conserving its natural values. A typical land trust is a not-for-profit corporation that is incorporated under statutory provisions that differentiate it from a for-profit business corporation. Both types of corporations are governed by a board of directors. However, rather than having shares and shareholders like a business corporation, a not-for-profit has members and they and the directors are forbidden from profiting from the activities of the organization, which in turn does not pay income tax. Most conservation land trusts apply under the Income Tax Act to become a charity so that donors can be provided with charitable receipts for income tax purposes. Moreover, the land trust must confine its activities to the pursuit of its mission of securing private properties and stewarding their natural values to benefit indigenous biodiversity.

The very first land trust was called the Trustees of Reservations, which was formed in 1891 to provide green space for the pleasure and health of the people of Boston and its vicinity.[1] Today, almost all land trusts have adopted a mission of conserving natural habitats, although some may focus on preserving cultural heritage or on keeping land in agricultural use in the face of urbanization pressures.

The land trusts that focus on biodiversity either purchase or accept donations of properties that support important natural values. The property can take the form of real estate or a conservation agreement such as an easement.[2] Once acquired, a property must be managed to maintain or enhance its ecological condition, an action that is called stewardship. To finance their activities, land trusts accept donations of cash, equities, life insurance policies, trade lands, and other valuable assets.[3] Land trusts receive much of their financial support from private individuals, but considerable funding may also be received from corporations, foundations, and governments.

There are now thousands of land trusts in North America and in other regions of the world. The largest such organization is The Nature Conservancy (TNC) in the United States, which was founded in 1951.[4] TNC works throughout the US and also internationally in more than thirty-two countries.[5] TNC has more than one million supporters and has contributed to the protection of more than 69,000 square kilometres in the US and greater than 473,000 square kilometres in other countries. In 2010 TNC had an annual revenue of $990 million, and it held assets of $5.7 billion. It should be noted here that NCC is not directly affiliated with TNC, although the two organizations work in similar ways on comparable missions and sometimes co-operate on projects of mutual interest.

In Canada, the largest land trust is the Nature Conservancy of Canada, which was founded in 1962 and works at a national scale. NCC has annual revenues of about $100 million (based on a range from 2007 to 2011[6]), and in 2011 held land and easement assets of about $478 million. The organization has more than forty-seven thousand donors and has contributed to the protection of more than one million hectares (2.6 million acres).

In the United Kingdom, a governmental agency also called the Nature Conservancy was founded in 1949.[7] However, in 1973 it was renamed the Nature Conservancy Council, and then in 1991 it was disbanded and broken up into three organizations: Scottish Natural Heritage, the Countryside Council for Wales, and Natural England. A Joint Nature Conservation Committee coordinates those national organizations.

Today, however, the vast majority of land trusts operate at a regional or even local scale. Land trusts in Canada have formed an umbrella organization known as the Canadian Land Trust Alliance (CLTA), which was created in 2006 to share information and coordinate partnerships among its members (which numbered 532 in 2011).[8] The CLTA was modelled after but separate from the Land Trust Alliance in the US, which was formed in 1981.[9]

A land trust is typically run by a board of directors, which consists of volunteer directors (sometimes referred to as trustees) that hold fiduciary responsibility. There may also be paid staff such as an executive director and other professionals, as well as a network of volunteers who assist with stewardship, fundraising, and other activities. Land trusts are independent, entrepreneurial, not-for-profit organizations that engage with willing landowners to achieve conservation results. They commonly work in partnership with like-minded organizations, including other NGOs, companies, foundations, and governments.

The largest land trusts, such as NCC, have a layered corporate structure. NCC has a national Board of Directors that holds fiduciary responsibility for the organization and sets national policy. Also, seven regional boards serve as committees of the national board and provide advice on policy development, planning, and fundraising within their designated region. The staff organization is also multi-tiered, being headed by a president and chief executive officer, who is supported by a team of vice-presidents with national responsibility for key functions such as conservation planning, communications, finance, and philanthropy. NCC has additional vice-presidents who run the regional operations of the organization. All of these executive positions are supported by staff professionals who work on conservation planning, acquisitions, stewardship, fundraising, and other activities of the organization.

Land trusts own property, with the ultimate responsibility for its appropriate management and potential disposition resting with the board of directors on behalf of the membership. In the case of NCC, the members consist of the national and regional directors. A much larger number of supporters of NCC provide the organization with funds. But, as is the case in almost all large charities, supporters are not members and so do not vote for slates of directors or otherwise direct the policies or activities of the organization.

Land trusts make progress in their conservation mission by undertaking a number of key activities, including the following:

• They undertake conservation planning to identify the most important sites that, if protected and properly stewarded, would make the greatest difference to conserving biodiversity in the region where the trust is working.
• They conduct research to identify the best ways of stewarding habitats to achieve conservation objectives.
• They inform all sectors of society about the importance of conserving biodiversity, including by the direct-action means of habitat acquisition and stewardship.
• They raise funds to pay for the preceding actions.

Conservation by Land Trusts

The first land trusts worked only by purchasing or accepting donations of real property, raising funds for that purpose from sympathetic donors. Often, a targeted property was opportunistically identified as being important for conservation, usually because it was well known to naturalists and perhaps under threat from a proposed economic development. Once secured, the property might have been passed to a third party for stewardship, usually a governmental agency.

Today, however, the operations of land trusts have matured to a much higher level of integrated conservation action, especially in larger organizations such as NCC. Advanced conservation science is now a core aspect of strategic planning for both the acquisition and the stewardship of properties. In addition, most projects now involve retention of the title of acquisitions, so the trust keeps the responsibility for ongoing stewardship.

Of course, the most frequently used tactic to conserve habitat is to acquire private land by a fee-simple purchase or donation (or by a combination of these, known as a split-receipt transaction, which may be accompanied by issuance of a tax receipt for the difference between the appraised value and the purchase price).

In many cases, however, the real property remains in private ownership, but biodiversity is protected by means of a conservation agreement (CA) that controls the kinds of activities that can be undertaken.[10] A CA has monetary value that can be legally appraised and then acquired by a land trust through purchase or donation. Note that depending on the jurisdiction, a CA may be referred to as an easement, covenant, or servitude. The rules, however, are not identical among these types and across jurisdictions. The term *conservation covenant* may also be relevant, although it is more commonly used in reference to commercial agreements.

A CA can provide important benefits in terms of conserving biodiversity:

• Ecological objectives can be met with a smaller expenditure of money.
• The land remains in private ownership, and the landowner continues to contribute to the local tax base.
• This flexible tool can be written in a way that meets the objectives of both conservation values and the needs of the landowner.
• A CA is registered on title and it runs with the title.
• A landowner who donates a CA may obtain tax advantages.

CAs are a relatively new instrument in the conservation toolkit and problems have arisen because of misunderstandings about their terms and conditions. These problems have sometimes resulted in legal actions. In general, CAs work best in proscribing certain land uses, such as subdivision or the construction of roads or buildings. CAs may be less useful in affecting land management according to the best practices needed to maintain natural values, which in some cases have proven difficult to specify. The true utility of easements will not be definitely known until a body of case law accumulates that demonstrates the strength with which these property rights can be specifically identified and legally enforced. In practice, the most frequent cause of problems with easements is when an encumbered property passes to a new owner, who may not be as sympathetic to conservation as the owner who entered into the legal agreement.

There are also cases in which certain acquisitions are passed on to a third party for management. These transactions may involve lands that were specifically acquired to enlarge an existing protected area owned by a governmental agency, such as an inholding or peripheral land to an established park. In such a case, an acquired property would be passed to the responsible governmental authority for the park, but with a landholding agreement attached to the deed to ensure that the owner undertakes appropriate stewardship. The land trust would still have a need to monitor that the stewardship was executed, but that is an assumed responsibility that is not embedded in the terms of the landholding agreement.

Sometimes land trusts sell property to a private interest, but subject to a conservation agreement that includes restrictions and specified stewardship activities. The purchaser is referred to as a conservation buyer. The transaction might involve a tract of native prairie for which appropriate stewardship could include the grazing of livestock at an appropriate density. In such a case, the land trust retains a responsibility to monitor the ecological condition of the property to ensure that the terms of the conservation easement are being met. The resale of conservation lands in this way relieves the land trust of many costs of stewardship and may also return the property to the local tax base (in cases where there was a tax exemption for conservation ownership).

Land trusts raise their funds for operations and land acquisition from individual donors, corporations, foundations, and governmental agencies. Donations can take the form of money, bonds, securities, the proceeds of expectancies from life insurance policies or bequests written into individual wills, and other kinds of equity. All of these sources of revenue are growing because increasing numbers of people are worried about damage being caused to biodiversity and are thus more generously supporting efforts to conserve the natural world.

Land trusts are also increasingly cognizant of the fact that their mission is more likely to be successful if people living in the neighbourhood of protected areas are supportive of local conservation actions. In this sense, the best-intentioned conservation projects may not work out well if the needs and aspirations of the local community are not sympathetically integrated into management plans to the degree that is possible. Nevertheless, the bottom line must remain focused on conservation objectives.

Another key characteristic of modern land trusts, especially the larger ones, is the great effort that they make in conservation planning. This systematic process is closely advised by ecological, environmental, and conservation science, and uses the rapidly developing tools of information technology. Ultimately, the aim of conservation planning is to identify the most important places that should be set aside to conserve biodiversity, within the context of a comprehensive network of protected areas. The conservation plan should indicate areas that support the highest priority biodiversity values, while ensuring that all indigenous elements are conserved in the ecological region. Part of the process includes a gap analysis that identifies tracts that have already been designated as protected, as well as key areas that do not yet have that kind of conservation status. For land trusts, the conservation plan must also show the privately owned areas that, if conserved by acquisition and stewardship, would most strategically contribute to the overall success of conserving biodiversity. In addition, conservation planning must account for the stewardship needs of protected areas, which is also heavily advised by relevant scientific knowledge and insight.

The ascendant role of science in the work of land trusts and other conservation organizations has had a hugely beneficial influence on their direct-action initiatives. It allows for systematic planning for conserving biodiversity in Canada and around the world. Nevertheless, land trusts such as NCC are not primarily science organizations. Rather, they use science to advise their operations in order to work efficiently and effectively in identifying and meeting their conservation objectives.

In the following chapters, we will examine the history of the Nature Conservancy of Canada. This organization celebrated its fiftieth anniversary in 2012, when it held pride of place as Canada's largest land trust.

7

The Beginning of the Nature Conservancy of Canada, 1962–71

In the first half of the twentieth century many Canadians became seriously worried about damage to the natural environment. There was alarm about many species that had suffered precipitous declines of range and abundance, and of comparably severe damage to certain ecological communities, such as older forests, prairies, and wetlands. It was well known that Canada had already seen some extinctions, such as the great auk (*Pinguinus impennis*), Labrador duck (*Camptorhynchus labradorius*), and passenger pigeon (*Ectopistes migratorius*), as well as near losses, such as the whooping crane (*Grus americana*), plains bison (*Bison bison bison*), and trumpeter swan (*Cygnus buccinator*).

Many of these concerned people were naturalists, hunters, and ecologists, all of whom had a profound respect and love of the natural world. They believed that society needed to mobilize itself to prevent further degradation of Canada's natural heritage, and even that of global ecosystems. They knew that the key actions to achieving that goal were in the realms of education, advocacy, and habitat protection.

Educational programs were developed to inform the public about environmental degradation. Governments at various levels, especially federal and provincial, were beginning to establish protected areas, such as national and provincial parks. This started in 1885 with Banff National Park, followed by Yoho National Park and Glacier National Park in 1886, Algonquin Provincial Park in 1893, Waterton Lakes National Park in 1895, Mont Tremblant National Park (in the Quebec system) in 1895, Jasper National Park in 1907, and many others since then. The creation of these and other parks was well supported by the public, but progress in establishing additional ones was slow.

Another important initiative began in 1946 when the Government of Ontario established a series of arm's-length conservation authorities (CAs) to conserve parts of the watersheds of larger rivers in southern parts of the province.[1] This action was part of a post-war effort to address widespread damage caused to game habitats and flooding in river valleys. The work began as watershed-based mapping studies of flooding risks and important game habitats. However, the impetus for the CAs was increased in 1954 because of damage caused by Hurricane Hazel in the Greater Toronto Area.[2] That immense storm dropped twenty-nine centimetres of rain in twenty-four hours, causing massive flooding that washed out low-lying roads, bridges, and buildings. About four thousand families were made homeless, eighty-one people were killed, and the total damage was about $100 million ($850 million in 2011 dollars).[3] In response, land-use regulations were enacted to prevent housing development in areas vulnerable to flooding, and the CAs were mandated and funded to acquire and conserve many low-lying properties.

Despite this sort of progress in conservation being made across Canada, most naturalists and conservationists were alarmed at the rate at which natural habitats were still being destroyed by conversion to agricultural or urban use or being damaged by timber harvesting and other industrial activities. They feared that governmental agencies were moving too slowly to protect natural habitats and that public advocacy was needed to encourage the authorities to pick up the pace. They also believed that there was a pressing need for non-governmental organizations to create nature reserves, as was beginning to happen in the United States and in Britain.

Canada, however, had no private organizations whose primary mission was to foster the acquisition and stewardship of natural properties across the country. This was a critical deficiency for conservation, because most of the imperilled species and their habitats occur in southern reaches across our country, where the land ownership is overwhelmingly private. Clearly, if the needed private-sector conservation was to be done, it was necessary to establish some of the new kinds of not-for-profit organizations, now referred to as land trusts. These groups are specialized in identifying privately owned natural properties that are at risk of being degraded by economic development and in taking steps to protect those lands if possible. Their fundraising capability gives them the ability to compete with other private interests so that natural properties can be purchased and set aside as nature reserves. The new land trusts might also accept donations of natural land, but a key requisite was their capability to make competitive offers on imperilled properties.

These big ideas were new at the time, and conservationists were contemplating them across Canada. In Ontario, a number of influential and activist members of the Federation of Ontario Naturalists (FON) decided it was necessary to quickly move forward with private actions to conserve natural lands. The FON is an umbrella organization for natural-history clubs across the province (in 2004 it was renamed as Ontario Nature).[4] It was founded in 1931, substantially through the efforts of John R. Dymond, who was director of the Royal Ontario Museum of Zoology and later a professor at the University of Toronto. He worked with several other dedicated naturalists, notably A.F. Coventry, H.C. Nunn, T.F. McIlwraith, and W.E. Saunders, who was the first president of the FON.

These dedicated naturalists wanted to promote the conservation of nature through the establishment of parks and other protected areas, while also encouraging outdoor activities and nature education. At the time, however, the FON did not want to create and manage its own nature reserves. Rather, it engaged in public and behind-the-scenes advocacy to encourage governments to designate protected areas on public lands. Still, the FON leadership knew that conservationists in Britain and the US had recently organized land trusts to create nature reserves, based on public lands in the UK and private lands in the US. There was clearly a pressing need for comparable organizations to undertake direct conservation work in Canada.

After considerable informal discussions beginning in the late 1950s, the FON began formal deliberations to create a land trust. To study the issue, an ad hoc committee was established in 1961 by David Fowle, the FON president. There were six members, all of whom were well-known naturalists and members of the FON board of directors:

- J. Bruce Falls, a graduate student of ecology at the University of Toronto and later a long-serving professor at the University of Toronto;
- David Fowle, the head of wildlife research for the Government of Ontario and later a professor of ecology at York University;
- William W.H. Gunn, the FON vice-president and later the president of LGL Ltd., an environmental consulting firm;
- Aird Lewis, a lawyer and later a partner in LGL and an employee of the Nature Conservancy of Canada;
- Kenneth Mayall, a civil servant in the Government of Ontario who conducted the wildlife parts of the watershed surveys that were eventually the organizational basis of the CAs; and

- Walter Tovell, a geologist specializing in the Pleistocene who taught at the University of Toronto.

The committee examined the operational and business models of the governmental Nature Conservancy in the UK and the private-sector Nature Conservancy in the US. Their investigation of the UK conservancy was mostly based on work by Bruce Falls during a post-doctoral sojourn at the University of Oxford.[5] The research into the US organization was conducted through correspondence and advice offered by Richard Pough of The Nature Conservancy (US) during a helpful visit he made to Toronto.

The FON group decided that problems of conservation were Canada-wide and that an independent non-governmental conservancy working at a national scale was required. They recommended that a new organization be founded to pursue the acquisition of protected areas throughout Canada, rather than one working only in Ontario. The FON accepted this advice in the autumn of 1962 and under the leadership of Bruce Falls, who was its president at the time, took immediate steps to found a national land-trust organization.

Aird Lewis drafted a document that described the purpose of the new land trust and served as the template of an application for a federal charter for the new organization. The text was vetted by other interested people in the FON and then an application was made to the federal government for the necessary letters patent. On November 28, 1962, the Nature Conservancy of Canada became duly constituted as a trustee-governed, no-share capital corporation (a not-for-profit corporation), incorporated under the Canada Corporations Act, with charitable status under the Income Tax Act.

The letters patent named five inaugural trustees of the new organization: Antoon de Vos, David Fowle, William Gunn, Aird Lewis, and John Livingston. (de Vos was a professor of wildlife ecology at the University of Guelph, and Livingston was a writer, broadcaster, manager of the Audubon Society of Canada, and later a professor of environmental studies at York University.) These people, along with Bruce Falls, Kenneth Mayall, and Walter Tovell, are the far-sighted conservationists who founded the Nature Conservancy of Canada.

The objectives of the new organization had to be stated in the letters patent in order for the new organization to be given charitable status. At the time, the conservation mission in itself would not have been sufficient to satisfy this criterion. The objectives were stated as follows:[6]

1. To educate the Canadian public toward the conservation of the landscape, including its flora and fauna, and to cooperate with other Canadian and international organizations having similar aims, and to encourage such organizations in their activities.
2. To establish, maintain, develop, and manage Nature Reserves in Canada, including the maintenance of physical features of scientific interest; and to encourage scientific research and educational services related thereto.
3. a. to acquire by purchase or otherwise real estate and property;
    b. to solicit or otherwise acquire donations of money or property;
    c. to hold, manage, improve, develop, exchange, or sell property; and
    d. to enter into any arrangements with any authorities, public, academic, or otherwise that may be conducive to the Conservancy's objectives.

William Gunn published an article in *The Ontario Naturalist* in 1963 to introduce the nascent NCC to the wider community of naturalists in Canada. He explained the objectives as specified in the letters patent, which were to educate the public about nature and to conserve natural lands all across Canada, often by working in collaboration with partners in government and other organizations.

Interestingly, the educational mandate as expressed in the letters patent was crucial to NCC acquiring tax status as a charitable organization. Under the legislation of the time, the direct-action conservation work of NCC was not sufficient to obtain that kind of charitable status, while education was. In actual fact, NCC never did pursue educational initiatives very strongly, leaving that mandate to other environmental NGOs that focus more on that sector of public literacy. Instead, NCC developed and maintained a focus on direct conservation action through the creation and stewardship of protected areas.

Gunn's article also spoke to a need for NCC to be engaged in public advocacy for protected areas. However, NCC never much used this tactic. Essentially, the organization has stayed out of the arena of public advocacy and environmental controversy, leaving that task to other kinds of environmental charities that do it effectively. Instead, NCC has always focused on direct conservation action through conservation planning and the acquisition and stewardship of natural properties.

During the first phase of NCC (defined here as the time of its founding to 1971), the work of the organization was almost entirely led and undertaken by a small group of volunteer trustees. These people recognized the pressing need to take direct conservation action and worked toward making that happen. At the time, these ardent conservationists saw their mission as saving individual properties of high natural value. Today this perspective is sometimes referred to as an "islands of green" view, and it is seen as being somewhat disengaged from consideration of disruptive land uses that may be taking place on the surrounding landscape. Moreover, the initial model was to act as a helpful partner that makes key financial contributions to the acquisition of properties, rather than necessarily providing all the necessary funding. Once acquired, the properties would be routinely turned over to another responsible organization for management, usually a governmental agency or a CA.

During the early years, the lists of potential NCC projects were mostly based on the knowledge of naturalists, planning studies that had been made by CAs and other governmental agencies, and information available from the International Biological Program (IBP). The latter was an international effort of somewhat coordinated studies in ecology and environment, which ran from 1964 to 1974. In Canada, the IBP had a program to identify lists of sites of high conservation value, meaning they supported species or ecological communities that were unusual or rare in the country.

However, the first projects that were taken on by the emerging NCC were prompted by high-profile conservation issues of the day: important natural places that were imminently threatened by economic development. Interestingly, the first project that NCC attempted had only limited success. Despite an enthusiastic campaign the Conservancy was unable to raise sufficient funds to purchase the property in question, a wetland west of Toronto called Rattray Marsh, although much of it was eventually conserved by other means (as will be discussed later in the chapter). This initial disappointment underscored the vital message that direct conservation is not an easy thing to accomplish. Strong opposing forces and insufficient resources make it difficult to do the job. Nevertheless the volunteers of the embryonic NCC persevered. They soon found success in several acquisitions and learned how to adapt in order to pursue their goals.

The Organization, 1962–71

As is typical of most charities in their emergent phase, NCC activities in its first years depended entirely on the efforts of a small but dedicated ensemble of volunteers. The inaugural meeting of the Board of Trustees was held on April 4, 1963. The meeting was chaired by Aird Lewis, who went on to serve as the chair of the Board until 1969. Other attendees were Antoon de Vos, David Fowle, and William Gunn, all from the Toronto area (John Livingston, another local trustee, was unable to attend this first gathering). At the meeting, three additional trustees were elected from other parts of Canada: Roderick Haig-Brown (Campbell River, BC), George Ledingham (Regina, SK), and George Montgomery (Montreal, QC). Additional trustees who joined the NCC Board during the next several years were William Harris (1965; Toronto), Bruce Falls (1966; Toronto), H. Albert Hochbaum (1966; Winnipeg), John MacKenzie (1966; Toronto), Charles Sauriol (1966; Toronto), Alan Steiner (1966; Toronto), and Robin Fraser (1969; Toronto). Fraser served as both trustee and solicitor to the Board, and in fact became NCC's longest-serving director, remaining active on the Board until 2002 (see appendix 1 for the terms of members of the Board).

The minutes of the meetings of the first two years indicate that the trustees were mostly dealing with such pressing issues as fundraising, identifying and prioritizing sites to conserve, networking with naturalist groups across Canada, and developing pamphlets and other materials to publicize the new Canadian land trust.

The trustees considered the ways and means of spreading the reach of NCC across the country. In May 1967 they discussed the possibility of establishing local NCC organizations across Canada, with provincial trustees serving as links to a national board. This corporate structure was viewed as an important way forward for the organization, although it took several decades until the financial situation of NCC allowed the organization to fully implement it. Although from the early 1970s NCC had part-time representatives or key volunteers in various regions of Canada, it was not until 1990 that the first staffed provincial office and regional council were established, in Alberta. By the late 1990s, staffed offices had been launched across Canada.

The funding climate was quite tough for several years. NCC's first application to the Canadian National Sportsmen's Show Conservation Fund was declined, although soon afterwards that source became a reliable supporter (its first donation of $3,000 in 1967 was to be used for administrative purposes by the fledgling NCC). To help in these early years The Nature Conservancy (US) offered a loan, but the NCC trustees turned it down to maintain the independence of their embryonic organization.

The first dramatic improvement in the funding environment occurred when NCC assumed a leadership role in a high-profile project to acquire

Rattray Marsh near Clarkson, west of Toronto (see the next section for project details). During 1965–66 NCC had revenues of $98,000, of which 81 percent was for the Rattray campaign. Although that project was not successful, NCC was not blamed for the outcome, and the networking that NCC had undertaken while trying to raise money provided an initial base of an expanding community of supporters. Money is always a problem for land trusts, but from these modest beginnings NCC became extremely skilled in attracting a supportive foundation of donors. In recent times, this donor base has included tens of thousands of individual Canadians, companies of all sizes, private foundations, and governments at levels.

After a few years, NCC started to accumulate some undesignated funds—that is, monies that had not been donated specifically for a particular land acquisition. In the "business" of land trusts, undesignated funds are vital to operations because they can be spent in ways that are most immediately beneficial to the organization. The minutes of a board meeting in November 1965 reveal that the trustees were sufficiently confident about their fiscal situation to authorize the hiring of their first staff person as a part-time administrative director. This was Charles Sauriol, an experienced supporter of conservation projects in Southern Ontario and a strong presence at NCC until 1985. In 1969, Aird Lewis, a lawyer who had drafted the first terms of reference for NCC, resigned as chair of the board to take up a staff position as the first executive director, with Sauriol remaining as the administrative director. Interestingly, these employees continued to serve as trustees of NCC, a practice that the Board did not discontinue until 1983. After that date, senior employees would attend meetings of the Board to advise the trustees, but they did not move motions or vote on them.

Initially, these two employees were paid only nominal salaries. Combined, they earned $10,000 a year and worked with no office support and a measly travel budget of $5,000. However, this arrangement turned out to be temporary because these staff and the trustees soon began to raise more funds to support the work of NCC. This allowed the organization to pay its personnel a more reasonable wage for their steadfast work on behalf of conservation. In 1970, Lewis was awarded a three-year contract at $18,000 per year.

In 1967, NCC issued its first public report, a four-page document titled *The Nature Conservancy of Canada Report*. The front page features NCC's vision statement of the time: "A Canadian charitable organization formed to acquire and preserve natural areas throughout Canada for the benefit of future generations." This statement is not quite the same as the present vision statement, which boldly states that NCC works to conserve nature for its intrinsic value, as well as to benefit people (see chapter 1). Financials were not reported in the document, but minutes of the board meetings show that the total revenue for 1966 was $9,900, of which a remarkable $5,400 had been earned as interest.[7] NCC's capital assets in land had a value of $10,000 in 1966, related to the acquisition of Marshall Woods (which is described in the section below).

In comparison, the annual revenues for the 1971 fiscal year, when NCC was ten years old, showed proceeds of $184,000. NCC was involved in the acquisition of four properties totalling 1,796 hectares (4,434 acres) that year, all of which were passed to partner organizations for stewardship. At the time, NCC still held only $10,000 worth of property, plus a nominal $1 for a donated property at Sight Point in Nova Scotia.

In an October 1971 board meeting the trustees were sufficiently confident in NCC's medium-term financial stability to authorize the purchase of a $50,000 Canada Savings Bond as a money-holding vehicle. There was even discussion of establishing a trust fund whose yield through investments could provide a degree of predictable cash flow. However, it took decades for NCC to become large enough to actually establish its first endowment fund. As we will see in a later chapter, this National Land Conservation Fund was set up in 1997, initially using monies from undesignated bequests.

Having several employees devoted to the work of NCC was vital to accelerating the development of sympathetic relationships with private companies, family foundations, and other potential sources of funding. In 1969, NCC received its first "donation" of national media support when the Canadian edition of *Time* began to run small advertisements on the inside back page of its weekly magazine. In 1971, NCC prepared its first piece of filmed advertising, a sixty-second commercial that was shown gratis on the CBC network.

In November 1970, Lewis and Sauriol reported to the Board about their first long-distance junket, which they had made to Vancouver, Edmonton, and Calgary to meet with leading naturalists and potential funders of NCC in western Canada. This was the inaugural peregrination by NCC staff outside of Ontario. The trip was a harbinger of many additional trips by staff and volunteers to all regions of Canada. From such limited initial travels, a full-blown national organization has grown.

The minutes of early board meetings also make note of initial contacts made with several donors who went on to be enthusiastic long-term supporters of NCC. For example, the minutes of September 1970 describe a potential undertaking with the Weston family. The minutes of September 1971 record that contact with "Mr. Weston . . . was a valuable experience . . . and it is likely we will be involved with him . . . at some point in the future." Very happily for conservation in Canada, that did indeed turn out to be the case, and The W. Garfield Weston Foundation went on to be an extremely generous private supporter of the work of NCC.

Similarly, the minutes of November 18, 1970, mention support provided by Richard Ivey for the acquisition of a Carolinian woodlot. The Ivey family has been a consistently generous supporter of NCC since then, having a particular affinity for projects that conserve woodlands in Southern Ontario. In 1971, negotiations involving the Richard Ivey Foundation, the Ontario Ministry of Natural Resources, and NCC resulted in a ten-year program to acquire forested properties on the Niagara Escarpment, which greatly accelerated conservation actions on that extensive landform. The minutes of a board meeting of April 1977 contain the following resolution: "The Trustees of The Nature Conservancy of Canada at their Annual Meeting . . . acknowledge the support of the Richard Ivey Foundation . . . and further recognize the profound impact of this support on the capacity of the Conservancy to pursue its objectives."

The Conservation Program, 1962–71

The Nature Conservancy of Canada was founded in response to the realization that it is necessary to have a private-sector organization with the capability of protecting natural areas throughout Canada. In its first decade, NCC began to do this mostly by contributing to securement projects that were being led by other organizations, usually by governmental conservation authorities or by local land trusts or naturalist groups.

Interestingly, the first private action to create a nature preserve in Canada was in 1937 by the Province of Quebec Society for the Protection of Birds (PQSPB; Société Québecoise de protection des oiseaux; now Bird Protection Quebec or Protection des oiseaux du Québec). This involved the acquisition of Île aux Perroquets on the Lower North Shore, a twelve-hectare (thirty-acre) island near Blanc-Sablon that supports a rookery of Atlantic puffin

(*Fratercula arctica*) as well as breeding by ten additional species of seabirds.[8] That island was bought for only $185 from the estate of a local ship's captain.[9] Acquisition of the island was a high priority for the Canadian Wildlife Service (CWS), but the agency had no funds to buy it, so Harrison Lewis, the head of the CWS at the time, asked Lewis Terrill, the founder and president of the PQSPB, to buy the island, and so it was done.

The second private conservation action in Canada took place in 1961 when the Hamilton Naturalists' Club purchased thirty-nine hectares (ninety-five acres) of older woodland in Norfolk County for $4,500 to create the Spooky Hollow Nature Sanctuary (a 1991 addition increased its area to 66 hectares [165 acres]).[10] The third project was undertaken by the FON in 1962, at Dorcas Bay on the Bruce Peninsula.[11] That undertaking had to be quick because the $20,000 deal needed to close in August, and although the incorporation of the FON-sponsored NCC was imminent, it had not yet been completed. The project at Dorcas Bay conserved one of the last surviving dune-and-slack wetland habitats on the Bruce Peninsula, a site of eighty-one hectares (two hundred acres) that is extremely rich in wildflowers. It had been threatened by subdivision for a cottage development. The FON quickly mounted a campaign, acquired the site, and established the Dorcas Bay Nature Reserve. It was later expanded to 130 hectares (320 acres), and in 1995 was incorporated into the Bruce Peninsula National Park.

The first big effort NCC led was a campaign to preserve high-quality wetlands in Rattray Marsh, which was the last relatively intact lakeside marsh between Toronto and Burlington.[12] In this case, residential and proposed marina development was threatening a 61-hectare (150-acre) property, including 14 hectares (35 acres) of marsh that provided critical habitat for breeding and migratory birds and other wild life. The Rattray property was well known to naturalists as a good place to visit and as important to biodiversity. It had first become available in 1959 after its long-term owner died. There were proposals to develop the area for housing and commercial use, and local opposition to that scheme arose, led by the naturalist Ruth Hussey. At that time the provincial government considered purchasing the property for $750,000 to create a park, but that did not happen. In 1964, a new owner asked $875,000 for the property, and NCC participated in a campaign to acquire it to develop a residential nature school, while protecting the wetlands. The most active partners in the campaign were the Rattray Estate Preservation Committee and the

South Peel Naturalists' Club. Unfortunately, during two years of fundraising NCC managed to accumulate only about $159,000 in cash and pledges for this project, and so the deal fell through. Soon after, in 1966, the owner managed to have the property rezoned for residential development, which resulted in a major revaluation of its wetland portion to $2 million, pricing it far out of the reach of NCC at that time.

Over the years much of the land adjacent to Rattray Marsh was converted to residential development, although the proposed marina was never built. However, much of the natural property was acquired by the City of Mississauga in collaboration with the Credit Valley Conservation Authority, which established the thirty-eight-hectare (ninety-four-acre) Rattray Marsh Conservation Area. Although residential development occurred along much of the shoreline, relatively little of the marsh itself was filled in, although some degradation of the natural habitat occurred as a result of the conversion of adjacent habitats and invasions by alien species. In a larger sense, because much of the wetland habitat was eventually conserved, the Rattray project should be viewed as an "incomplete success" of conservation.

Nevertheless conservationists were disappointed when they were unable to secure the entire natural property. It was also a rude awakening to the financial struggles of private-sector conservation. Still, the ardent volunteers in the new NCC were buoyed by the fact that almost all the donors to the Rattray project were forward-thinking and allowed their monies to be retained and used for other conservation projects. In fact, donors requested the return of only 5 percent of the Rattray donations.[13]

The first completed NCC project was a 1967 collaboration with a conservation authority in the purchase of a nine-hectare (twenty-one-acre) woodlot known as Marshall Woods, located near Meaford, Ontario, immediately below cliffs of the Niagara Escarpment. This property supports a rare surviving tract of never-logged mixedwood forest with old-growth tree trunks that are up to 1.2 metre (4 feet) in diameter, and a diverse understorey of calcium-loving vascular plants and bryophytes. This property was purchased for $10,000 and passed to the North Grey Region Conservation Authority for ownership and stewardship. In 1971, two adjacent properties were purchased by NCC. The terms of transfer of the properties were that the forest was to be kept in a natural condition, without the development of major recreational infrastructure such as horticultural landscaping or picnic tables, and that public access could occur only by foot. NCC used this model for most of its early projects—that is, it participated in the acquisition of a property but then passed title to another organization for stewardship, such as a governmental agency. NCC's ongoing responsibility was to ensure that appropriate management would be undertaken by the title-holding conservation partner.

Another early NCC project was undertaken near Peterborough, Ontario, in the Cavan Bog, an exceptional complex of bogs and other wetlands covering about 1,378 hectares (3,400 acres). NCC purchased the first property there in 1968, in part using funds remaining from the unsuccessful Rattray campaign. By 1986, NCC had contributed to the acquisition of sixteen properties totalling about 470 hectares (1,160 acres).[14] This site is now the Cavan Swamp Wildlife Area, owned by the Otonabee Region Conservation Authority (ORCA) and well known for its richness of wild life, including a profusion of twenty-two native species of orchids. The funding arrangement in this case was that NCC contributed 50 percent of the project cost, with those monies being matched by the Government of Ontario. This took advantage of a program in which funding provided by a conservation authority for an acquisition would be matched by the provincial government; in this case, NCC provided the funds that the ORCA put toward the project.

Remarkably, prior to this deal, NCC was not very aware of these sorts of possibilities for matching funds for conservation acquisitions. According to Charles Sauriol in his memoirs, the potential opportunities of matching funds were revealed during a meeting with Christine Nornabell, chair of ORCA, held to discuss the Cavan project.[15] In the meeting, Sauriol told Nornabell that NCC had monies that could be drawn upon for land purchases at Cavan Bog. Nornabell then said, "It is strange that this should happen because we have been talking about the Bog for some time. Herb Crown of ARDA [a regional development agency] wants to give the Authority [i.e., the ORCA] $50,000 to purchase land in the Bog, but only if we can match his funds, which the Authority is unable to do. Now supposing you gave the Authority $50,000, we could then get the ARDA or a Ministry grant to match it and we could buy $100,000 of land."[16]

Knowledge of this prospect was an epiphany for Sauriol, who recorded his own thoughts as follows: "Yes, of course. This was why the Conservancy had been born. Its role was that of a catalyst, a facilitator; being a purveyor of funds and matching grants was its raison d'être. Christine [Nornabell] had discovered the formula, the modus operandi, the open sesame, the 'approach' which was to shape the Conservancy's future and my own. How utterly simple. That meeting was perhaps the most important single meeting of my twenty-one years with the Conservancy."[17] The matching funds available for work done through a conservation authority, which were not available elsewhere in Canada, were a key reason why NCC did many of its projects in Southern Ontario at this time.

NCC's first project outside of Ontario was a land donation in 1971 at Sight Point, Cape Breton. Jean Rosner, an American owner of this property, had spent many pleasant summers there and wanted to ensure that it would remain in a natural condition. To do this, she donated 175 hectares (432 acres) at Sight Point to NCC to create a protected area. Subsequent acquisitions have enlarged this area to 417 hectares (1,030 acres), to which NCC has retained ownership. The Nova Scotia Nature Trust is also active in this project area, having secured an easement of 111 hectares (275 acres) in an ongoing assembly.[18] The properties conserved by the trusts include well-known scenic and heritage viewscapes, including one at MacKinnon's Brook that inspired a symphony written by Scott Macmillan, a Nova Scotian composer.[19]

The Spruce Grove (Wagner) property in Alberta, located just west of Edmonton, was the first NCC project outside of Ontario that involved the provision of cash. The partners in this 1970 project of 130 hectares (320 acres) were the Alberta Wildlife Foundation (now the Alberta Sport, Recreation, Parks and Wildlife Foundation) and the Government of Alberta, with NCC providing partial funding of about $12,000 that was essential to the success of the acquisition. The Wagner Natural Area is now a 219-hectare (540-acre) provincial reserve that conserves a calcium-rich fen wetland, while allowing low-intensity use by hikers and naturalists. In 2006, NCC purchased an additional thirty-two hectares (eighty acres) adjacent to the Wagner Natural Area, but it has retained the title to that adjunct habitat.

The minutes of early meetings of the NCC Board contain mentions of important conservation projects that NCC subsequently went on to undertake even decades later. For example, in February 1965, the trustees discussed an important conservation need in southern Saskatchewan, close to the southern border with Montana, at a place they referred to as Prairie Dog Town. Many years later, in 1988, NCC committed to helping with the assembly of prairie lands in that region for the new Grasslands National Park. This park conserves some of the best remaining short-grass prairie in Canada, and so provides habitat for many species-at-risk that depend on that imperilled natural eco-system. Further details on this national park are provided in chapter 10.

Similarly, in a meeting in January 1968, the possibility of a land assembly at Minesing Swamp, located west of Barrie in Southern Ontario, was dis-cussed. This land is one of the most impressive "true" swamps in Canada. It has an extensive area of bottomland forest that receives a deluge of flood-water in the springtime when the Nottawasaga and Mad Rivers overflow their banks. There are not many places in Canada where you can canoe for kilo-metres through a wilderness of mature flooded forest, but Minesing is one such wonderful swamp. The area supports twenty-eight species-at-risk listed at the federal level by COSEWIC, six globally rare species, and three globally rare ecological communities.[20] The rivers are also important migratory routes for the threatened lake sturgeon (*Acipenser fulvescens*). The present Minesing Wetlands Natural Area has been designated an Area of Natural and Scientific Interest and a Provincially Significant Wetland. It is also on the Ramsar List of Wetlands of International Importance (named after the city in Iran where this international convention was negotiated).[21] NCC started to acquire nat-ural properties in the area in 1971, in collaboration with the Nottawasaga Valley Conservation Authority (NVCA), the Canadian National Sportsmen's Show Conservation Fund, the Ontario Ministry of Natural Resources, and other partners. In that year, the first 879 hectares (2,170 acres) were acquired in the Minesing Swamp. As of 2011, the assembly of conserved habitat in the Minesing Wetlands Natural Area had increased to an impressive 4,684 hec-tares (11,567 acres) of rare hardwood swamp, other wetlands, and adja-cent terrestrial communities. The major landholders are the NVCA with 3,935 hectares (9,717 acres) and the Government of Ontario with 545 hec-tares (1,347 acres). All lands acquired by NCC in the Minesing wetlands have been transferred to NVCA for ongoing stewardship.

In May 1971, the Board authorized negotiations to purchase a key prop-erty from the Morton Salt Company to add to the Ojibway Prairie Park of the city of Windsor in southwestern Ontario. This is the best tract of tall-grass prairie to survive in eastern Canada, rivalled only by those in southeastern Manitoba, where NCC began to work about fifteen years later. These assem-blies of rare tall-grass prairie are described in later chapters.

By the end of this initial period of its development, the Nature Conservancy of Canada was successfully undertaking an increasing number of projects with diverse partners. As a result NCC was becoming widely recognized within the conservation community as a successful "go to" organization to work with when ecologically important private lands had to be acquired in Canada.

8

A Freshening Breeze, 1972–80

The Nature Conservancy of Canada's next stage of development is characterized by steady momentum. The Conservancy was attracting several relatively
wealthy donors and corporate supporters, in addition to growing numbers of
smaller-scale contributors. The improved cash flow meant that the few staff
members could be better paid and several additional people could be hired,
allowing NCC to take on more conservation projects across the country. In its
choice of projects, however, the Conservancy was still mostly responding to
ideas that were brought to its attention by other organizations, and the operational model was to provide partial support and rely on a trusted partner to
own and steward the conserved land.

The Organization, 1972–80

In 1972, thirteen members made up the NCC Board of Trustees. Most were
from the Toronto area, but several represented other regions of Canada. The
organization had three employees in Toronto, and donations were being
received from several hundred people. NCC's first public document, and its
first *Annual Report,* was published in 1972.[1] This report proudly noted that
the organization had raised about $246,000 in that year, of which 60 percent
was from private foundations, 12 percent each from corporations and the
Canadian National Sportsmen's Show Conservation Fund, 8 percent from
individual donors, 4 percent from governments, and 4 percent from interest earned on cash equity. Of the total monies raised, 66 percent was spent
on projects. However, the overhead rate was not 34 percent; instead, some
funds were carried forward to the next year. In fact, the operating budget for
the three employees was only $12,800. Nevertheless, the overhead costs of
the time were high in comparison with those of today, because a relatively
large allocation to staff and their expenses is typical of organizations that
are in the lag phase of their historical growth. The 1972 report also noted
that the $100,000 used to purchase lands in partnership with conservation

authorities had leveraged about $300,000 in matching funds from the Government of Ontario.

Moreover, 1972 marked a major step forward in terms of corporate support for NCC. That year, Xerox Canada entered into a ten-year funding agreement with the Conservancy to acquire properties across Canada. The contribution of Xerox under that arrangement eventually totalled more than $285,000 and provided a model for long-term corporate patronage of NCC's work that was subsequently "copied" by many additional companies.

During the first board meeting of NCC's second decade, in March 1972, Aird Lewis and Charles Sauriol reported on a visit they had made to visit key people at The Nature Conservancy (US) in Arlington, Virginia. They had meetings there with the TNC president and his senior staff, and came back to Canada with a vision of an organizational structure and operational model that NCC might adaptively follow to elevate its own conservation business to a higher level of activity.

The corporate structure of TNC involved a national board of directors that set broad policies and held fiduciary responsibility for the organization. TNC also had an underlying stratum of state chapters that raised funds at their geographic scale and set land-acquisition priorities. Senior employees in the head office of TNC in Arlington were responsible for national financial management and policy implementation, and those in the state bureaus were accountable for the design and implementation of most of the conservation projects that were undertaken. Lewis and Sauriol were impressed with this sensible and effective corporate model, and to a substantial degree it was emulated when NCC eventually developed its regional operations across Canada.

At the time, the revenues of TNC were about ten times larger than those of NCC. Although the scale of operation of both organizations has grown enormously since then, the ten-to-one ratio has remained fairly steady. For example, during the two-year period of 2009–10, TNC revenues averaged 8.3 times those of NCC.[2] These differences of scale are not mysterious. They mirror the relative sizes of the economies of Canada and the United States. In 1972, the US population was 9.6 times that of Canada, and its gross domestic product was 13 times larger.[3] Those ratios remained similar in 2010, when the US population was bigger by 9.3 times and the GDP by 13 times.

In 1973, Charles Sauriol's staff position changed from administrative director and secretary of the conservancy to that of projects director. This important change allowed Sauriol to identify key projects for consideration by the Board, and if approved to implement them. Sauriol had a special affinity for projects in the watershed of the Don River near Toronto, as well as nearby regions of Southern Ontario. Those personal interests and enthusiasms, as well as close ties with the conservation authorities in the province, meant that Sauriol was particularly effective at developing projects in that region.

The minutes of a meeting in February 1974 contain the first discussion of a need for the NCC Board to form committees that would deal with the details of certain key responsibilities. By May, several committees—including Finance, Public Relations, and Natural Areas—had been established and trustees were assigned to serve on them. The initial idea was that the committees would advise NCC employees, rather than make recommendations to the Board. Soon after, however, the Finance Committee operated in a more appropriate way by providing recommendations on policies and specific actions to the NCC Board, rather than directly to the staff (although certain kinds of advice could be given directly to employees). In September 1974, a Nominating Committee was added to identify potential new trustees. It consisted of the chair of the board, the executive director, and an additional trustee. Although today NCC employees may assist committees with advice and logistics, they are never members of them; in 1974, however, the executive director was also a trustee, and in that context it made sense for that main staff person to serve on the Nominating Committee.

From its very beginning NCC had aspirations to have a physical organizational presence in the regions of Canada beyond Southern Ontario, and in 1974 the Board authorized initiatives to begin to develop that structure. In May, trustee John Woodworth of Kelowna was appointed as an executive trustee for British Columbia with a focus on fundraising in the region, and for that service he was provided with an annual sum of $4,000, including any expenses. Woodworth would be assisted by Derek Arnold of the Okanagan Similkameen Society in south-central BC, who would develop project briefs for NCC staff to consider for action. He was paid $1,000 annually to cover his expenses. At the same meeting, Pierre Taschereau of Halifax, a new trustee, was appointed as a representative in the Maritime provinces. He received $2,500 a year, including expenses. A year later, trustee Hans Hochbaum of Winnipeg was given permission to establish a local committee to support

NCC's work in Manitoba, and trustee George Ledingham of Regina was asked to form a similar committee in Saskatchewan.

In September 1974, the NCC Board received a formal presentation from its auditors on NCC's annual report. NCC had been employing Clarkson Gordon & Co. as auditors since 1966, but this company had not previously made a verbal presentation of the results of an audit to the Board of Trustees. This new procedure represented an important move forward in terms of meeting fiduciary responsibility and the need for fiscal transparency. In any event, NCC received an unqualified audit of its 1973 finances, meaning there were no significant variances or contraventions of proper accounting practices. This result has been typical of all NCC audits.

Also in September 1974, the Board established a Natural Area Fund to hold monies that donors had given to support specific projects. (These are known as restricted funds because they cannot be diverted to other uses without first obtaining permission of the donor.) Typically land trusts have difficulty raising unrestricted funds to pay for salaries and other aspects of operations. To help in this regard, the Board authorized that a 15-percent administrative charge be levied on the appraised value of NCC projects.

NCC's new Natural Areas Committee was made up of several trustees who had a science background, plus a few additional ecologists who did not sit on the Board. Their principal mandate was to review proposals developed by NCC staff and partners in other conservation organizations to vet the embedded information and confirm the conservation value. The committee was also to help with policy development if requested to do so by the Board. The minutes of a board meeting in February 1975 record that this new committee had diligently reviewed the merits of seven projects on the Niagara Escarpment, recommending that they all move forward if funds were available. It also noted that from that time on the scientists and trustees were to be provided with formal project analyses according to a new template, which was always to include a map of the targeted site (remarkably, this was missing from some earlier projects).The minutes of a board meeting in April 1975 include the first discussion of a formal process of strategic planning by NCC. The main intent of NCC's first multi-year action plan was to develop a capacity for conservation planning within the Conservancy. This plan was needed to more strategically identify places and regions where private-sector land securement would achieve the greatest benefits for conservation. From this small beginning, NCC increasingly focused on conservation planning, rather than relying mainly on other organizations to bring projects forward in an opportunistic manner. In large part, the growing attention to building capacity in conservation planning emerged from the recent efforts of the International Biological Program, the global effort mentioned earlier that was intended to identify sites vital to supporting at-risk species and ecological communities.[4] Although the new action plan for NCC was also intended to enhance the effectiveness of fundraising, its core priority was to develop an in-house capacity for conservation planning. One year later, in April 1976, a working plan for 1975–85 was presented to the NCC Board, discussed at some length, and approved for implementation.

A September 1975 meeting discussed matters related to fundraising, including the touchy fact that some trustees were not donors to NCC. Some of the trustees expressed the opinion that the most important contribution they could make was from the benefits their volunteerism brought to the organization, rather than money they might contribute. Depending on the trustee, those received benefits might be related to professional services, standing in the community, and the ability to help with fundraising by marshalling personal relationships with companies, foundations, or wealthy patrons. However, the minutes record that some other trustees felt that all trustees should be donors to NCC at some personally appropriate level. This mildly contentious issue was resolved as follows: "It was felt that it was not necessary for any Trustee to financially contribute to the Conservancy and the Trustees' contribution was in terms of time and attendance at meetings. However, the contribution of any Trustee, should he feel it desirable to do so, would be welcome." This rather ambivalent policy lasted for several decades, until 2004, when the Board established a new framework for the roles and responsibilities of its members, which included an explicit requirement to be an annual donor to NCC at a level commensurate with personal capacity.

In January 1976, Jennifer Shay of Winnipeg was appointed as a trustee. She was a plant ecologist and professor at the University of Manitoba, and the first woman to serve on the NCC Board. Shay served as a trustee for eleven years and is still an advisor to the organization. In 1997, she and her husband made a personal statement about conservation by giving the provincial government a seven-hectare (seventeen-acre) property that supports rich floodplain forest on the Red River south of Winnipeg. That site is now the Jennifer and Tom Shay Ecological Reserve.

In 1978, NCC established a regional presence in Quebec, initially represented on a volunteer basis by Louise Beaubien Lepage of Montreal and
working under the name of Société canadienne pour la conservation de la
nature. Lepage went on to serve as a trustee from 1980 to 1990 and is still a
supporter of NCC's work in Quebec. She was also a driving force in a long-
term property assembly known as Un Fleuve, Un Parc to conserve islands
along a stretch of the St. Lawrence River east of Montreal (see the next section
for details on this project). Several years later, in May 1981, the French name
was changed, including in the letters patent, to Société pour la conservation
des sites naturels du Canada.

In October 1978, NCC printed its first newsletter, which was intended to
keep its trustees and employees informed of projects and other developments
in the organization. The newsletter was to be published on a quarterly basis
and was an internal document rather than one intended for donors or the
broader public.

In December 1978, Aird Lewis, the executive director, presented the first
annual budget to be formally submitted for consideration by the Board.
Lewis prepared the budget in collaboration with the Finance Committee, and
from then on, an annual budget was submitted to the Board for consideration in January.

At a board meeting in April 1979, Robin Fraser, a trustee and the NCC
solicitor, told the surprised group that, under the laws of Ontario of the time,
a charity was allowed to hold real estate only for a two-year period. The relevant legislation, he explained, was the Mortmain and Charitable Uses Act.
That legislation specified that an acquisition of land by a charity, by either
purchase or donation, required immediate possession of the property for its
direct charitable use.[5] That might include use of a building as a house of
worship required by a church or as a residence for a charity helping orphans.
According to the act any other lands not used in such direct ways must be
sold or turned over to the Crown within two years. However, it was unclear
in legal precedent as to whether the ownership of natural properties by a land
trust fulfilled the legal requirement of direct use. The principal intent of the
act was to prevent charities from holding collections of land for investment
purposes. Although the Crown could potentially issue a licence to a land trust
to hold natural lands, a licensing agreement of that sort had never been asked
for by a conservancy, and there was a risk of the request being refused. The
issue became moot a few years later in 1982, when the act was repealed.

In April 1980, the Board held its annual meeting in Simcoe, a town close to the north shore of eastern Lake Erie. At that meeting, long-serving trustees William Gunn and William Harris retired from the Board and were awarded commemorative plaques. From then on, all retiring trustees have been awarded framed certificates in remembrance of their volunteer service, usually featuring a picture of an NCC project with which they had a personal affinity. Afterwards, the Board held its first-ever field trip, to the nearby marshes and associated habitats of the Long Point Peninsula. This area is famous for the diversity and abundance of migratory birds during spring and fall migrations, as well as other rich biodiversity values. Over the years it became a focal point for NCC conservation efforts in Southern Ontario, as we will examine in later chapters.

In October 1980, the Board considered and approved a roster of new projects, and for the first time relatively detailed "project analysis" documents were received and included in the minutes of the meeting. This formalization of the approval process strengthened the administrative processes and transparency of documentation of the scientific merits of NCC projects. The reported details of each project included its recognized name, location, area, ecological region, estimated property and associated costs (including the fraction borne by NCC), the key natural features of the site, a description of threats by development or other stressors, and the eventual ownership of the property after it had been acquired. Remarkably, little or nothing was written about the proposed stewardship measures for the projects, other than a broad statement about its protection from economic development. These early project-analysis documents were usually only one page long, plus a map. The latter might only be a marked-up photocopy of a roadmap of the type used by motorists at the time, or at best, a relevant portion of a one-to-fifty-thousand-scale topographical map. Compared with the standards of NCC science of today, these project analyses were light on details related to species, habitats, and other ecological criteria. However, they were considered adequate at the time and in fact were an important step forward from earlier practices.

The meeting of the Board of Trustees in October 1980 was a well-attended national one held in Toronto, and a major activity was the review of a strategic planning document that an ad hoc committee had prepared. This *Forward Planning Report* is described in the minutes as a "coming of age" document in which optimism is expressed for the future of the organization and its conservation work. However, a number of important caveats were noted, including that the financial base of NCC was not yet secure and predictable, and that staffing and management needed improvements, including job descriptions to clarify roles and responsibilities. It was further specified that the Board of Trustees should consist of twenty to twenty-four members, with one national meeting per year and an associated field trip to a nearby NCC project. It was also recommended that a new Executive (or Management) Committee be established that would meet more frequently and would hold the delegated powers of the full Board.

It was also proposed that NCC employees should no longer be allowed to serve on the Board of Trustees, because of the possibility of a conflict of interest between the two roles (however, exceptions were given for the current staff/trustees, Aird Lewis and Charles Sauriol). It was further specified that the staff position of executive director should be a full-time commitment and its holder should not have any other employment (as Lewis did at the time). It was also suggested that about half of the trustees should be ecologists or other relevant professionals, and the rest lawyers, accountants, doctors, and businesspeople with an abiding interest in the conservation of nature. In addition to a full-time executive director, the report listed other necessary staff positions: a projects director to develop projects for consideration by the Board, a research director to undertake proactive ecological planning for strategic projects rather than only relying on partners to bring proposals forward to NCC, a public relations officer to arrange for publicity and grow the NCC brand, and an office manager. These recommendations were all adopted by the Board.

The trustees also worked to refine the vision and mission statements of NCC. In the annual reports for 1977 through 1979, it was noted that

The Conservancy sees its objectives and national role to:

- preserve land areas for biological diversity and for their outstanding natural features,
- preserve land for scientific observation and research, education, pleasure, and predominantly passive recreation,
- restore land to its natural condition,

- improve techniques of land preservation by developing and disseminating methods of acquisition and preservation,
- advance the cause of nature preservation and ecological concern in Canada through education in the schools and by other means.

It was further noted that "To accomplish this the Conservancy's policy is to act as a catalyst in drawing the various concerned groups and people together, plan an acquisition or educational programme, and supply a portion of the money to start the procedure. It successfully works with private groups and individuals, government departments, corporations, and foundations."

In the 1980 annual report, however, and until 1985, the vision and mission were identified more succinctly, as follows:

The Nature Conservancy of Canada is a national non-profit organization, dedicated to the preservation of ecologically significant natural areas, unique natural features, and places of special beauty. The Conservancy does not hold the properties it purchases, but transfers them to other conservation organizations for management and protection. Wetlands, shoreline properties, and areas which provide habitat for a wide diversity of flora and fauna, especially rare and endangered species—these are the priorities of The Nature Conservancy of Canada in the Eighties.

This mission has remained substantially intact, although in the mid-1980s NCC began to undertake many more projects that it would then own and steward, rather than routinely pass on to another conservation organization to undertake those longer-term responsibilities. Also, the term *natural beauty* is no longer specifically mentioned. Although all NCC projects are gorgeous in many aesthetic respects, the declared focus of conservation planning, securement, and stewardship is now almost entirely science-based.

The Conservation Program, 1972–80

In 1972, NCC contributed to its first project in British Columbia, the Mud Bay Nature Reserve near Surrey. This important estuarine area on the Pacific Flyway has invertebrate-rich mudflats and eelgrass beds that are well used by large numbers of migrating shorebirds and waterfowl. NCC holds partial title to this 59-hectare (145-acre) property, but leases it to the provincial government for stewardship. It is now a designated Important Bird Area[6] and is within one of only six designated Western Hemisphere Shorebird Reserve Network (WHSRN)[7] sites in Canada (the Boundary Bay section of the Fraser River Estuary WHSRN site).[8]

Also in 1972, NCC participated in the securement of five properties on the Niagara Escarpment. This dolomite-over-limestone ridge is the most prominent geographical structure in Southern Ontario. It runs northward from the Niagara Peninsula to Tobermory, then submerges beneath Georgian Bay, and re-emerges on Manitoulin Island. Because the Escarpment has steep topography and shallow and rocky soils, it is still relatively well forested and supports extensive natural habitats. Nevertheless, the area is threatened by residential development, quarrying for limestone and gravel, and timber harvesting. NCC and its partners had long regarded the Escarpment as a high priority for conservation, and these initial five acquisitions were the beginning of many more on that landform, where land assemblies are still ongoing in various places. The initial work on the Escarpment was greatly stimulated by funds provided by the Richard Ivey Foundation to establish a program to acquire forested properties. In those projects, $1 of Ivey funds was to be matched by $3 provided by the Ontario Ministry of Natural Resources through a conservation authority. NCC administered this land-acquisition program and received a 5-percent fee for providing that core service. This was the first programmatic funding provided by a Canadian government and foundation to a land trust, and over its ten-year duration, the financial support resulted in the securement of 2,057 hectares (5,080 acres) on the Escarpment at a total expenditure of $4.1 million.[9]

The minutes of a board meeting in October 1972 note that NCC made an offer of $125,000 to the Morton Salt Company to purchase its land in the Ojibway Prairie, located within the bounds of the city of Windsor in southwestern Ontario. Unfortunately, that offer was not accepted by the vendor. However, the next year a larger sum provided directly by the Ontario Ministry of Natural Resources was successful in acquiring the property. Although NCC did not make that specific purchase, the organization went on to consistently help with the preservation of this rare tall-grass prairie, making it the first of a number of purchases of contiguous properties in 1977. The Ojibway Prairie is now a complex of about 350 hectares (865 acres) of parks and nature reserves within Windsor.[10] It includes some of the finest tracts of tall-grass prairie that have survived in Canada, and has impressive late-summer stands of grasses and forbs that grow up to two metres tall. The area also has rare stands of Carolinian forest and southern wetlands, and these various ecological communities support a disproportionately large number of species that are rare and endangered in Canada. Over the years, NCC has acquired a number of properties to add to the Ojibway Prairie Complex, totalling about 115 hectares (285 acres).[11]

In 1973, NCC participated in its first project in Quebec when it helped to create the Réserve écologique de Tantaré, located about forty kilometres north of Quebec City and now owned by the provincial government.[12] This protected area covers 1,450 hectares (3,582 acres) and conserves a representative landscape of hilly granitic bedrock, covered by mature forest ranging in character from boreal to temperate, as well as peaty wetlands.

The minutes of an April 1975 meeting note that a plan was discussed to work in the Gulf Islands, located in the Strait of Georgia between Vancouver Island and the Lower Mainland of British Columbia. This ecoregion supports a great richness of rare biota and ecological communities, including exceptional stands dominated by Garry oak (*Quercus garryana*), whose presence is related to climatic conditions of winter rains and summer drought. Beginning in 1975, the Conservancy participated in a field survey of the ecological features of the Gulf Islands. Its first purchase was in 1978, when NCC acquired Cabbage Island, a 4.5-hectare (11-acre) island located off the east end of the much larger Saturna Island. Cabbage Island was transferred by NCC to the British Columbia Department of Parks for stewardship, and that group later passed it to Parks Canada. Both Cabbage and about half of Saturna Islands are now managed by Parks Canada as part of its Gulf Islands National Park Reserve, which was proclaimed in 2010 and consists of 3,600 hectares (8,900 acres) on fifteen larger islands and many islets and reefs, plus 2,600 hectares (6,400 acres) of marine reserves.[13] In total, NCC has acquired property totalling 52 hectares (129 acres) on four islands to add to this national park reserve, and the organization still hopes to do more.

The minutes of a board meeting in January 1976 contain the first mention of the possibility of acquiring property in a famous tract of rare hardwood forest known as Backus Woods. This is the largest and best-quality stand of older forest to have survived in the Carolinian ecozone of Southern Ontario. The tract supports many rare animals and plants, including twenty-three species that are listed by COSEWIC as being at risk and many others that are provincially rare.[14] Backus Woods has long been well known to naturalists and a focus of conservation efforts. This plan resulted in the acquisition of some of the forest by the Long Point Region Conservation Authority (LPRCA) as early as 1956, plus additional properties at various other times. The tract specifically known as Backus Woods is 263 hectares (650 acres) and represents the largest and ecologically best part of the rare forest. Conservation action has also taken place in an adjacent area, which was purchased by LPRCA in 1956, and for which NCC helped acquire an 80-hectare (198-acre) parcel in 1975. However, in 2011 LPRCA sold to NCC a 354-hectare (875-acre) tract consisting of Backus Woods plus two adjacent properties.[15] In addition, NCC already owned several properties contiguous with those purchased from the LPRCA, areas that are being restored from farmland to a forested condition. The area owned by NCC is now 728 hectares (1,799 acres). This land adjoins the 1,214-hectare (3,000-acre) St. Williams Conservation Reserve owned by the Ontario Ministry of Natural Resources, so the aggregate protected area is about 1,903 hectares (4,700 acres). The Conservancy is still hoping to acquire additional properties adjacent to its new Backus Woods protected area.

In 1977, NCC launched its first project in Manitoba, which resulted in the Brokenhead River Ecological Reserve, located northeast of Winnipeg and just south of and draining into Lake Winnipeg. This project conserves 64 hectares (158 acres) of rare floodplain mixedwood forest dominated by ash, elm, oak, and spruce, with a rich understorey of wildflowers.

Also in 1977, NCC acquired Main Duck and Yorkshire Islands in easternmost Lake Ontario. These islands are located just before Lake Ontario begins to flow into the St. Lawrence River, in the Thousand Islands region east of Kingston. These islands were purchased using funds provided by the Government of Canada, with the intent of transferring the land for incorporation into the St. Lawrence Islands National Park. The federal money was to come in three annual instalments, but if the government changed in an election the funding was not guaranteed.[16] To offset that potential risk, NCC took out an insurance policy under which, if the government did not pay all three instalments, the insurer would make good. The federal government paid the premium for the insurance, which proved not to be necessary, as the original pledge was honoured. Main Duck Island is 209 hectares (518 acres) and Yorkshire Island, located just a short passage to the east, covers 19 hectares (48 acres). These and the many nearby islands in the region have biologically rich offshore waters that may eventually be designated as a marine conservation area. The islands are in a well-used migration corridor for a great variety of birds, both aquatic and terrestrial species, as well as various rare plants. Main Duck and Yorkshire Islands are now managed by Parks Canada as ecological reserves. Visitation is allowed, but no infrastructure has been developed to support tourism.[17]

The minutes of an April 1977 meeting refer to the donation of a large area of natural habitat at Long Point, a forty-kilometre-long sandspit located on the north side of Lake Erie, to the Government of Canada for management as a wildlife sanctuary. This extensive tract of exceptional wetlands and southern forest and savanna is well known for supporting an impressive diversity and abundance of birds that are drawn to the peninsula because it shortens their migratory transit across Lake Erie.[18] There are also many species of rare plants and animals of southern affinity. Most of the area had been owned since 1866 by the Long Point Company (LPC). Although this private hunting club had stewarded the habitat well, NCC and other conservation-minded organizations had long been seeking to acquire the area to ensure the long-term protection of its important natural features. The 1977 donation involved about 3,200 hectares (7,900 acres) of natural habitat, although the LPC did retain another 3,239 hectares (8,000 acres) of the marsh to ensure continued hunting privileges for its members.[19] In essence, the LPC was a joint venture owned by various people, both Canadians and Americans. The Canadian members donated their portion of the assets directly to the Government of Canada, receiving a tax credit in exchange. However, under the tax laws of the time, the US owners could not do this; instead, they donated their assets to The Nature Conservancy (US) in exchange for tax benefits in the United States. TNC then donated the property to Canada to incorporate into the new Long Point National Wildlife Area, which was proclaimed in 1978. Although NCC was not directly engaged in these transactions, the organization had been deeply involved in many of the behind-the-scenes conversations and negotiations. However, embedded in the lands transferred to Canada was a thirty-six-hectare (eighty-eight-acre) block known as the Anderson Property, whose title was unclear because certain people outside of the LPC also had legal rights to "hunt, course and fish" there.[20] Because the Government of Canada would not accept a property with such unclear title as a donation, the LPC gifted that tract to NCC. Soon after the 1977 donation, in April 1978, NCC partnered in its first project at Long Point that involved a purchase. The organization has since acquired other properties adjacent to the Long Point National Wildlife Area and its vicinity, and plans to continue to do so.

The board meeting minutes of June 1977 refer to a project at Oak Hammock Marsh, which is located at the southwestern corner of Lake Winnipeg.[21] The site is listed as a Wetland of International Importance and an Important Bird Area. About two thousand hectares (five thousand acres) of open marsh plus additional fringing pasture and forest have now been conserved there, including extensive tracts that have been converted from agricultural use into well-functioning wetlands. Most of the conservation work at Oak Hammock Marsh has been undertaken by Ducks Unlimited Canada (which has located its national office there), in partnership with the Governments of Canada and Manitoba, but NCC also provided funding for some of the property acquisitions.

The same meeting minutes also refer to a project at Mer Bleue in the Ottawa area. That site is now protected as the Mer Bleue Conservation Area, a tract of about 3,331 hectares (8,225 acres) that is designated as a Wetland of International Significance and managed by the National Capital Commission (a federal agency).[22] This protected area is well used by many people from the Ottawa area, who can stroll on excellent boardwalks through marshy and boggy wetlands to see diverse species of orchids and other uncommon plants, and perhaps admire an endangered spotted turtle (*Clemmys guttata*) sunning itself on an emergent log. The engagement of NCC in the initial purchase of large tracts in the Mer Bleue was mostly related to advice in conservation planning and in land negotiations. In 1980, however, NCC did provide funds to assist in a land purchase to further enlarge the protected area.

The NCC annual report for 1977 refers to planning for the conservation of natural habitat in the Oak Ridges Moraine, an extensive region of drumlins located north of Toronto.[23] In 1978, NCC contributed to the acquisition of the Warwick property, the first of many securements in the moraine. NCC was a major partner in the process that resulted in the Oak Ridges Moraine Conservation Plan of 2002, which had a great influence on land use in the region, including the establishment by the Government of Ontario of a conservation-friendly greenbelt. As of 2011, NCC had contributed to the securement of more than 1,012 hectares (2,500 acres) in the Oak Ridges Moraine, including 113 hectares (280 acres) in a focal area known as the Happy Valley Forest.[24] That tract is one of the largest surviving areas of hardwood forest on the moraine, and NCC has a long-term goal of managing a heritage woodland there of about two hundred hectares (five hundred acres).

In 1977, the first discovery in Canada was made of a globally rare orchid, the small whorled pogonia (*Isotria medeoloides*). This endangered wildflower of the understorey of humid, acidic, open-canopied, southern mixedwood forest is known only from one location in Canada, the 213-hectare (526-acre) Calton Swamp in southwestern Ontario.[25] In 1980, NCC participated in a project to secure the only known habitat of the rare orchid, a property that is now part of the 72-hectare (178-acre) Calton Swamp Wildlife Management Area owned by the Catfish Creek Conservation Authority. This case of the rapid acquisition of the habitat of a newly "discovered" rare plant showed that NCC and its partners in conservation could move quickly when the circumstances required fast and effective action. Unfortunately, this ability must be tempered by the fact that the endangered *Isotria* has not actually been observed flowering at that site since 1998.[26] However, certain species of orchids sometimes enter prolonged resting phases and so it may still be present in the Calton Swamp.

Later in 1977 and 1978, NCC made its first of a number of important acquisitions on Manitoulin Island. These projects involved two parcels of 698 hectares (1,724 acres), acquired in partnership with the Ontario Ministry of Natural Resources. The coastal areas of these properties support large numbers of rare plants that inhabit wetland complexes of marsh, fen, and bog, as well as areas of limestone pavement (known as alvar) and forested habitat. The first to be acquired was the Robertson Property (165 hectares; 407 acres) in 1977, and then in 1978 the Sifferd Property (534 hectares; 1,320 acres). Both of these were subsequently transferred to the Government of Ontario to be stewarded within Misery Bay Provincial Park.[27] NCC continues to secure natural areas on Manitoulin Island and, as of 2011, has acquired about 8,300 hectares (20,496 acres) there through a leading or supportive role in nineteen projects. Of this total, NCC continues to hold title to about 3,015 hectares (7,446 acres) at five sites.[28]

The Sifferd acquisition was the most complicated transaction that NCC had undertaken up to that time. The Sifferds were conservation-minded American school teachers who had assembled their Manitoulin property over a number of years. They were not wealthy, and the land purchases and architecturally distinctive home they had built on the property had been expensive for them. Their desire was to retire there, sever the house lot from the balance of the property, hold a life interest in the house and its lot, and convey the balance of the land to a conservation owner who would pay them an amount equal to their expenditures to acquire the property over the years without any profit to them. They also did not want to lose money by paying capital gains or other taxes arising from the transaction. The eventual deal was complicated by many circumstances. For one thing, the family's job earnings were American-sourced, and there was a possibility the land deal could trigger further US taxes. In addition, severance of the house lot raised problems under Ontario's Planning Act, and capital-gains tax had to be dealt with. Also, the land was to be transferred to the province for a provincial park and because it would no longer be assessed the local municipality could not collect realty taxes, thus eroding its tax base. Moreover, some local residents were upset because if the lands were integrated into a park they would no longer be able to hunt there, so they objected to what they viewed as "foreigners" (the Sifferds) and "Torontonians" (the Conservancy) interfering with their traditional land use by tying up large tracts of land. On the other side, conservationists were impatient and had trouble understanding why what appeared to be a simple procedure to secure an important property was taking so long to implement. Eventually the transaction was completed, but only after the expenditure of many hours by lawyers and accountants specializing in Canadian tax law, American tax law, and Ontario real estate law. Those legal bills were paid for by the Government of Ontario, which also agreed to offsetting payments to the municipality in lieu of municipal taxes.

In 1978, NCC participated in its first project on Prince Edward Island. This venture involved partnering with the Island Nature Trust, a new provincial conservancy, to acquire a tract of 67 hectares (165 acres) at Blooming Point on the north shore of the island. This area of seashore, wetlands, sand dunes, shrubby habitat, and mature forest has been an ongoing focal area for conservation, and by 2011 about 248 hectares (613 acres) had been set aside at Blooming Point and nearby Deroche Point.

In 1978, NCC made its first property acquisition, Île aux Moutons, in a long-term assembly of islands in Quebec known as Un Fleuve, Un Parc. However, planning for this project had begun in 1971, and there had already been a few purchases of islands by the federal and provincial governments. The planning had taken a landscape-scale approach to the conservation of natural habitats. In that sense it was an early model for NCC's increasing focus on large-scale projects, often involving an assembly of contiguous natural properties. Trustee Louise Lepage was an early champion of this project, with a great deal of help from Tony Le Saulteur, Monique Beauchamp, and

Bob Carswell. Over the years, Un Fleuve, Un Parc has created an assemblage of conservation properties involving islands along a seventy-kilometre stretch of the St. Lawrence River, extending from Montreal eastward and downstream to Lake St. Pierre, that being a fluvial expansion located between Sorel and Trois-Rivières. As of 2011, this project had acquired thirty-two properties on twenty-one islands, totalling about 1,592 hectares (3,932 acres).[29] It is helping to conserve the largest freshwater floodplain in Quebec, including critical habitat for migratory and breeding waterfowl and other wildlife.

In 1979, the Conservancy purchased a property at Oak Lake, located near Brandon in southern Manitoba. This 769-hectare (1,900-acre) tract supports extensive wetland complexes that are well used by waterfowl and other birds, as well as sand dunes, forest, and prairie. The previous owners were dedicated conservationists who agreed to continue to steward the property as a nature reserve on behalf of NCC. NCC has gone on to emulate this kind of project many times. It involves working with landowners who are passionate about conserving the natural world, and helping them to realize their own vision of ensuring that a property they had loved and carefully stewarded would remain in a natural condition, ideally forever. By working with NCC, these conservation-minded people could realize a glowing satisfaction from the fact that they had contributed to a natural legacy that would be sustained beyond their own lives.

9

Steady Progress, 1981–89

The Nature Conservancy of Canada entered this decade making substantial changes to its leadership and organizational structure. The executive director position saw considerable turnover and was held by five different persons during these years. Nevertheless, the Conservancy made steady progress. Additional full-time employees were hired to deliver such crucial functions as fundraising and project development. Moreover, during the period the salaries paid to employees became increasingly competitive with those in the broader marketplace, which allowed the Conservancy to attract and retain talented specialists. The changes in staffing and the work environment represented a significant enhancement of the professionalism of the organization. There was also a clarification of governance structures, with the roles and responsibilities of trustees and staff becoming more clearly defined than they had been previously. NCC also began to be engaged in some large individual projects and long-term land assemblies, which was a harbinger for its more recent approaches to conservation.

The Organization, 1981–89

In 1981, the NCC Board consisted of sixteen trustees from all parts of Canada. There were five NCC employees in Toronto and three part-time representatives in other parts of Canada (Halifax, Montreal, and Victoria). A few hundred donors were supporting the Conservancy. Its total revenue for 1981 was $597,000, of which 41 percent had been raised from foundations, 11 percent from corporations, 18 percent from individuals, 22 percent from interest on cash and deferred accounts, and 9 percent from governments and other sources.[1] The seemingly large interest income was partly because of high inflation rates in 1981, when the prime interest rate averaged 14 percent.[2] NCC's capital assets in land had a value of $698,000 in 1981, up from $277,000 in the previous year, reflecting the beginning of NCC's trend of retaining title to more of the acquired properties. The administrative costs at the time, which are related to the costs of salaries, office space, and other necessary expenses, was about $250,000 annually.

The minutes of a board meeting in April 1981 make note of several important changes that had been implemented in the governance of NCC, based on recommendations of a strategic-planning document that had been ratified the previous October (as described in the previous chapter). One of the new organizational strictures was that the executive director must be a full-time employee of NCC. This was a problem for existing executive director Aird Lewis, because he was a principal in LGL Ltd., a well-regarded environmental consulting firm that had been founded in 1971 by himself, William Gunn, and John Livingston (all were also founding trustees of NCC, serving on the Board for nineteen, nineteen, and fourteen years, respectively). Partly as a consequence of this change, Lewis resigned as the executive director of NCC, but he was invited to remain on the Board of Trustees, which he did for another eight years. Meanwhile, the Board convened a search committee to find a new executive director.

In June 1981, the Board approved a bylaw to establish its first Executive Committee, which would consist of the chair, vice-chair, past-chair, and three additional trustees, to be appointed on an annual basis. At the same meeting, Wilfred Bigelow, a trustee and well-known heart surgeon, noted that The Nature Conservancy (US) had recently developed a computerized filing system for their project and financial information. He said that NCC should investigate doing something similar—at this point, the world of NCC did not yet include any computers.

Those minutes also refer to a discussion of various problems that had been "experienced as a result of transferring properties to governments versus the Conservancy holding them." However, there was a dissenting opinion on the issue, and it was also noted that "strict controls are demanded in writing before any property is transferred" and that "no difficulty has been experienced to date." Clearly, some important issues related to stewardship were discussed during the meeting, likely related to cases in which lands transferred to partners were not being managed in ways that properly conserved the lands' natural values, at least not to the satisfaction of all trustees. However, the examples were anecdotal and the conversation was not recorded in detail. It is likely that the cases discussed involved certain conservation-authority partners allowing some logging, or excessive development of trails or other infrastructure on lands that NCC had helped to acquire. In actual fact, hindsight reveals that some of the early property transfers by NCC to governmental partners did result in problems with respect to the stewardship of natural values. The Conservancy now effectively avoids those problems by requiring the conservation partner to enter into a landholding agreement, or in some circumstances, a conservation agreement, to ensure that the lands will be properly stewarded.

The minutes of a board meeting in August 1981 record that Charles Sauriol, who had been a trustee since 1966 and an employee since 1968, had been chosen to serve as the new executive director. The NCC annual report for 1981 notes that Sauriol is sometimes known as Mr. Conservation in Ontario because of his sixteen years of engagement with the Conservancy, with conservation authorities before that, and for his popular writing and frequent media interviews. During a meeting in September 1981, Sauriol made the first recorded mention (i.e., in the minutes) of NCC's goal of "preserving Canada's natural heritage." This evocative phrase has subsequently become well embedded in the corporate culture of NCC. It is often repeated in the vernacular and other communications of the organization and is an excellent way of simply communicating the intent of NCC's conservation actions.

In September 1981, the Board of Trustees held its first annual meeting outside of Ontario. After the meeting at the Four Seasons Hotel in Calgary, a reception was held in the Glenbow Museum, providing NCC with an excellent opportunity to showcase its mission and accomplishments and to network with conservationists and influential people in the region. The attendees proved to be highly supportive, and the event helped to spark the extensive work that NCC has gone on to do in Alberta and elsewhere in western Canada.

At that board meeting, the trustees examined a conservation planning study focused on wetlands that had been done for lands surrounding the Great Lakes. NCC had funded that work, and it represented NCC's first serious effort to use large-scale ecoregional planning to identify the most important places where private-sector action could achieve the best conservation results.[3] The research project was titled the *Great Lakes Biogeographical Study* and was undertaken by Craig Campbell, David Fowle, and George Francis, the latter two being academic ecologists and NCC trustees. The study proved to be quite helpful in prioritizing conservation actions around the Great Lakes. Within a few years, however, the study was superseded by more detailed research that took advantage of rapidly developing computerized methodologies for information handling, data analysis, and mapping.

During a meeting in December 1981, the trustees discussed a potential project at Oak Lake, Manitoba. The minutes noted that "ownership of land is a major departure from policy and the practice should be given serious consideration before any further property is considered for Conservancy ownership and management." Later on in that meeting, while discussing a potential donation of a property in Quebec, members discussed that it would be difficult for NCC to accept the land as a gift if a source could not be found to "provide maintenance funding." These conversations are representative of the beginning of a major policy change for NCC—a shift to greater emphasis on properties that would be owned and stewarded by the organization, rather than its initial model in which NCC helped various partners to acquire and manage conservation properties. At the meeting, Lloyd Mayeda, the NCC general manager, was asked to develop a land management policy for consideration by the Board.

At the time, the funding for the operational spending of NCC was raised mostly by the 15-percent levy that had been imposed on the appraised value of land purchases: money that had to be raised to complete any project. But unrestricted funds were always in short supply, and during a board meeting in November 1982, the possibility of raising an endowment fund of $1 million to help provide stable funding for running the organization was discussed (as we will see, this fund was never established). A few months later, the NCC offices moved from their cramped location on Yonge Street in Toronto to a somewhat larger space one building farther north. The staff now had 24 percent more space in which to do their work, but the rent was 17 percent more costly. In 1986 another move was made, to an even larger space on Broadview Avenue, but this new office was located above a dry-cleaning business so there was some distracting noise and an occasionally odoriferous ambience.

In 1983, a coalition of conservation organizations called the Ontario Natural Heritage League (ONHL) was established. NCC was one of the fifteen member groups, along with the Federation of Ontario Naturalists, Sierra Club, World Wildlife Fund, and other ENGOs that were concerned with the perils faced by the biodiversity of Ontario. Governmental partners, including the Ontario Ministry of Natural Resources, also took part. The ONHL was supported administratively by the Ontario Heritage Foundation, a

Crown corporation of the Ministry of Citizenship and Culture. The ONHL was founded to provide a coordinating body to encourage efforts to protect natural habitats. The ONHL and its partner organizations undertook conservation planning and developed action plans for important ecoregions or habitats, in particular the Carolinian Canada program for southern forests, another for the Niagara Escarpment, and another for wetlands. It also developed systematic procedures for contacting landowners of high-priority sites and engaging them in voluntary conservation, worked to build public awareness of the need to conserve biodiversity, and collaborated with governments and the private sector to find conservation solutions. Within this larger context of the mission of the ONHL, the Conservancy restricted itself to activities related to conservation planning and land acquisition. The ONHL terminated its activities in 1994.

During a meeting of the Executive Committee on May 7, 1983, Charles Sauriol and other employees were asked to recuse themselves. The ensuing in-camera discussion was likely about staffing issues, including the extraordinary workload of NCC employees. That and subsequent discussions resulted in a resolution that was passed during the following board meeting in July, which directed that a new projects director be hired. This new position was intended to give Sauriol some much needed relief; even while undertaking the many tasks of the executive director, he remained heavily engaged in the development and implementation of conservation projects. An additional intent was to increase the activity of NCC in regions of Canada beyond Southern Ontario, the latter having been the focus of Sauriol's interests.

Despite that staff enhancement, the minutes of a following board meeting in August reveal that Sauriol had resigned from NCC, as both the executive director and a trustee. Sauriol did this with the expressed intent of devoting his time to nature writing and the development of new conservation projects in the Toronto area, in several places for which he had a great personal affinity. However, Sauriol agreed to remain available to NCC as a special advisor, which turned out to be a significant ongoing commitment to the organization. He continued to serve in that capacity until 1987. In NCC's annual report for 1983, Sauriol wrote, "With the growing acceptance of the ethic that crucial natural-area land must be saved while it is still possible to do so, it is imperative that we continue to work together to add new laurels to the Conservancy's first twenty years of noteworthy achievement."

Lloyd Mayeda, the general manager of NCC, was then appointed as the executive director for a two-year term. With the retirement of Sauriol, however, no employees of NCC would ever again concurrently serve as a trustee of the organization, because of the possibility of a conflict of interest between the roles.

At a meeting in November 1982, the Board had discussed the idea of raising an endowment of $1 million to help support the operating expenses of NCC. Toward that end, a funding proposal was submitted to the Canadian National Sportsmen's Show Conservation Fund, which had been a consistent supporter of the work of NCC. However, in August 1983, the Sportsmen's Fund declined the request for $500,000 that would have been used as an operating endowment. NCC countered with a second proposal to the Sportsmen's Fund for five years of capital funding, at $50,000 per year, but that proposal was also unsuccessful. The trustees did not pursue this matter further, and it was not until 1987 that the Conservancy established its first endowment—a trust fund to support operations of the Ann and Sandy Cross Conservation Area near Calgary. NCC's first general-purpose fund was the National Land Conservation Fund, initiated in 1997. It was capitalized using monies from undesignated bequests and used to provide rotating bridge funding for conservation projects. However, NCC never did go on to establish an endowment fund to support its general operating expenses, the costs of which are still paid for by the allocation of much of the undesignated donations to the organization and by charging staff time to projects.

On November 21, 1983, NCC hosted a public fundraising event in Ancaster, Ontario. It featured an illustrated lecture by Robert Bateman, who at the time and still today is a widely acclaimed wildlife artist and conservationist. That event was attended by more than eight hundred people. It raised some immediate funds for NCC and also helped to raise awareness about the organization and its vital mission of conservation.

At a board meeting in January 1984, trustee Wilfred Bigelow reported on his recent visit to the offices of The Nature Conservancy in Arlington, Virginia. As he had similarly reported several years previously, Bigelow was impressed with the fact that TNC had established a computerized databank to support its analysis and presentation of financial information and fundraising activities, and to develop and track conservation projects. He strongly recommended that NCC implement a comparable system, and the trustees were highly supportive of that proposal. The minutes of the discussion say,

"It is agreed that a computer would be required." More than a year later, at a board meeting in April 1985, it was announced that an order had recently been placed for word processing equipment based on microcomputer hardware and software manufactured by Xerox, a supporter of NCC. It was expected that the system would be delivered to NCC in six weeks. Today, of course, computers, wireless communication devices, information technology, and advanced software applications are deeply integrated into all operations of NCC, and indeed in the very culture of the organization. In those early days of 1984, however, it took more than a year to implement a Board decision to purchase the Conservancy's first computer, and more than six weeks to receive it after it had been requisitioned from the vendor!

On April 3, 1984, a new Canada-wide, not-for-profit conservation organization known as Wildlife Habitat Canada (WHC) was announced.[4] It was established as a collaborative venture by Environment Canada, wildlife agencies in the provinces and territories, and several ENGOs. WHC works by developing partnerships among landowners, local communities, governments, NGOs, and private corporations to find conservation solutions for problems involving the habitat of wild life in Canada. It does this by providing funds for projects that conserve and restore natural habitats and by promoting coordinated efforts among conservation organizations. WHC has been provided with funds from governments and private donors, and it also raises money by selling Canadian wildlife habitat conservation stamps, which are released annually and based on an original piece of Canadian artwork. Almost all the stamps are purchased by waterfowl hunters as a necessity for the validation of their federal game-bird hunting permits, but many are also sold to philatelists and naturalists. From its beginning in 1984 to 2011, WHC has granted more than $60 million to hundreds of habitat conservation projects across Canada. It has been a key participant in important collaborative initiatives, including Carolinian Canada (see below) and the North American Wildlife Management Plan (see below). WHC has been an important supporter of NCC projects, providing a total of $1.56 million of funds between 1984 and 2011.[5] Louise Lepage was a founding member of the board of directors of WHC, and represented NCC in that capacity.

From its beginning, Wildlife Habitat Canada was highly supportive of the Conservancy undertaking more projects to own and manage conservation land, in addition to acting as a partner in acquisitions by other organizations. This important change in the business model altered NCC's predominant way of operating. In fact, in 1984, NCC had retained title to only 12 of the 250 properties that it had helped to acquire and it was actively managing only one of those (Oak and Plum Lakes in southwestern Manitoba). Because of the large implications for responsibility and expenses related to stewardship, this business model change generated a great deal of discussion during subsequent board meetings. Today, most projects undertaken by NCC involve the organization retaining ownership of acquired properties and having a perennial responsibility for stewarding their defining natural values. NCC has become Canada's leading ENGO in terms of the ownership and stewardship of privately owned conservation lands, rivalled in that respect only by Ducks Unlimited Canada.

Matching funds provided by WHC have also been helpful in allowing NCC to tap into funding available from the US to conserve wetland habitat for migratory waterfowl. In Canada, projects associated with the North American Waterfowl Management Plan (NAWMP) can receive US funding through the North American Wetlands Conservation Act (NAWCA).[6] That act requires that funding from the US federal Fish and Wildlife Service must be matched at least one to one by donations from non-federal US sources, and their sum must be at least matched by Canadian funds. As of June 2011, NCC had received a total of $120.5 million under the NAWCA program, of which $19.6 million was from the US Fish and Wildlife Service, $21.8 million was from non-federal US sources, and $79.1 million was from various Canadian sources, including Wildlife Habitat Canada.[7]

Considerable time was spent during a board meeting in September 1984 discussing several documents that had been prepared to improve fundraising by NCC. This included ways of achieving a higher public visibility for the mission and accomplishments of the Conservancy, and a potential campaign to celebrate its twenty-fifth anniversary in 1987. The minutes note that "in actual fact, the Conservancy's primary role is not saving land, it is raising money which results in land being saved." It may have seemed that way to the trustees of the time, but today it is more usual to think of NCC's role as being a fusion of those two vital functions of a non-governmental conservation organization: the integrated needs of raising money to undertake planning studies and to protect and steward large tracts of natural lands.

It was noted during that same meeting that "NCC is really not as effective as it could be" at raising money, and there was a need to plan for more strategic fundraising initiatives. To that end, some of the trustees favoured a realignment of the composition of the Board, to be achieved by appointing more people who would be effective in raising funds for the organizations, as well as more women and a somewhat younger demographic. It was also suggested that the Board might need fewer scientists as trustees, and that instead those specialists could serve on an advisory group, whose chairperson could be on the Board. However, rather than pursuing that relatively stark option, a middle way was followed that continues today: a larger number of trustees help to bring funds and business expertise to NCC, and typically three or four trustees are scientists, usually ecologists or high-level naturalists. Moreover, since 2000, NCC has gone on to establish regional Science and Stewardship Committees to review planning documents and project proposals. Those groups, along with the science trustees, ensure that due diligence is met with respect to ecological criteria for high-quality conservation work.

In 1984, a collaborative project known as Carolinian Canada was announced. This joint project of the Conservancy and World Wildlife Fund (Canada) was intended to develop a conservation strategy for the imperilled biodiversity of southwestern Ontario. The Carolinian ecozone accounts for less than 1 percent of the land area of Canada but supports a much larger fraction of the biodiversity of the country, especially species and ecological communities that are typically more abundant to the south in the eastern United States.[8] In fact, this relatively small ecozone supports a larger number of species of both plants and animals than any other in Canada, including about twenty-two hundred species of herbaceous plants and seventy species of trees. About four hundred species of birds have been observed, representing more than half of those occurring in Canada. Because only about 3 percent of the Carolinian ecozone is still in a natural condition, there are many imperilled species and ecological communities. This includes more than 130 species that COSEWIC lists as being at risk on a national basis and more than four hundred species considered rare in Ontario. The following communities are some of the fifty-eight natural communities considered rare in the ecozone: tall-grass prairie, savannah woodland, southern hardwood forest, and various kinds of wetlands.

The initial funding for the Carolinian Canada program was $400,000 over two years, equally sponsored by the Richard Ivey Foundation and the Ontario Heritage Foundation. The initiative still survives as the Carolinian Canada Coalition.[9] Now, however, it has a wider base of funding, receiving support from various foundations, governmental agencies, corporations, and individuals. The initial planning studies for the program identified thirty-six sites as critical natural areas that should be conserved, with the total estimated funding for the necessary securement actions being about $1.3 million (or about $2.5 million in 2011 dollars).[10] In hindsight, this amount was enormously underestimated, in view of the much larger sums that NCC and other conservation organizations have already spent to acquire natural lands in the Carolinian ecozone. By 2011, NCC alone had purchased land worth about $36 million, and donations had helped NCC acquire land and easements worth an additional $3.5 million (a total of seventy-seven properties and 4,131 hectares [10,200 acres] in southwestern Ontario).[11]

Nevertheless, that study helped to focus the development of projects for the various conservation organizations that were involved. NCC's particular role was the acquisition of privately owned lands, for which the Conservancy was expected to raise about $250,000 during the first three years of the program. Between 1984 and 1994, Carolinian Canada funded projects that resulted in the acquisition of about 810 hectares (2,000 acres) by conservation groups, plus more than six thousand hectares (fifteen thousand acres) of voluntary stewardship by private landowners. Since then, the organization has focused on a "big picture" project to develop a system plan for the Carolinian ecozone, using the best available conservation science and computerized mapping technology. This plan is now widely used to develop partnerships and undertake conservation actions.

In 1984, George Francis, a trustee and chair of the Projects Committee, presented a discussion paper to the Board titled *The Nature Conservancy of Canada and Its Projects/Scientific Advisory Committee*. The document states the position that the well-established business acumen and practices of NCC must be balanced against high-level scientific advice and oversight on strategic planning and acquisitions. The paper examines the direction and actions the Scientific Advisory Committee was taking to identify the best places where NCC should be working, while also scrutinizing proposed projects for their ecological merit. In addition, the working paper explored the needs for stewardship, although at the time NCC tended not to hold lands.

In 1985, NCC modified its vision statement in its annual report, with the key change being the removal of a sentence that had stated: "The Conservancy does not hold the properties it purchases, but transfers them to other conservation organizations for management and protection." This important modification reflected the growing emphasis on NCC undertaking projects that it would then own and manage instead of routinely passing them to conservation partners that would be responsible for the stewardship.

The minutes of a board meeting in January 1985 include the first recorded mention of the acronym *NCC* to represent the Nature Conservancy of Canada. More importantly, during that meeting the trustees received a draft report from their Projects Committee titled *Proposed Site Assessment Criteria for Recommending Natural Heritage Areas for NCC's Involvement*. This document represented an important step forward in terms of setting a high and consistent bar of ecological standards for conservation projects. The key criteria included whether the site had representative or rare/exceptional ecological communities, the richness of habitats or communities, the level of ecological integrity (this is related to the natural condition of the area; see endnote 4 in chapter 2), the presence of rare or unusual species, and any other special wildlife or ecological features.

Also at that meeting, trustee Robin Fraser presented a memo "in regard to the structure and makeup of the Board of Trustees and Committees" that clearly specified the roles and responsibilities of those key volunteer groups. This important document clarified the terms of reference for these persons within NCC's corporate structure. Fraser recommended that the Board be composed of a maximum of twenty-four trustees, with a quorum of five, and that appointments should be for two renewable three-year terms. A trustee could serve for longer but would have to retire from the Board for at least one year before being renominated. The term for officers of the Board (chair, vice-chair, secretary, and treasurer) was to be one year, on the basis of annual appointments, but the chair could not serve for more than two years. The secretary and treasurer did not have to be trustees, and staff persons of NCC could not also be trustees. The Executive Committee was to be elected annually by the Board, and it was to consist of the chair, vice-chair, immediate past-chair, and at least three but no more than nine additional trustees. The Board had the power to appoint committees as it deemed appropriate.

At a meeting in July 1985, Lloyd Mayeda's retirement from the executive director position was announced. He would be temporarily replaced by Darryl Peck, the national projects director, who would serve as the acting executive director while a search was mounted to fill this vital position. At the next meeting of the Board, in October, Peck provided the trustees with a substantial report in which he presented the recent business results and made numerous recommendations for improvements to operations. In addition, the trustees congratulated Peck for having organized a successful donor recognition dinner the night before the meeting. The Inn-on-the-Park in Toronto hosted this event, which was attended by two hundred invited guests. The dinner recognized the many supporters of NCC as well as the extensive contributions of Charles Sauriol. It was also a platform for the announcement of a $3-million fundraising goal to celebrate NCC's twenty-fifth anniversary in 1987.

Tom McMillan, the federal environment minister, was a keynote speaker at that event. The meeting minutes after the event quote him as saying, "If I do my job as well as you [NCC] are doing yours, generations of Canadians will enjoy the richest, most varied and most valued environment anywhere in the world." McMillan also announced an accord between his department and the Conservancy called the Nature Conservancy of Canada Trust Agreement, which appointed NCC as a trustee in the acquisition of donated land for use as part of a national park or national wildlife area. This program involved a greatly enhanced tax benefit to encourage the donation of such lands, allowing NCC to issue a tax receipt for 100 percent of the appraised donated value of qualifying properties. This was the first programmatic engagement of NCC with the Government of Canada.

Also at that event, NCC unveiled its first graphical logo, an impressionistic green-coloured image of Canada that was intended to evoke the dynamics of wind, water, and landforms as seen from a high-altitude view of the entire country. McManus and Associates designed the logo and donated it to NCC. The new motto of NCC was "Conservation for Life," which was explained in the 1985 annual report as being intended to evoke "our belief that land is the basis of life and that Canadian land preserved by NCC will remain so in perpetuity." Interestingly, the name of NCC in French had reverted to la Société canadienne pour la conservation de la nature.

Also in 1985 the Board organized a task force of six trustees with Tom Beck as chair to investigate the question of the organization retaining ownership of large numbers of properties, rather than routinely passing them on to other organizations for ownership and management. Their report concluded that "Although the funding and manpower requirements for The Nature Conservancy of Canada to become more involved in land ownership and land management are substantial, it is inevitable and a logical step in the growth and maturation of this organization to move into these activities. The question remains, however, as to how quickly we can organize the planning, finances, staffing, and volunteer involvement to deal with this new program thrust." At the time, NCC owned only ten properties totalling 1,261 hectares (3,114 acres) and having a book value (at acquisition) of $392,000.

At a board meeting on February 11, 1986, it was announced that Gerry Glazier had been hired as the new executive director. Glazier had been attracted to NCC and the not-for-profit sector from previous employment in the "oil patch," where he had worked for Petro-Canada as a senior manager dealing with environmental issues. The Glazier appointment represented a step forward in the increasing professionalism of NCC operations, and within that context Glazier was paid a competitive salary.

The previous evening, William Blair, the president of The Nature Conservancy (US), had given an address to a gathering of NCC supporters at the University Club of Toronto. At that meeting, Charles Sauriol was again feted, being introduced as "the heart and soul of the Conservancy." Blair's speech about TNC was intended to provide a model that NCC, a much smaller organization, might consider emulating. He noted that TNC revenues in 1984 were $53 million (US), of which 60 percent was raised from foundations, 34 percent from individuals, and 6 percent from corporations (for comparison, NCC's revenues that year were $785,000, or only 1.5 percent those of TNC, with 57 percent received from foundations, 25 percent from individuals, 9 percent from corporations, and 9 percent from governments, interest, and other sources).[12] TNC spent about 10 percent of its revenues on fundraising (an indicator of its overhead costs), 14 percent on stewardship, and the remaining 76 percent on acquiring conservation properties. At the time, TNC owned about 122,000 hectares (300,000 acres) in eight hundred nature preserves. Meeting minutes record that Blair also noted that, at TNC, "everyone is a fund-raiser . . . that is the name of the game . . . we are the best conservation organization in the country."

During a meeting of the trustees in July 1986, it was noted that only half of the trustees were current donors to NCC. However, during the ensuing discussion it became clear that some trustees felt that their time was enough of a contribution to the organization. There was further discussion of this recurring issue during the next meeting, in August, and the following policy was adopted: "It is not a requirement that a Board member make a financial contribution. On the other hand, those Board members who are able and willing to donate funds in addition to the donation of their time, talents, and expertise should be encouraged to do so." Wilfred Bigelow, the chair of the Board, followed up by writing a letter to all trustees in which a cash donation was solicited. In the letter, the suggested range of a suitable donation was $1,000 to $5,000 per year for five years, with the "scientific members of the Board" being asked for a smaller amount.

In 1986, the Conservancy entered into an important collaboration with The Nature Conservancy (US). The goal was to use biodiversity-inventory software and other methodology developed by TNC to establish a network of conservation data centres (CDCs) in Canada. This new initiative would greatly improve the capability for conservation planning by NCC and many partner organizations across Canada. It was moved forward by NCC signing a memorandum of understanding with The Nature Conservancy (US) to use its *Natural Area Inventory Program* software and related methodologies to establish a network of CDCs in Canada.

The purpose of a CDC is to conduct systematic inventories to find and document populations of rare species, and to study and classify ecological communities within some designated region, such as a province or territory.[13] A CDC also provides reliable information about the locations of rare biodiversity to specialist interest groups as well as the broader public, which is mostly done through an Internet portal. Many CDCs began as a partnership involving governmental and non-governmental organizations, but once established they are usually housed and operated by a government agency. If fully staffed, their employees typically include specialists in biodiversity, ecology, geographic information systems, and data management.

The initial goal of NCC in this partnered venture was to establish a CDC in one or two provinces, and to then work to complete a network of the facilities across Canada, including a national CDC. To help stimulate the process, Sue Crispin, a TNC employee and specialist, moved to Toronto to work with NCC on the CDC file. The first CDC to be established was the Centre de données sur le patrimoine naturel du Québec, which was launched in 1988. The next was the British Columbia CDC in 1991, then the Saskatchewan CDC in 1992, the Ontario Natural Heritage Information Centre in 1993, the Manitoba CDC in 1994, the Alberta Conservation Information Management System in 1996, the Atlantic Canada CDC in 1997 (which covers all four provinces in that region), and the Yukon CDC in 2002. In 1999, NatureServe Canada, a national not-for-profit organization, was established as a network to help the various CDCs engage in collaborative projects.[14] NatureServe Canada is the Canadian affiliate of NatureServe, an international organization that also includes fifty-three CDCs in the US and eleven in Latin America.[15] The establishment of a network of CDCs in Canada is a success story of conservation, although one that is tempered by perennial underfunding and other constraints on the operations of the system.

Also in 1986, the popular magazine *Nature Canada* ran an eight-page article about NCC, titled "A Gift to Last." It was illustrated with colour images by Freeman Patterson, a well-known photographer from New Brunswick, who a few years later became an NCC trustee. The article celebrated NCC's conservation achievements in various parts of Canada and described the key role of the Conservancy in building partnerships to raise funds for projects that were often quite complex. It also profiled NCC's tough, business-like approach to the development and execution of its conservation projects.

The minutes of a board meeting in May 1987 refer to a modification of the letters patent of NCC. The "purposes and objects of the Conservancy" were modified as follows: "(a) To identify, preserve and manage lands and the flora, fauna and natural features thereof, in Canada and elsewhere, having significant natural values; and (b) To educate and inform the Canadian public in regard to such aims and to co-operate with other Canadian and international organizations having similar aims and to encourage scientific research and educational services in regard to such lands and aims." In the original purposes and objects, the terms (a) and (b) had been listed in the reverse order, so the change represents NCC's greater emphasis on direct action through the acquisition and stewardship of lands, more so than on education and cooperative ventures. Overall, however, the changes represented only a modest refinement of the mission in response to changing environmental and societal contexts. The amendments to the letters patent also dealt with the new bilingual name of the organization: The Nature Conservancy of Canada – La Société canadienne pour la conservation de la nature.

Also at that meeting, the trustees were presented with a draft of the first strategic plan for NCC, which was to cover the period from 1988 to 1993. This action plan was intended to encourage more rapid progress of achieving the conservation mission, which was stated as "the identification, protection and management of natural area lands important for the maintenance of biological diversity." Following several months of discussion, the strategic plan was adopted by the Board at a meeting in December 1987.

An important new initiative late in this decade was a plan to rapidly build the number of NCC "members," who were in actual fact non-voting supporters. The key tactic in this strategy was a new recruiting effort by direct mail, with secondary actions being a limited amount of advertising in mass-media outlets, along with personal networking by trustees, staff, and the existing supporters of NCC. Many friends of NCC were pleased when, in early 1989, the Canadian Broadcasting Corporation devoted an entire edition of its popular newsmagazine *The Journal* to a description of the mission and accomplishments of the Conservancy.

In effect, this initiative was NCC's first national fundraising drive. Trustees Gordon Chaplin and Wayne Wright were particularly enthusiastic advocates of this strenuous—and costly—effort to increase the number of supporters of the Conservancy.

The direct-mail initiative involved sending a brochure and solicitation to a large number of people who had been selected as likely to be supportive of the work of NCC. Of course, the key to success in such a mailing rests in the list itself. For its first effort, NCC was given access to the subscriber lists for *Equinox* and *Harrowsmith* magazines, which provided about 300,000 prospects, as well as a list from Mountain Equipment Co-op, which supplied another 115,000 names. The first test mailing was undertaken in September 1988, with a budget of $10,000. It was timed to take advantage of the approaching Christmas season, during which many people donate to charities. The success rate for that first direct-mail solicitation was about 1.7 percent, which was considered a relatively good rate of return. At a meeting in July 1988, the Board decided to invest $75,000 in a second membership campaign of two hundred thousand direct-mail solicitations. At the April 1989 board meeting, the campaign results were announced: it had achieved a return of 2 percent, and the total number of NCC supporters had grown remarkably to about seventy-five hundred.

Of course, as the numbers of NCC supporters grew larger, more had to be done to track these donors and service their needs for information about conservation. Staff needed to be hired to manage the lists and design and produce newsletters, pamphlets, and other evocative materials.

In May 1988, NCC hosted a dinner to celebrate its twenty-fifth anniversary at the Caledon Mountain Trout Club, located in the Oak Ridges Moraine north of Toronto. The event was attended by forty-six trustees, staff, and a select group of high-end supporters of the Conservancy.

The next day, the trustees and staff got back to business at their annual board meeting, where the Board modified the NCC vision statement: "The Nature Conservancy of Canada is a national non-profit organization dedicated to preserving biological diversity. We identify, protect and maintain ecologically significant natural areas, and places of special scientific and educational interest." The important change was the simplification of the vision of working to preserve biological diversity, as opposed to the previous "preservation of ecologically significant natural areas, unique natural features, and places of special beauty . . . Wetlands, shoreline properties, islands, and areas which provide habitat for a wide diversity of flora and fauna, in particular for rare and endangered species, are priorities in the Conservancy's acquisition program." This statement remained in place until 1996 (with only a minor modification in 1990 to "the only national organization dedicated to"). Interestingly, the phrase *special beauty* was taken out of the mission statement, reinserted in 1997, and then permanently removed in 2001 in favour of non-aesthetic, science-based criteria for projects.

In December 1989, NCC and The Nature Conservancy (US) received collaborative funding from the Joyce Foundation of Chicago to undertake a binational survey of wetlands throughout the periphery of the Great Lakes. This was to be a two-year project to establish conservation priorities in the study region, as well as surveys of biota to determine ecological damage caused by pollution. The design of the project was appropriately ecoregional, meaning that its spatial limits were based on boundaries set by ecological and environmental factors, rather than those of political units such as provinces and states. The study was to involve all eight CDCs in the US, whose study regions included the Great Lakes watershed plus the Ontario CDC.[16] This Great Lakes project set a precedent for a suite of ecoregional projects undertaken by NCC, which it either completed itself or with a partner organization, that were binational in scope, where the ecoregion intersected with the Canada–US border. Moreover, NCC, TNC, and other partners went on to carry out additional binational projects in the Great Lakes ecoregion, including some relevant to the conservation of alvars,[17] islands,[18] and conservation blueprints for aquatic and terrestrial biodiversity.[19]

At a board meeting in April 1989, the trustees learned that Gerry Glazier, the executive director, would be resigning. He had been asked to head up a large project to train environmental professionals in Indonesia, run by Dalhousie University and funded by the Canadian International Development Agency. The Board quickly struck a committee to find the next executive director of the Nature Conservancy of Canada. After a wide-ranging search that attracted considerable interest within the conservation community of Canada, John

Eisenhauer was hired. Eisenhauer had held the position of executive director of Trout Unlimited Alberta. His assertive personality was well suited to taking NCC to a higher level of development on its mission of working to conserve the biodiversity of Canada.

The Conservation Program, 1981–89

A major project in 1981 was the acquisition of Great Manitou Island in Lake Nipissing, close to North Bay, Ontario. That 81-hectare (200-acre) island has an unusual volcanic geology and supports a large colony of great blue heron (*Ardea herodias*) and breeding osprey (*Pandion haliaetus*). The island was purchased at a cost of $310,000, provided by an anonymous donor.[20] It was later transferred to the Government of Ontario as the anchor property for Manitou Islands Provincial Park.[21]

In 1982, NCC helped to secure a property known as the Qu'Appelle Coulee, which was the organization's first project in Saskatchewan. This 64-hectare (157-acre) site near the town of Wolseley conserves a fabulous steep-walled canyon, or coulee, up to seventy-five metres deep, that was formed by erosion caused by fast-flowing water. (The region is relatively dry now, but in immediate post-glacial times there was abundant surface water from rapidly melting ice sheets.) The vegetation in the canyon is diverse, with mixed-grass prairie on drier south-facing slopes and woody vegetation on cooler, more mesic north-facing aspects. The property was purchased by NCC with funds provided by an anonymous donor who was living in Ontario but had heritage roots in Saskatchewan. The site is now owned by the province, and in 1991 was designated as the Qu'Appelle Coulee Provincial Ecological Reserve.

In 1984, the NCC Board approved the purchase of a property of 486 hectares (1,200 acres) on Brier Island, Nova Scotia. The acquisition proved to be rather complicated and did not close until 1988. This project involved a private American owner, who sold the property to the Maine chapter of The Nature Conservancy (US), but at a price of about one-half of the appraised value so that a US tax receipt could be received from the TNC. In turn, the Maine Chapter sold the property to NCC, which had raised funds from Wildlife Habitat Canada, the Government of Nova Scotia, Ducks Unlimited Canada, and several other donors. The property conserves coastal heathland, forest, and wetlands, including habitat for an endangered plant, the eastern mountain avens (*Geum peckii*), which at the time was only known from Brier Island and a disjunct site in the White Mountains of New Hampshire.

Although most plentiful on Brier Island, the rare *Geum* has since been discovered on nearby Long Island. The NCC property is co-managed with a stewardship group from the local community of Westport. The management plan allows for access to the site for picnicking, hiking, and even riding all-terrain vehicles, although passage is not allowed through sensitive habitat, such as that of the rare *Geum*. NCC also allows public camping on a restricted area of the property, to accommodate some of the many ecotourists who come to Brier Island for its famous whale-watching tours (it is one of the few places in the world where sightings are routinely made of the endangered northern right whale [*Eubalaena glacialis*]), excellent birding during the migratory periods, and botanizing during the growing season.[22]

In 1984, NCC became involved in the conservation of South Moresby Island in the Haida Gwaii (Queen Charlotte) archipelago off the northern coast of British Columbia. The protection of habitat in the region had become a high-profile environmental issue, with national- and international-scale advocacy led by the World Wildlife Fund Canada (WWF). The controversy focused on commercial logging of the remaining old-growth forest in the area as well as the traditional rights of the Haida, the First Nation of Haida Gwaii. Within this milieu, the key role of NCC was to quietly approach forestry interests, particularly Western Forest Products, in order to acquire timber rights in ecologically important and scenic habitats so they could be set aside as protected and ultimately be incorporated into a new national park. Eventually the conservation efforts by various interests resulted in the designation in 1993 of the Gwaii Haanas National Park Reserve and Haida Heritage Site, covering about 147,000 hectares (363,000 acres), based on an agreement between the Government of Canada and the Council of the Haida Nation.[23] Because the islands of Haida Gwaii have long been isolated from the mainland, a number of endemic taxa occur (endemics are especially frequent on isolated islands). These include the extinct Queen Charlottes Islands caribou (*Rangifer tarandus dawsoni*), six additional subspecies of mammals, three subspecies of birds, fifteen subspecies of sticklebacks,[24] four full species of insects, five species of vascular plants, and six species of bryophytes.[25] Later, in 1997, NCC (working with WWF) also secured a donation of about 130,000 hectares (321,000 acres) of rights to explore for offshore petroleum from several oil companies, which were retired and made it possible for Parks Canada to designate the Gwaii Haanas National Marine Conservation Area Reserve and Haida Heritage Site in 2010.[26]

In 1985, the Conservancy participated in its first project on the island of Newfoundland. NCC worked with the provincial government to acquire properties in an area known as Flat Island near Stephenville on the southwest coast. This area and its greater vicinity at Sandy Point have the most valuable breeding habitat in Newfoundland for the piping plover (*Charadrius melodus*), an endangered shorebird.[27] As it turned out, the title for Flat Island was uncertain, and because of the disputed ownership, the project did not go through on the first attempt. However, because of the important ecological values of the Sandy Point area, particularly to the rare plovers, NCC maintained its interest and in 2001 it began to assemble properties there. As of 2011, NCC had acquired a total of twenty-eight hectares (sixty-eight acres) of coastal properties in that focal area.

In 1986, NCC was a partner in a purchase within a wetland complex known as Alfred Bog, located about seventy kilometres east of Ottawa. The initial acquisition was 81 hectares (200 acres), and it was later followed in 1988 by another much-larger property of 1,539 hectares (3,800 acres). The key natural feature of Alfred Bog is an extensive raised (or domed) bog that has developed on an ancient but defunct channel of the Ottawa River.[28] Mer Bleue, an earlier NCC project, is a smaller nearby wetland that has a similar ecogenesis.[29] Alfred Bog is the largest bog of the raised sort in Southern Ontario, with an original area of about seventy-seven hundred hectares (nineteen thousand acres). However, large parts of the wetland have been affected by drainage for agricultural development or by horticultural peat mining, and its conservation had become a high-profile issue. Alfred Bog provides habitat for a variety of species-at-risk, including the bog elfin butterfly (*Callophrys lanoraieensis*), Fletcher's dragonfly (*Williamsonia fletcheri*), spotted turtle (*Clemmys guttata*), white-fringed orchid (*Platanthera blephariglottis*), and Atlantic sedge (*Carex atlantica*).

The engagement of NCC in this project had actually begun in 1983, when a meeting was held among the Conservancy, the Ottawa Field-Naturalists' Club, and representatives of the federal, provincial, and municipal governments. The 1988 purchase was for $725,000, with an unenforceable, but honoured promise from the vendor to donate $100,000 of that amount to NCC. However, at the time of the purchase's closing, NCC experienced a large funding shortfall because the Alfred Bog deal was happening at the same time as another big project (see below for information about the Brackman Island project in BC). NCC's financial capability was being stretched. The funding gap was covered by low-interest bridge-financing loans from the Ontario Heritage Foundation, the Long Point Waterfowl and Wetlands Research Fund, and the Laidlaw Foundation, plus a commercial loan from the Canadian Imperial Bank of Commerce. CIBC needed to be repaid within two years, and that loan was backstopped by the equity of the property as well as sureties provided by several of the NCC trustees, who put some of their personal wealth on the line. The NCC family experienced some nerve-racking times until eventually a successful fundraising campaign for this purchase allowed the various loans to be retired.

A number of subsequent acquisitions have increased the amount of protected area in Alfred Bog, including a large purchase by NCC in 2001 of 1,300 hectares (3,200 acres), at a cost of about $2.5 million. Today, the Alfred Bog is a protected area of 3,057 hectares (7,550 acres) that is managed by Ontario Parks as a natural environment class park. The success of the initiative to conserve the best natural habitats of Alfred Bog was celebrated in a 1988 article in the nature magazine *Seasons*: "For all of those who soldier on, looking for a breakthrough in other seemingly hopeless causes, the story of the protection of Alfred Bog should be an inspiration."[30]

Also in 1986, NCC acquired a property of twenty-two hectares (fifty-four acres) on Wilson's Lake in southwestern Nova Scotia. This was NCC's first securement in an ecoregion that hosts an assemblage of about ninety-one rare and at-risk plants known as the Coastal Plain flora, which in Canada is most well developed in the valley of the Tusket River.[31] Many of these species are listed as being at risk in Canada, including the pink coreopsis (*Coreopsis rosea*), thread-leaved sundew (*Drosera filiformis*), water pennywort (*Hydrocotyle umbellata*), and Plymouth gentian (*Sabbatia kennedyana*). Most of the coastal-plain species occur on the shores of lakes and rivers that draw down during the summer drought, exposing cobbled shores that the rare plants favour. As of 2011, NCC and its partners had accumulated about 1,602 hectares (3,957 acres) in that assembly area, most of it as an extremely large acquisition from J.D. Irving Ltd. that involved a combination of fee-simple purchase and donation. The Nova Scotia Nature Trust is also acquiring conservation properties in this assembly area.

In 1987, rancher Sandy Cross donated to the Government of Alberta about 810 hectares (2,000 acres) of prime foothills habitat, located only ten kilometres (six miles) southwest of the city limits of Calgary. Although owned by the province, the property was to be managed on a lease basis by NCC using monies from a $2-million endowment fund established by the Conservancy through a public campaign. In 1991, the site ceremonies were held to dedicate a newly constructed facility that would provide nature and outdoor education to schoolchildren from Calgary and its vicinity. This project is a dream realized by the Cross family, which, according to the meeting minutes, stipulated that the land "be used for conservation education" and "its habitat be preserved in perpetuity." At the time, the Cross donation of private land was the largest that had ever been made for conservation purposes in Canada. This property is now the Ann and Sandy Cross Conservation Area; it has an area of about 1,950 hectares (4,800 acres) and is operated by its own not-for-profit organization.[32] Each year it offers outdoor nature programs to thousands of schoolchildren (roughly five thousand kids participated in 170 programs in 2011), while also hosting day-walks for many visitors from nearby Calgary.

In December 1988, a single-issue meeting of the trustees was held. On the table was an innovative deal that resulted in NCC and the Nature Trust of British Columbia acquiring Brackman Island, located about 3.5 kilometres northwest of Sidney on southern Vancouver Island. The island was an important conservation target, but its owner was not willing to sell it at a price close to its fair-market appraisal. To move the project forward, a company owned by a NCC supporter purchased the mortgage of the island at a sheriff's sale and then initiated foreclosure proceedings. That tactic helped to persuade the island's owner to negotiate its sale at a price that reflected its market value. To further assist NCC in the purchase, one of its trustees, Eric Earnshaw, agreed to bridge-fund some of the costs. Once the island was acquired, a ninety-nine-year lease was entered into with the Government of British Columbia, which would manage the property as an ecological reserve. The province would pay $100,000 for the long-term lease, which helped to offset some of the cost of the purchase. Although only five hectares (twelve acres) in area, the island supports pockets of old-growth forest and thirteen plants that are designated as rare in British Columbia. This island was designated as a provincial ecological reserve in 1999 and then donated to the federal government for incorporation into the Gulf Islands National Park Reserve.[33] Note that at the same time that Brackman Island was being acquired, NCC was heavily engaged in the acquisition of Alfred Bog near Ottawa, all of which pushed the Conservancy's obligations to a level not seen before and gave the Board some anxious moments until the necessary funds were raised.

In 1989, NCC hired Larry Simpson as its regional director for Alberta. Simpson is still with NCC, and he is renowned for his ability to foster good relationships with landowners and to find ways that they can realize their personal vision of conservation by working with NCC. Over the years Simpson has helped to develop a remarkable number of conservation projects, some of them involving enormous assemblies, such as the ongoing Waterton Front Project that was about 12,133 hectares (29,970 acres) in size in 2011, as well as other extremely large projects, such as the 6,477-hectare (16,000-acre) conservation easement on the OH Ranch in 2009. More details are provided about these massive Alberta projects in following chapters.

In 1989, NCC acquired its first property in New Brunswick. This involved partnering with the Nature Trust of New Brunswick (NTNB) to acquire a small property of 1.2 hectares (3 acres) that supports a population of a globally imperilled plant, the Furbish's lousewort (*Pedicularis furbishiae*).[34] This site is now the George Stirrett Nature Preserve, named after a botanist who did fieldwork to document the populations of the rare plant, which occurs only at a few places on the upper St. John River in New Brunswick and Maine. At this particular site, the lousewort grows at the base of steep forested banks above the lower riverbank, a habitat that is naturally disturbed by ice-scouring and flooding in the springtime. This project had a cost of $7,000, with funding provided by the New Brunswick Naturalists, Xerox Canada, and the Canadian Wildflower Society. In 1992, NCC deeded the site to the NTNB, with a landholding agreement on title that commits the owner to necessary stewardship.

Also in 1989, NCC undertook its first project in the Yukon, which was a joint initiative with the territorial government, the Liard First Nation, and Foothills Pipelines (Yukon) Ltd. The project resulted in the establishment of the Coal River Springs Territorial Park, a protected area of 1,600 hectares (3,952 acres) in southeastern Yukon.[35] This site contains extensive terraces of an unusual surficial geology that sometimes develops in regions of limestone bedrock, in which groundwater rich in dissolved alkalinity erupts to the surface and deposits a crystalline veneer of tufa, an aquatic precipitate of calcium carbonate, over the ground, plants, and organic debris.[36] The cool-water Coal River Springs flow year-round through an extensive network of natural terraces of tufa, and a great richness of species is associated with the varying chemical conditions, which range from alkaline to acidic. The area also supports numerous plants of relatively southern distribution that are otherwise rare in the Yukon and abundant populations of larger mammals.

10

Working from Coast to Coast to Coast, 1990–97

In 1990, the Nature Conservancy of Canada was poised to achieve substantial growth in its operations. Its new executive director, John Eisenhauer, had a great deal of personal energy and expansive corporate ambitions. He immediately worked to find ways of ramping up the funds raised by NCC and the number and scale of the projects that the organization was undertaking. Additional employees were hired, further professionalizing the organization and advancing its goal of having staff and offices in key places across Canada. Some of the new employees enhanced the fundraising by direct-mail and other means, while others were engaged in landowner contacts and additional elements of project development in regions where the Conservancy was working most intensively. A science advisory network was formed and was routinely engaged to scrutinize the conservation value of proposed projects and to consider matters of stewardship. There was also strong NCC-assisted growth in the network of conservation data centres across Canada. Some impressively large projects were undertaken, such as Gowlland and Mount Broadwood in British Columbia and Old Man on His Back in Saskatchewan, as well as the beginning of an impressive property assembly in the Waterton Front region of southwestern Alberta (all of which will be discussed in more detail below).

For a while the improvements of staff capacity enabled the Board of Trustees to step back further from relatively direct engagement in many aspects of the operational activities and to focus more on the Board's core mandate of policy development, strategic planning, and oversight of finances and the scientific quality of projects.

The Organization, 1990–97

In 1990, the Board had twenty-one trustees from across Canada. Six NCC employee led by the newly appointed executive director, John Eisenhauer, were in Toronto. Other representatives of NCC were working in satellite offices in Victoria, Calgary, Burlington, Montreal, and Halifax. Of the regional staff, however, the only full-time employee was Larry Simpson, who worked out of donated office space in Calgary. NCC's total revenue in 1990 was $1.23 million,[1] including $53,000 in land donations. Of the cash revenue, 55 percent had been raised from governments, 23 percent from foundations, 17 percent from corporations, 2 percent from individuals, and 3 percent from interest and other sources. Although individuals provided only a small part of the total revenues, these donations were being given by a historically impressive 7,300 supporters. NCC's capital assets in land had a value of $2.45 million in 1900. The general and administrative costs were about $360,000 annually.

In May 1990, the trustees moved to implement an improved process for the approval of conservation projects undertaken by NCC. It consisted of the following steps: (1) project staff would develop a proposal based on the ecological merits and projected costs of a potential acquisition; (2) the Science Advisory Committee (SAC) would review the proposal with respect to its ecological values and provide a recommendation to the Board; (3) project staff would make changes required by the SAC and also prepare a plan to raise the necessary funds; and (4) the project would then go to the Board or its Executive Committee for approval. To ensure that the SAC could carry out its due diligence with respect to science review, its membership was expanded by recruiting additional ecologists and expert naturalists from across Canada, and its chair was asked to participate as a member of the Executive Committee of the Board.

During a strategic-planning session held in October 1990, the trustees decided that NCC should implement regional boards for the following areas: British Columbia, the Prairie provinces, Ontario, Quebec, and the Atlantic provinces. Within that organizational structure, the national board would hold fiduciary responsibility for NCC, and the regional boards would in effect be committees having responsibility for the identification and initial vetting of projects and the necessary fundraising. Each regional board would have at least one national trustee, including its regional chair. The expectation was that this regionalization would allow for more effective fundraising because of the efficiencies of local networking, and the intent was for it to be in place by the end of 1991. However, things moved rather slowly, and by that date only two regional boards were active: one in Alberta supported by Larry Simpson as a regional employee and another in Atlantic Canada, dealing with four provinces, with trustee Bill Schwartz serving as the volunteer regional director. In 1993, additional progress was made when a regional board was formed in Quebec, with trustee Louise Lepage serving as the volunteer regional director.

At a meeting in November 1993, the Executive Committee again determined that it was a "high priority" for NCC to make more rapid progress on regionalization. A motion was passed that specified that a staffed regional office should be quickly established in Victoria. At the next executive meeting in February 1994, John Eisenhauer presented a national development plan to complete a system of regional offices by 1997.

During another discussion in the strategic-planning meeting of October 1990, some trustees expressed unease about the increasing stewardship responsibilities of NCC. The minutes contain the following text: "All acquired properties will be transferred to local authorities, except for special cases, such as the Ann and Sandy Cross Conservation Area" and "NCC acquires a stewardship responsibility upon acquiring land. A stewardship program, involving our conservation partners, for properties owned and then transferred, will be established by the end of March 1991." For a while these policies had the effect of greatly slowing the rate at which the Conservancy accumulated properties to which it retained title.

At a strategic-planning session, held in Cambridge, Ontario, in November 1990, a revised mandate was confirmed; NCC would now be known as "the organization in Canada that is in the business of acquiring lands of special value for conservation." In this context, the notion of *special value* was interpreted in terms of a property supporting some or all of the following attributes: native biodiversity, critical habitats, rare or threatened species, representative landscapes, prospects for educational activities, and high public profile. This expressed mandate for NCC clearly differentiated it from other conservation NGOs working at a national scale, such as Ducks Unlimited Canada, whose mandate at the time was focused on conserving the habitats of hunted waterfowl.

At a meeting in August 1991, Wayne Wright, then chair of the Board, proposed that NCC should use its contacts with senior bureaucrats and politicians to pursue tax changes that would be favourable to conservation actions by land trusts, and it was decided to move forward with that useful initiative. At a meeting in June 1993, the trustees received a report from an ad hoc group of NCC volunteers who had been studying the tax implications of land donations, with the intent of meeting with representatives of governments to propose improved legislation. A major problem at the time was associated with capital gains, in the sense that if a conservation property had appreciated in value during the tenure of an owner, then tax was payable on that capital gain, whether the property was being sold or donated to a charity. The fact that a landowner could not just "give it away," and in fact would be liable for a significant cost if that was done, was an enormous disincentive working against donations of ecologically important lands to land trusts in Canada. Interestingly, at the time there were no capital-gains taxes for works of art that were donated to a charity even though art can be subject to substantial variations of appraisal value, generally more so than those for land. Another problem was that the use of a receipt for a charitable donation was restricted to a maximum of 20 percent of the net income of the donor in the year of the gift, rather than 100 percent of the land value (if the 20-percent limit was not reached, the differential could be carried over for up to six years, but to the same 20 percent cumulative maximum). Discussion of these and other tax issues had been greatly stimulated by the recent publication of a document titled *You Can't Give It Away: Tax Aspects of Ecologically Sensitive Lands.*[2] NCC was determined to work with governments to change the situation in ways that would be sympathetic to conservation. Because NCC does not engage in public advocacy to encourage changes in governmental policy, it pursued its goal by meeting with senior bureaucrats and politicians, rather than by criticizing anyone in an open forum. As we will see later, this quiet approach eventually bore fruit.

At the spring meeting in May 1992, the Board ratified NCC's new logo. This graphical symbol, rendered in an appropriate green colour, featured the name of the Conservancy in large block letters, with a stylized bird soaring above it and a single maple leaf on the right side. This logo is still being used today.

At a meeting of the Executive Committee in May 1992, Robert Carswell, a trustee from Montreal, informed the Board that a legally arm's-length organization had been established to assist NCC with its work in Quebec. It was named La Société canadienne pour la conservation de la nature (Québec)/The Nature Conservancy of Canada (Quebec). On December 4, 2002, the name was modified to its present one: Conservation de la nature—Québec, referred to by the acronym CNQ. In essence, the creation of CNQ was required because the laws of Quebec limit the ability of organizations not located in the province to own land exceeding 1.6 hectares (4 acres) in an "agricultural zone." To meet this condition, CNQ, a corporation that is legally independent of NCC, entered into a service agreement with NCC under which CNQ receives funding and administrative support from NCC to achieve its objectives. In turn, CNQ leases to NCC the lands it has acquired with NCC funding.

Soon after CNQ was established, but also in 2004, an arms-length organization was established in Prince Edward Island to assist NCC with its work in that province. This was necessary because non-residents of the province (of which NCC, a company incorporated under the federal Corporations Act, was one) were not permitted to hold more than two hectares (five acres) of owned or leased land. As a resident corporation, NCC (PEI) Inc. can hold up to 1,215 hectares (3,000 acres). It achieves its objectives through the funding and administrative support of NCC under a service agreement similar to that entered into between CNQ and NCC.

Also in 1992, the NCC office in Toronto moved from its space above a dry-cleaning business to a more commodious and less odoriferous workplace in an office building on Eglinton Avenue. The employees working out of the national office were appreciative of this move, and the new space was considerably more suitable for habitation by a leading conservation organization.

In March 1993, NCC hosted the first-ever workshop of its national Science Advisory Committee (SAC). That volunteer group was chaired by trustee Bill Freedman, an academic ecologist, and at the time it consisted of about fifty expert naturalists, biologists, and ecologists from universities, governments, and the private sector. From time to time, those people would be asked to assist NCC with conservation planning, site assessments, stewardship, or other volunteer tasks relevant to their local or professional expertise. Major themes of discussion during the workshop were the meaning and measurement of ecological integrity, stewardship, advocacy, conservation in northern areas, and the ways that scientists could play a more useful role in the Conservancy. The report resulting from the workshop made twenty-one consensus-based recommendations to the NCC Board about the roles and responsibilities of scientists and science within the organization. After several rounds of discussion by the trustees over about a year, the recommendations were adopted by the NCC Board for implementation in the organization. Some of the key ideas were to reconfigure the volunteer science group as a science advisory network (SAN), to impose a three-year renewable term on the members, to continue to have NCC focus its conservation efforts on southern regions of Canada, to work in the north only on an opportunistic basis, and to routinely use the services of persons on the SAN on an as-needed basis for science-related work. At the time, NCC did not have any scientists as employees, so the use of these expert volunteers was critical to ensuring that projects were credible with respect to conservation science.

The minutes of the September 1994 board meeting reveal the first recorded discussion of the need for NCC to establish an entity in the United States that would be capable of accepting donations of cash or land in Canada against a US tax receipt. At the time, NCC could receive donations of Canadian property from American owners only in an indirect manner. The donation had to first be made to The Nature Conservancy (US), which would issue a tax receipt to the donor, and then TNC would pass the title or other gift to NCC. This procedure could be awkward and slow, and TNC was not always enthusiastic about co-operating in such deals because it did not want to run the risk of being seen as a conduit of US tax benefits to a non-US organization. The minutes of a meeting in June 1996 record that a new charity, The Friends of the Nature Conservancy of Canada, had just been incorporated in New York but had not yet received its charitable status from the US Internal Revenue Service. It took some additional years for this new corporate entity to eventually become established and operational, as we will learn in a following chapter.

Also at that meeting in September 1994, the Board learned that the Georgian Bay Land Trust (GBLT) had approached NCC with a proposal for co-management of a new $2-million trust fund that a donor had established to purchase and steward lands in the eastern coastal region of Georgian Bay, Ontario. This resulted in a long-lasting and productive collaboration involving the two land trusts and the provincial and federal governments. As of 2011, the trusts had secured 788 hectares (1,947 acres) of high-quality lands, almost entirely in the southern part of the region, where ownership is mostly private and development pressures are intense. In addition, governments have set aside 97,900 hectares (241,725 acres) of Crown lands as parks and conservation reserves, mostly in the northern part of the coastal region of Georgian Bay.

At a meeting of the Executive Committee in February 1995, the issue of stewardship responsibilities was again discussed. At the time, NCC was holding more than one hundred properties, and the stewardship needs of many of those lands were becoming increasingly problematic given a lack of funding to undertake them at suitable levels of diligence. It was clear that NCC had to ramp up its policies and capacity relevant to the stewardship of its properties, and this conundrum was gripping the attention of the Board and senior staff.

However, some uplifting information was also received at that meeting: NCC had just received a generous bequest of $850,000 to support projects in British Columbia. This particular gift was a significant event, as it marked the beginning of substantial revenue flows from these kinds of legacy gifts, which have since developed into a key income stream. Because of the large amounts of cash that were now being held by NCC, partly as a result of the bequest from BC, the trustees discussed the need to implement a portfolio of medium-term investments.

At the spring meeting of the Board in May 1995, the trustees authorized some important changes to the financial system. One was to convert the fiscal year-end from the end of the calendar year (i.e., the end of December) to the end of October. This was done to reduce the anxiety that was habitually associated with unpredictability of the flow of donations during the Christmas season—with the changed year-end those monies would be received and tallied earlier on. In addition, the accounting system moved from tracking two separate funds, the General Fund and Natural Area Fund, to a single one. This change simplified the accounting system, which had sometimes been complicated by the need to transfer money between the funds.

At that same meeting, the issue of stewardship was again discussed, once more prompted by problems that had arisen with respect to some properties that had been transferred to other organizations. They involved such issues as timber harvesting and excessive development of trails and other infrastructure, which threatened the natural values that NCC had sought to conserve when the properties were acquired. That discussion highlighted a dilemma faced by NCC at the time: the great obligations inherent in the stewardship responsibilities of properties whose ownership NCC retained versus the opposite tack of turning them over to other organizations for management, some of which did not have sufficient funding to do the necessary work.

In September 1995, the annual meeting of the Board was held at Tadoussac, Quebec. It featured a discussion of potential fundraising models for NCC. At the time, NCC was receiving gifts from a slowly increasing number of supporters, and the average donation amounts were also growing. The Board considered three budget scenarios that each varied in the assertiveness of the fundraising effort. It made the decision to pursue a relatively aggressive model by hiring additional fundraisers to assist the executive director with that core aspect of the operations, while also better using key volunteers to network with potential high-end donors. The ten-year budget scenario had the following strategic elements: (1) substantial growth of the overall conservation business of the Conservancy, (2) a move to larger assemblies of contiguous properties in focal areas vital to conserving biodiversity, (3) greater emphasis on the retention of secured properties, and (4) building of the capacity for conservation planning and on-the-ground stewardship. In addition, there was to be an improved property database, better financial planning, vitalization of a planned giving program to attract bequests, an empowerment of regional offices and their boards, and development of a portfolio of showcase properties across the country that could demonstrate the conservation work that NCC was doing.

Some of these initiatives were already moving forward and began to do so even more quickly. For example, at a meeting in December 1995, the trustees were presented with an advanced draft of a document titled *Guidelines for Regional Councils*, which was intended to define the roles and responsibilities of those entities. Also, a regional office had just been established in Manitoba (in 1994), located in office space donated by supporter Bill Loewen. The first employee of this office was Gene Fortney, who served as the regional director (he still works with NCC in land securement and stewardship, particularly in the tall-grass prairie ecoregion). In April 1996, at the spring meeting in Sidney, BC, the Board undertook additional strategic-planning exercises. The trustees examined the possibility of a large-scale campaign, to be called Nature Legacy 2000 and intended to celebrate the beginning of the next millennium in the year 2000. That campaign would be designed to attract larger numbers of high-end donors to the work of NCC, while also building the base of individual supporters. If successful, the campaign would lift NCC to a higher but sustainable level of conservation operations. The model was to follow the recent success in the recent Eagles of Brackendale campaign, which NCC had undertaken to conserve critical habitats used by large numbers of bald eagles (*Haliaeetus leucocephalus*) near Squamish (this is described in the following section on projects). Although it was to be a national campaign, in the sense that it would occur across Canada, Nature Legacy 2000 would largely be regionally based. It would be a campaign of regional campaigns, with high-end volunteer leadership and an exciting portfolio of important conservation projects. This April meeting was invigorating for all who attended, and NCC employees were directed to engage in the necessary feasibility studies and planning for the potential Nature Legacy 2000 drive.

After the strategic-planning sessions of the meeting of April 1996, the trustees turned to other matters of business. They talked about conservation agreements, a relatively new and increasingly used legal mechanism that was becoming enabled as the provinces passed legislation that allowed for conservation easements (also known as covenants and servitudes) that would attach to the title of a property.[3] Because a conservation easement could be acquired at relatively small cost compared with a fee-simple acquisition of the same real estate, their use might allow for large increases of conserved lands. However, conservation easements also carried some legal and conservation risks, especially in terms of their long-term security and enforcement. The key to their success is to have appropriately written and enforceable agreements.

The minutes of April 1996 also contained the first recorded mention of the term *carbon credits* in the context of conservation projects. These are associated with the fact that natural habitats store large amounts of organic carbon in their biomass, and thereby provide offsets against anthropogenic emissions of carbon dioxide and other greenhouse gases.[4] The theme was introduced by trustee Bill Freedman, who had recently published research concerning carbon credits in forest biomass for the Tree Canada Foundation. The topic of carbon credits came up many times in subsequent meetings, and in 2011 the Conservancy engaged in its first sale of this monetized ecological service, as is described in a later chapter.

The minutes of a meeting in June 1996 show that monies held in the Long Point Waterfowl and Wetlands Research Fund had been transferred from NCC to the Long Point Bird Observatory. Similarly, in September 1996, all endowment funds associated with the Ann and Sandy Cross Conservation Area were transferred to an independent foundation that had been established to run that conservation area and its activities. By undertaking these transfers, the Conservancy and its partners recognized that those two collaborative ventures had reached a sufficient maturity that they no longer required significant engagement from NCC.

In September 1996, the Board held its annual meeting in Baddeck, Nova Scotia. A key item on the agenda was discussion of the proposed Nature Legacy 2000 campaign, the biggest fundraising effort that NCC had ever considered undertaking. Some of the initial planning had been aided by new trustee Mel Cooper of Victoria, who had achieved considerable fundraising success in conjunction with the international Expo 1986 in Vancouver. During the meeting, Cooper said, "What we are doing is for Canada—forever." There were to be five theme areas to the proposed campaign: threatened habitats, imperilled species, ancient forests, wildlife concentrations, and community-based initiatives. Several trustees advocated for the addition of two more themes—marine and international projects—but this idea was not widely supported. The initial target of the Nature Legacy 2000 campaign was to raise $46 million by the year 2000, which was not a particularly aggressive goal considering that it was only about a $10-million stretch from the Conservancy's base revenues at the time.

John Eisenhauer left the organization in February of 1997. In light of his departure the Board decided not to move forward with a Nature Legacy 2000 campaign until a new executive director was hired, and perhaps not even then. Meanwhile, a search was launched to find an executive director for the Conservancy. While that played out, the organization was supervised by an ad hoc Management Committee of senior trustees, who spent considerable time in the Toronto office on a rotational basis and also on other tasks needed to keep the Conservancy running well. Three trustees living in the Toronto area spent much time in the office helping to run NCC: Robin Fraser played a lead role, aided by Ted Boswell and George Francis, and they were assisted with certain tasks by Bob Carswell, Bill Freedman, and Bill Schwartz.

Bill Schwartz lived on St. Margaret's Bay near Halifax, and for several months he made occasional commutes to Toronto to help supervise NCC operations during its interim without an executive director. Schwartz was an experienced businessman and was passionate about the conservation mission of NCC, and he was needed and well suited to help run the organization during the interregnum. Tragically, one morning as he was leaving his rural home to drive to the airport to make a flying commute to the NCC office in Toronto, he suffered a heart attack. He died almost immediately, and having just put his truck in reverse gear, the vehicle drove backwards until it stalled against a tree. Several minutes later, Schwartz's partner, feeling that something was amiss, discovered him slouched in his truck. Bill Schwartz passed away in the midst of doing something that he felt was important and beneficial to the natural world and to Canada.

In late 1996, Jan Garnett was hired as a land-securement officer for British Columbia, joining BC director Kirk Davis, who had been hired in 1993. Together they worked to speed the rate at which projects were undertaken in BC, including the beginning of a series of acquisitions in the Cowichan Garry Oak Preserve and in the Campbell River Estuary. Garnett became the regional director in 1997 and remained with NCC until 2011, building up the numbers and capabilities of the BC staff. The region implemented some remarkable projects during her tenure, many of which are noted in following chapters. They include ventures at Darkwoods, Frolek Ranch, Kumdis Estuary in Haida Gwaii, Rocky Mountain Trench, Swishwash Island, and Tatlayoko Lake, as well as eight well-regarded ecoregional plans that have had a great influence on conservation actions in British Columbia.

At a meeting of the Executive Committee in December 1997, the Board approved proposals to acquire two properties in the foothills along the eastern boundary of Waterton Lakes National Park, on the eastern slope of the Rocky Mountains. These acquisitions were the first in a huge focal region that became known as the Waterton Park Front Project area,[5] where NCC has undertaken what for many years was Canada's largest private assembly of conservation lands. (About a decade later, it was surpassed by another NCC project, Darkwoods in British Columbia;[6] see chapter 12.) NCC is still working in the Waterton assembly area to create an extensive conserved landscape that will support large wide-ranging mammals and other biodiversity below the national park. This is an ecologically vital section within the context of the Yellowstone to Yukon Conservation Initiative (Y2Y),[7] a binational networking effort to maintain an ecologically viable corridor of natural habitats extending from the vicinity of Yellowstone National Park in Montana and North Dakota, all the way north to the coastal plain of the Yukon in northwestern Canada. A key objective of Y2Y is to maintain the necessary habitat conditions for large animals with extensive ranges, such as grizzly bear (*Ursus arctos*), cougar (*Puma concolor*), and timber wolf (*Canis lupus*), as well as large-scale ecological functions related to hydrology and carbon storage. The work by NCC in the Waterton Front area proceeded relatively quietly until 2004, when it was publicly announced as a project assembly of about 10,900 hectares (27,000 acres) of grassland and riparian habitat, the largest ongoing conservation project on the eastern slopes of the Rocky Mountains in Alberta. As of 2011, NCC had secured 9,751 hectares (24,078 acres) of fee-simple lands and 2,385 hectares (5,890 acres) of conservation easements in the Waterton Front region. Most of the funding for this large-scale project has been generously provided by The W. Garfield

Weston Foundation, with additional support from the Poole Foundation, and of course local ranchers.

Also in late 1997, NCC and several other environmental organizations made a joint application to the federal government for substantial funding to establish an initiative called Natural Legacy 2000. The intent was to celebrate and advance the conservation of Canadian nature in the impending millennial year of 2000. The participating organizations were the four leading conservation NGOs that were working at a national scale in Canada: the Canadian Nature Federation, Ducks Unlimited Canada, the Nature Conservancy of Canada, and the World Wildlife Fund (Canada). This group made a forceful pitch to upper-echelon strata of the political and bureaucratic reaches of the federal government, so much so that then Minister of the Environment Sheila Copps jokingly referred to it in a media interview as the "Gang of Four." Essentially, the project was designed to support a comprehensive program of research, planning, and land acquisitions that would significantly advance the conservation of Canadian biodiversity. Within that context, the special role of NCC was to engage in conservation planning and especially in property acquisitions. In October 1998, Prime Minister Jean Chrétien announced funding for Natural Legacy 2000, with $10 million to be shared equitably among the four conservation organizations. By the time this program finished in March 2001, NCC and its partners had completed 225 projects, which protected 24,300 hectares (60,000 acres) of natural habitats through land donations and conservation easements.[8] Although this large federal investment in a partnered conservation initiative was unprecedented in its scale, the $10 million was much less than NCC and the other organizations had asked for. Nevertheless, the notion of a substantial federal investment to support private-sector conservation initiatives had become seeded within the federal government. In 2007, it germinated and grew into a much larger level of support for the programmatic work of land trusts, led by NCC. This particularly great boost to private-sector conservation is described in chapter 11.

In June 1997, Elva Kyle of Regina became the first woman chair of the NCC Board. This appointment was made in recognition of Kyle's particular capabilities, and it also reflected progress toward an increasingly diversified Board.

Also in the summer of 1997, NCC established its first office in Regina, Saskatchewan. The first employee, Kimberley Cunningham, had been hired only a few months earlier as a project officer, and when the office was set up she was joined by Jordan Ignatiuk as a land securement officer. With these employees in place, NCC's conservation activities started to move much more quickly.

Another important initiative was the establishment of the first revolving fund intended for use in NCC's core programs (as opposed to the endowment for the Cross project, which was specifically directed to its benefit). This new National Land Conservation Fund was capitalized using monies from undesignated bequests. Its purpose was to provide bridge financing for projects that had a tight closing date but not all of the funds had been raised. The regions were charged interest on their internal loans from the fund at a rate just above prime. The loans were to be repaid in a timely manner, thereby allowing the new fund to be accessed by the NCC regions on a revolving basis.

One of the key Board initiatives during the period between executive directors was directed toward improving relationships with The Nature Conservancy (US) and with regional Canadian land trusts, some of whose dealings with NCC had become rather tense during the past several years. To that end, the Board established a working group to develop better relationships with like-minded organizations, consisting of trustees Bob Carswell, Robin Fraser, Bill Freedman, and Jon Grant. At a meeting in Vancouver with TNC and several Canadian land trusts in 1997, Freedman proclaimed that "a sea change" had occurred at NCC with respect to collaborative relations with other conservation organizations. This improved attitude of NCC was also expressed at other meetings, including high-level ones that involved only NCC and TNC. It quickly resulted in much better relationships with some previously aggrieved partners, and also in more collaborative ventures in conservation.

At the annual meeting in Regina in September 1997, the working group presented a report on discussions that had been held with The Nature Conservancy (US). It noted that TNC had annual revenues of about $170 million, compared with $14.7 million for NCC (1996 data).[9] The group reported that recent discussions between the NCC trustees and senior TNC staff had renewed the enthusiasm for working together and that various collaborative scenarios had been explored. The conversation had mentioned the possibility of amalgamation, although the NCC trustees had quickly rejected that idea in favour of continued sovereignty of the Conservancy. The minutes of a meeting recorded a letter from John Sawhill, the TNC president and CEO, who outlined his vision of the basics of a deeper collaboration between the two national organizations in this way:

- Mutual respect for the corporate identity of each organization, while cooperating and working together towards the common purpose of protecting our biological heritage.
- Identification of conservation priorities in furtherance of our common mission to preserve biological diversity should be based on bioregional or ecoregional perspectives and should be informed by the best available scientific data.
- Focus on mutually beneficial, on-the-ground conservation projects. Both of our organizations have a long tradition of targeted conservation actions and we both desire to continue our cooperation around specific land conservation projects, particularly where such projects serve multiple conservation objectives.
- Efforts to bring resources and expertise to enhance the respective organization's capacities. Both of our organizations have special contributions to make to add value to our cooperative ventures. We will pursue those opportunities where, by our working together, we can make the "whole greater than the sum of its parts."

Ultimately, NCC was to take the lead in collaborative ventures within Canada. However, it was recognized that, because of NCC's limited capacity, some projects might progress more slowly than TNC might like. At the meeting in Regina, the NCC Board passed a motion to agree in principle with the Sawhill letter and to develop a memorandum of understanding to formalize the articles of collaboration. The enabling memorandum was signed in early 1998 and it committed NCC and TNC to establish a strategic relationship to protect natural areas whose distribution is binational.

The Regina meeting also involved a session that looked at the composition and role of the national and regional boards of NCC. This session was led by trustee Ted Boswell, who was heading an internal NCC committee on the issue and had engaged Coopers and Lybrand, a professional services firm, to provide assistance. At the time, Boswell was the vice-chair of the NCC Board, and he was leading the effort to bolster the organization in preparation for the anticipated growth of its national-scale operations. According to the minutes, the consulting report indicated the following:

- NCC is a strongly centralized organization;
- The organization needed to decide whether to maintain the status quo or to expand;
- There should be systematic expansion to the regions;
- The National Office should provide seed money and direction to the regions;
- There should be latitude given to the regional offices to aid in their expansion and empowerment;
- NCC should establish a foundation or fund for regions to finance the opening of offices and expansion of operations, but the regions must provide accountability; and
- NCC needs to focus more on fund raising.

In view of the prognosis of a substantial growth of the Canada-wide operations of NCC, Boswell noted that the Board needed a somewhat modified role and different responsibilities. The key improvements were greater attention to attendance at meetings and to other commitments, participation in strategic planning, approval and evaluation of the executive director, execution of fiduciary responsibility and oversight of good business practice, oversight of science aspects of the conservation programs, help in fundraising, personal contributions of monies at a level commensurate with individual circumstances, and oversight that the Board is effective in its governance and all other responsibilities. Boswell's points were made with his customary force and dynamism, were thrashed out in a highly engaged discussion, and were then all accepted by a motion of the Board. An additional minor change was that henceforth, the members of the Board would be referred to as directors rather than as trustees, an amendment that was in keeping with current language in business environments and somewhat less confusing as to meaning.

The Board also revisited NCC's vision and mission statements in the Regina meeting. The new vision statement was "The Nature Conservancy of Canada will protect areas of biological diversity for their intrinsic value and for the benefit of future generations." The vital change here was overt recognition of the notion that the foremost reason to conserve biodiversity is in support of its inherent value, with benefits to people being a secondary consideration. This idea is consistent with contemporary musings in environmental philosophy about the value and importance of indigenous biodiversity. The notion of intrinsic value was subject to a focused discussion during the meeting, with a key proponent being Bill Freedman, and it was ultimately adopted as part of the NCC vision by a unanimous vote of the directors.

The new mission statement was "A Nature Legacy through Partnership. The Nature Conservancy of Canada will lead and use creativity in the conservation of Canada's natural heritage by: securing ecologically significant natural areas, places of special beauty or educational interest, through outright purchase, donations, conservation agreements, or other mechanisms; achieving long-term stewardship through management plans and monitoring arrangements." This statement recognizes the entrepreneurial spirit and methods of NCC, as well as the role of science-based conservation planning to inform the choice of focal areas and methods of stewardship. In retrospect, it seems odd that the directors reinserted the criterion of "special beauty" into the mission statement after a hiatus of almost a decade. When the mission statement was next revisited in 2001, this aesthetic reason for creating protected areas was again removed in favour of more objective, science-based criteria.

The Board also renewed its commitment to a speedy establishment of regional boards across Canada, which would essentially function as committees of the national board. Their role and responsibilities were expressed as follows: "The National Office will provide centralized support services, site assessment criteria, and overall program management and development" and "Conservancy Regions (Chapters) comprised of volunteer boards and members, with staffed offices and given meaningful decision making responsibilities, should be formed to provide an extension and strengthening of The Nature Conservancy of Canada on a local level." There was much discussion of the model of regional boards, including how to initially fund them, the need for their chairperson to sit on the national board, the establishment of regional science advisory networks, and the development of regional bylaws.

Another key point that was widely agreed upon was the need to maintain the model of "one Conservancy" that reflected a confederation of regional boards collaborating in a national landscape with regional economic and ecological disparities, so that resources must to some degree be shared. In a sense, this model is comparable to that of the governmental confederation of Canada itself, including its mechanisms to achieve a reasonable degree of financial equitability among relatively wealthy and less-so provinces and territories. By the end of 1997, NCC had established seven regional offices supported by volunteer regional boards, allowing fundraising and conservation programs to be better tailored to meet local needs, while still respecting national standards.

In late 1997, the Government of Canada authorized NCC to issue Certificates of Ecologically Sensitive Land for qualifying properties that NCC had secured as fee-simple purchases or conservation easements. The right to issue these certificates was important because they permitted NCC to apply for certain sources of federal funding, while also allowing landowners a measure of relief from capital-gains taxes for donations of qualifying conservation properties. Previously, only the Canadian Wildlife Service or Environment Canada could issue these certificates. When NCC became the first land trust to be allowed to do so it signalled a high level of federal confidence in the Conservancy's ability to identify and document high-quality conservation lands.

In September 1997, after a wide-ranging eight-month search that considered many candidates, the NCC Board announced that John Lounds would be coming aboard as the new executive director of the Conservancy. Lounds had most recently served as the executive director of the Federation of Ontario Naturalists and is a dedicated conservationist. He has proved to be a terrific choice to fill this extremely important position in the Conservancy and in the greater community of environmental organizations in Canada. In December 1997, Lounds presented his first *Executive Director's Report* to the NCC directors. This represented a new reporting mechanism that is rich in key data and policy analysis. It has since been routinely used to provide the directors with the updated information they need to execute their responsibilities of oversight of the financial and science aspects of the operations of NCC.

The Conservation Program, 1990–97

In early 1990, NCC began to work with Ducks Unlimited Canada and the Ontario Ministry of Natural Resources to secure about fourteen hundred hectares (thirty-five hundred acres) in the vicinity of Matchedash Bay. This project was the first to be undertaken under the Eastern Habitat Joint Venture of the North American Waterfowl Management Plan. NCC served as the land acquisition agent in the assembly, Ducks Unlimited as the banker that held and distributed funds raised from various sources, and the Ministry of

Natural Resources was to hold title to the lands. Matchedash Bay is a semi-enclosed riverine embayment draining into southern Georgian Bay near the village of Waubaushene. It is a productive complex of wetlands, including the most extensive marsh along the Georgian Bay shore as well as swamp, fen, and open-water wetlands.[10] The area is located at an interface between the hard granitic and gneissic rocks of the Canadian Shield and softer limestone-rich bedrock to the south. The bay is surrounded by a variety of terrestrial habitats, ranging from hardwood forest to land uses for agriculture and cottages. Because such a diversity of habitats is present, the area supports many species of plants and animals, some of which are at risk in Ontario and even in Canada, including nesting by the least bittern (*Ixobrychus exilis*), black tern (*Chlidonias niger*), and perhaps king rail (*Rallus elegans*). Matchedash Bay has been designated as a Ramsar Wetland of International Importance (see chapter 7, endnote 21) and as a Canadian Important Bird Area.

In 1990, NCC participated in the first acquisition of real estate in a still ongoing assembly of properties that at the time was referred to as the Western Prairie White Fringed Orchid Project, named after *Platanthera praeclara*. This rare and beautiful wildflower had first been "discovered" in Canada in 1986 in a small area of southeastern Manitoba. Botanist Paul Catling made that find. He had suspected that the rare orchid might occur in that area because of its recent discovery in nearby habitats in North Dakota.[11] Not only did Catling find the biggest population of the rare *Platanthera* in the world, he also discovered the unusual tracts of tall-grass prairie in that region of southeastern Manitoba. Interestingly, on the same field trip and in the same place, he also discovered the first occurrence in Canada of the Powesheik skipperling (*Oarisma powesheik*), a rare and endangered butterfly of tall-grass prairie.[12] Later on, from 2004 to 2009, Catling served as a director of NCC.

Today, the ongoing assembly of properties near the villages of Gardenton and Vita is known as the Manitoba Tall-Grass Prairie Preserve (MTGPP).[13] That first property acquired in 1990 was only 32 hectares (80 acres), but today (in 2011) NCC has 3,956 hectares (9,768 acres) in fee-simple ownership, 65 hectares (160 acres) of conservation easements, and 129 hectares (320 acres) of conservation leases (these are agreements that last for five years but are potentially renewable). However, the total area of the MTGPP, including lands owned and protected by governmental agencies, is much larger than the NCC properties, and it has reached an impressive 45,490 hectares (112,400 acres). The rate of acquisitions in this assembly area picked up markedly in 1992, when Gene Fortney was hired as the first NCC employee in Manitoba. He initially played multiple roles, serving as the first regional director to establish direction and gain support for work in the province, while also working as the land-securement representative for the tall-grass partnership and coordinator of stewardship activities on the preserve. Governmental partners with NCC in this long-term project include Environment Canada, Manitoba Conservation, the Manitoba Habitat Heritage Corporation, and Nature Manitoba. There have been many sources of funding, including The W. Garfield Weston Foundation, the federal and provincial governments, the Manitoba Naturalist Society, and in the early years Wildlife Habitat Canada and World Wildlife Fund (Canada).

The tall-grass prairie once covered an extensive area of relatively humid regions of the prairies, extending from the vicinity of Winnipeg to as far south as Texas. Because of the impressive height of the grasses and other perennial plants of this ecological community, the early explorers described it as a "waving sea of grass." The ongoing assembly in southeastern Manitoba is conserving the largest surviving tracts of tall-grass prairie in Canada, thereby sustaining critical habitat for a diverse suite of species-at-risk.[14] The most prominent plants are tall grasses such as big bluestem (*Andropogon gerardii*), little bluestem (*Schizachyrium scoparium*), Indian grass (*Sorghastrum nutans*), and switch grass (*Panicum virgatum*), which typically grow to one to two metres, but on good sites can grow up to three metres. There are also various forbs for which these habitats are critical, including endangered orchids such as *Platanthera praeclara* and the small white lady's slipper (*Cypripedium candidum*), as well as taller species such as lead plant (*Amorpha canescens*), Nuttall's sunflower (*Helianthus nuttallii*), prairie lily (*Lilium philidelphicum*), and coneflowers (*Ratibida*).[15] The protected tall-grass prairie also helps to sustain a number of declining grassland birds, such as the bobolink (*Dolichonyx oryzivorus*), clay-colored sparrow (*Spizella pallida*), and western meadowlark (*Sturnella neglecta*). Because the soil of most of the original extent of tall-grass prairie was relatively fertile and deep, almost all of this grassland has been converted into agricultural land uses. Today, less than 0.2 percent of this community survives. Note that there is also a smaller area of tall-grass prairie in southwestern Ontario, which is being conserved in the Ojibway Prairie Complex in the city of Windsor.[16]

Interestingly, the climatic regime of the tall-grass prairie is moist enough to support the invasion of the habitat by shrubs and trees, which if they grow too dense and tall would shade out the plants of the rare grassland. The tall-grass prairie was once a fire-dependent ecosystem that was naturally maintained by wildfires ignited by lightning strikes, and then by the Plains Indians who regularly burned the prairie to improve its habitat for the hunting of deer and other game. However, during the past century or so it was a common practice to quench wildfires. This allowed shrubs and trees to become excessively abundant in some remnants of tall-grass prairie, degrading its suitability for many dependent species. To deal with this recent situation, stewardship of the community includes prescribed burning to kill the woody plants and rejuvenate the grassland. The first prescribed fire on the MTGPP with NCC's involvement took place in 1992. The burning is typically done on a rotation of two to four years.[17]

In 1990, NCC received an important donation from Amoco Canada of mineral rights for a tract of 297 hectares (733 acres) in southern Saskatchewan. These rights were then transferred to the Government of Canada as an essential step to adding those unencumbered lands to the assembly that would become Grasslands National Park.[18] In 1991, an additional 2,227 hectares (5,500 acres) of mineral leases were donated by Amoco Canada to NCC and were also transferred to Parks Canada. In 2002, NCC further assisted in expanding this park by acquiring adjacent lands at Rock Creek. The Grasslands National Park is conserving some of the best remaining areas of short-grass prairie in Canada, and it provides habitat for many species-at-risk. Remarkably, a program began in the mid-1980s to reintroduce the swift fox (*Vulpes velox*) to the park, and in 2009 the black-footed ferret (*Musetela nigripes*).[19] These carnivores had long been extirpated from Canada, but some of the reintroduced individuals appear to be surviving.

Another exciting gift from an oil company occurred in 1992, when Shell Canada donated two contiguous properties of 8,947 hectares (22,092 acres) near Fernie in the Elk Valley of the East Kootenays of British Columbia. The highlight of the tract is Mount Broadwood, whose peak is an inspiring 1,448 metres (4,750 feet) higher than its base on the property in Wigwam Flats. The site has impressively abundant populations of ungulates such as elk (*Cervus canadensis*), mule deer (*Odocoileus hemionus*), white-tailed deer (*O. virginianus*), bighorn sheep (*Ovis canadensis*), and mountain goat (*Oreamnos americanus*). Large carnivores are also relatively abundant, including grizzly bear (*Ursus arctos*), black bear (*U. americanus*), timber wolf (*Canis lupus*), and cougar (*Puma concolor*). The area sustains diverse habitats, including two small rivers and three kinds of mature forest communities on sites that vary in moisture availability.

The area owned by NCC has been designated as the Mount Broadwood Heritage Conservation Area (MBHCA). This area is protected from subdivision and other forms of development, but hunting at controlled levels is allowed on the tract and Tembec Industries continued to own timber rights that were passed on from the former ownership (these rights were sold to Canfor Corporation in 2012). Tembec continues to harvest the area on a sustainable basis, and its management plan is subject to review and approval by NCC to ensure that larger conservation objectives are not compromised. However, most of the area of the MBHCA is not part of the timber-harvesting land base, and NCC retains the right to remove additional lands from that use incrementally over time.

Moreover, in 2004, NCC negotiated conservation agreements with Tembec to protect an additional 40,500 hectares (100,000 acres) of private land in the Elk Valley against subdivision and development, although forestry use remains permitted on part of that land base. This agreement included the purchase of 1,213 hectares (2,997 acres) of private lands between the MBHCA and the Elk River, and in the vicinity of the town of Hosmer, and the donation of a further 3,002 hectares (7,413 acres) of conservation covenants adjacent to MCHCA and extending farther up the valley in the Crowsnest Pass area toward the Alberta border. At the same time, an additional 35,045 hectares (86,533 acres) were temporarily protected by way of a ten-year moratorium agreement with Tembec that restricts subdivision and development. Because of the large increase in the protected area outside of the original MBHCA, NCC now uses the name Elk Valley Heritage Conservation Area to refer to the collective landscape of Mount Broadwood and the Tembec lands protected in 2004. The total value of these various projects is about $11 million. In the meantime, NCC and Tembec are continuing to collaborate to place durable conservation measures over portions of the extensive moratorium lands.

In the summer of 1992, the Conservancy began to work on a new long-term initiative to assemble critical habitats in the upper Bay of Fundy of New Brunswick and Nova Scotia that are used by several millions of migrating shorebirds during their autumn migration. The first acquisition was in 1994 and involved a cottage lot of only 0.4 hectare (1 acre) in the vicinity of Johnson's Mills, NB. However, this project has involved several focal areas, all in the upper Bay of Fundy, where huge expanses of mudflat are exposed during low tide where migratory shorebirds feed voraciously on small invertebrates in the surface mud.[20] The birds stay long enough to approximately double their body weight and then undertake the next stage of their migration, which is a non-stop 4,500-kilometre trip taking more than ninety-six hours to reach northern South America. However, when the shorebirds are feeding in the upper Bay of Fundy, and the tide is high, they must roost on sand-and-cobble shores. Because these are an uncommon habitat, the few good sites may become densely packed with the birds as they wait for the tide to fall. The most populous bird is the semipalmated sandpiper (*Calidris pusilla*), but other species also occur.

NCC has been progressively assembling the critical habitats used by the roosting shorebirds, especially at Johnson's Mills near Dorchester Cape, and also at Mary's Point and Daniel's Flats, all of which are listed as Important Bird Areas, as Ramsar Wetlands of International Importance,[21] and as Western Hemisphere Shorebird Reserves.[22] As of 2011, NCC had assembled 191 hectares (472 acres) at Johnson's Mills, 8 hectares (19 acres) at Mary's Point that are a key part of a managed area of 110 hectares (272 acres) owned by the Canadian Wildlife Service, and 235 hectares (580 acres) at New Horton just southwest of Mary's Point. In 2000, NCC launched a seasonal education and ecotourism centre at Johnson's Mills, which helps visitors to see and understand the shorebirds without disturbing them.

In February 1993, the Conservancy did its largest deal to date, in terms of the area conserved. This project involved receiving a donation of 670,599 hectares (1,655,800 acres) of mineral permits in the Old Crow Flats of the northern Yukon. By acquiring those extensive development rights, and then transferring that form of private property to the Government of Canada, NCC enabled the establishment of the new Vuntut National Park, which was proclaimed in 1995.[23] Its name means "between the lakes" and is reflective of the many shallow waterbodies that occur over much of the low-lying landscape. As many as three hundred thousand waterfowl breed in the region, with numbers increasing beyond that in the post-breeding period as birds gather from farther away to moult, feed, and stage prior to the southern migration. The area also includes some of the richest archaeological sites of early human habitation in North America. Vuntut National Park, along with the adjacent Ivvavik National Park and the Arctic National Wildlife Refuge in Alaska, also represent a binational effort to protect the extensive habitat of a large migratory population of caribou (*Rangifer tarandus*), known as the Porcupine caribou herd.

At a meeting of the Executive Committee in December 1994, the trustees had their first of many discussions of a coastal project in the Squamish Valley of British Columbia. This area, known as Brackendale, is located beside the busy Sea-to-Sky Highway that connects Vancouver to Whistler, a large skiing and resort destination. The key natural feature to be conserved is a part of the Cheakamus River that is seasonally used by as many as four thousand bald eagles (*Haliaeetus leucocephalus*), which congregate during November to February to feed on abundant runs of migrating salmon, particularly chum salmon (*Oncorhynchus keta*).[24] This feeding concentration of eagles is one of the largest in North America, but various development pressures were threatening aspects of the local critical habitat, such as riverine forest and large snags used for roosting. This project involved a partnership with the North Vancouver Outdoor School, and it included the protection of 170 hectares (420 acres) of habitat on the campus by way of a covenant (registered in 1997), the construction of a viewing and interpretation facility for the public, and the establishment of an endowment to provide for ongoing stewardship. The key sources of funds for this $3-million project were British Columbia Parks and a consortium of seventeen forestry companies known as the BC Forest Alliance. To celebrate the completion of that stage of the project, and to spread the word about the good work that NCC was doing in BC, a colourful magazine-style book was published, *The Book of Eagles*.[25]

Also in December 1994, the trustees discussed an exciting project near the town of Eastend in extreme southwestern Saskatchewan, involving an impressive 5,305-hectare (13,100-acre) property called the Butala Ranch. This property had been owned by the Butala family for a century, and they had carefully stewarded its natural values, maintaining almost all of it as native mixed-grass prairie. This type of ecological community has been extensively lost through conversion into cultivated agriculture or tame pasture,[26] to the extent that only about 30 percent of its original range in Canada is still extant.[27] The then owners, Peter and Sharon Butala, were contemplating retirement, but were loath to sell the ranch to anyone who might then damage its natural condition by intensifying the agricultural practices on the property. For some time they were in a quandary as to how to achieve their long-term conservation aspirations. Until one day, in 1993, Peter ran across a small advertisement in a magazine for the Nature Conservancy of Canada. He contacted NCC, and soon a deal was reached in which he would donate his property to conservation, with an endowment fund to be established to help provide for its stewardship, including the development of a facility for public education. The initial cost of this project was about $750,000, mostly to set up the endowment. In addition to the Butalas, partners who shared in the funding included Saskatchewan Environment, Saskatchewan Agriculture Food and Rural Revitalization, Environment Canada, Saskatchewan Wildlife Federation, SaskPower, TD Canada Trust Friends of the Environment Foundation, and the Eden Foundation.

This conservation deal was quite a relief for Peter, who loved the prairie and his well-stewarded family ranch. Sharon later wrote that Peter believed the ranch should be protected "because, riding it from spring to fall, day after day, year after year, he had come to understand his grassland as ecologically fascinating and, as it disappeared all around him, an increasingly precious property."[28] In July 1996, the Old Man on His Back Prairie and Heritage Conservation Area (OMB) was dedicated, and NCC officially took control of the property in 2001. Sharon described the meaning of this outcome for her husband in this way: "Peter Butala has become one of the lucky few in the world whose fondest dream and far, far more, has come true."[29] Sadly, Peter passed away in August 2007, but by working with NCC he was able to leave a natural legacy for the people and biodiversity of Saskatchewan and Canada, and he will be remembered as a champion of the prairies. Peter would have gotten a lot of satisfaction from knowing that, in 2009, wildlife biologists confirmed the presence of swift fox (*Vulpes velox*), an exceedingly rare native carnivore, on the OMB property.[30]

Stewardship of the OMB property has involved some forward-thinking measures, including the ecological restoration of about four hundred hectares (one thousand acres) of cropland to native grasses and forbs of the mixed-grass prairie. More famously, in 2003 NCC introduced a herd of fifty juvenile plains bison (*Bison bison bison*) to the property. This was done as an act of restoration, in the sense that bison were the original dominant large herbivore of the prairie ecosystem. However, it was also an appropriate stewardship action, because maintaining mixed-grass habitat in a healthy condition requires an appropriate level of grazing by big herbivores. The founder animals were obtained gratis from Parks Canada, which has periodic surpluses of bison in its ungulate-rich Elk Island National Park farther to the northwest in Alberta.

In March 1994, NCC acquired the 888-hectare (2,194-acre) Gowlland Property, located on the Saanich Peninsula near Victoria, British Columbia.

This property became a core part of the Commonwealth Nature Legacy, a park named after the Commonwealth Games that were held in Victoria in 1994. This protected area encompasses about 1,012 hectares (2,500 acres) of dry coastal Douglas-fir forest, as well as stands of Garry oak (*Quercus garryana*), both of which are natural communities that were once widespread in the region but whose old-growth stands now exist in less than 2 percent of their original extent. The area is now known as Gowlland Tod Provincial Park.[31]

In December 1995, NCC negotiated the surrender of mineral and timber rights and the donation of a tract of 1,701 hectares (4,201 acres) of wilderness in central Newfoundland. The timber rights were owned by Abitibi-Price, a forestry company, and the mineral rights by Noranda, a mining company. The tract is located north of Burgeo and consists of most of the watershed of the Lloyd's River, an area dominated by extensive shrubby barrens, conifer forest, wetlands, and riverine delta.[32] The diverse habitats support a richness of boreal species, including individuals of the endangered Newfoundland marten (*Martes americana atrata*). The area is also used in winter by many animals of the La Poile caribou herd. In 1996, the provincial government designated the tract plus some adjacent Crown land as the 1,893-hectare (4,674-acre) King George IV Ecological Reserve (named after King George IV Lake, which is within the area). This protected area conserves the largest undisturbed river-and-delta system in Newfoundland.

Also in 1997, NCC, working in collaboration with the World Wildlife Fund (Canada), secured an extensive area of about 130,000 hectares (321,000 acres) of private rights to explore for offshore petroleum in waters surrounding the Queen Charlottes (Gwaii Haanas) archipelago of coastal British Columbia. The rights were donated by several oil companies: Chevron Canada Resources, Mobil Oil Canada, Petro-Canada, and Shell Canada. NCC later turned the rights over to the Government of Canada, an action that was pivotal in allowing Parks Canada to eventually designate (in 2010) what is by far the largest marine protected area in Canada: the Gwaii Haanas National Marine Conservation Area Reserve and Haida Heritage Site.[33] These waters are famous for their marine biodiversity, which includes regular use by four species of large whales and other marine mammals, teeming seabirds, and a rich variety of fish and other aquatic biota. In 1993, Parks Canada had previously designated the Gwaii Haanas National Park Reserve and Haida Heritage Site.[34] As such, Gwaii Haanas is presently the only place on Earth to be protected from the top of its highest mountains to the depths of its regional sea floor. The announcement of the donation of exploration rights was made at a ceremony at Calgary's Palliser Hotel, attended by HRH Prince Philip, Duke of Edinburgh. Prince Philip, who was also the international president emeritus of the World Wildlife Fund, said the donation was "a very important gift to the Earth," adding that guests "see here today an unusual sight . . . four oilmen with budding haloes," in reference to the generous donation being made by the companies to support the conservation of such an extensive marine protected area.[35]

Also in 1997, NCC acquired another unusual kind of marine property consisting of 937 hectares (2,315 acres) of "water rights" in the Cole Harbour estuary, located just east of Halifax in Nova Scotia. This is a rare form of property that is sometimes held in coastal regions of eastern Canada, which includes the right to develop intertidal and marine habitats within the bounds of the estate.[36] In this case, NCC received a donation of the water rights for the entire estuary, a key habitat for migrating and wintering waterfowl and shorebirds on the Atlantic coast. The property was eventually turned over to the Province of Nova Scotia for incorporation into its Cole Harbour Heritage Park, which includes extensive areas of terrestrial habitat as well as the intertidal and subtidal habitats that NCC had acquired.

11

A Campaign for Conservation, 1998–2005

In 1998, the Nature Conservancy of Canada was poised to undertake substantial growth of its conservation operations. The progress was to occur in all aspects of the enterprise—in science-based planning for focal areas, in the number and scale of the projects that were taken on, and in the communications, fundraising, and partnership-building that are so vital to mission success. With strong encouragement from the Board of Directors, John Lounds, the new executive director, worked quickly to develop the Conservancy's capacity to attract the necessary levels of financial support to undertake more and larger conservation projects. He did this by hiring talented employees to take charge of the following vital sectors of the organization: financial and business management, fundraising, and conservation science and stewardship. Staffing and capabilities were also ramped up across Canada, and the network of regional boards was galvanized to move conservation forward within their domains. According to the new organization model, NCC regions had to raise most of the funding for their own projects. In a metaphorical sense, they could eat healthy meals only if they first cultivated and harvested the necessary food.

There were also timely investments in emerging technologies, particularly in geographic information systems that have become so vital to conservation science. In addition, the Conservancy began to embrace conservation agreements as a way to protect natural values while still allowing properties to directly serve the economy through compatible management, usually in agriculture. This new tool of conservation, used with particular measure in the western regions, can achieve meaningful results with much smaller expenditures than fee-simple purchases of real estate.

These various improvements resulted in impressive financial growth and momentum for larger individual projects designed to accommodate larger-scale ecological dynamics. There were also property assemblies to also achieve conservation at a larger scale, such as those at Johnson's Mills in New Brunswick, the Sutton Mountains of Quebec, and the Waterton Front of Alberta. The impressive enlargement of the conservation vision of NCC captivated several larger donors, most especially The W. Garfield Weston Foundation, whose generous support facilitated major securements across the country.

Increasingly larger fractions of the acquired properties were retained by the Conservancy. To help deal with the management obligations and support the expenses of core stewardship activities, a new endowment fund was established. An additional endowment known as the Weston Family Science Fund was used to establish a core science capacity in the national office, allowing procedures and standards to be determined and implemented across the country for conservation planning, site assessment, and stewardship.

On the whole, the outstanding qualities of this period of NCC's history resulted from John Lounds working with the Board to do the following things: energize and empower NCC staff to secure larger conservation properties, collaborate effectively with a range of like-minded partners, institutionalize ecoregional planning, and engage governments and Canadians in supporting the work of NCC across the country. Because so many competent employees were hired during this period, the Board was able to become much less engaged in NCC's operational activities, while more strongly formalizing its governance structure and diligently executing its base functions of policy development and oversight of finances, business operations, and the scientific quality of conservation planning, projects, and stewardship.

Notwithstanding all of that progress, the defining attribute of this phase of NCC's history was its first national-scale fundraising venture, called The Campaign for Conservation. This endeavour had an expansive vision that drove the Conservancy toward increasingly larger projects, while developing an improved capability for science-based planning, acquisition, and stewardship of properties. To achieve these benefits, NCC developed better communications and marketing systems, and learned to engage the support of highly influential Canadians in those vital functions, including through the new facility of a high-level campaign cabinet.

The Organization, 1998–2005

In 1998, the NCC Board had eighteen directors from across Canada. Eleven NCC employees worked in the corporate office in Toronto and twenty-six additional staff members were in Victoria, Vancouver, Calgary, Red Deer, Regina, Winnipeg, Guelph, Montreal, Fredericton, and Halifax. NCC's total revenue in 1998 was $13.4 million, including $5.2 million of donated conservation lands and easements.[1] Of the donated cash revenue of $8.2 million, 41 percent was given by foundations, 27 percent by about seventy-nine hundred individuals, 22 percent by governments, 9 percent by corporations, and 2 percent was earned in interest and other sources. NCC's capital assets in land and easements had a value of $24.3 million in 1998, and its endowment funds totalled $1.3 million, almost all in the National Land Conservation Fund. The general and administrative costs at the time were about $898,000 annually.

As was noted in the previous chapter, NCC and The Nature Conservancy (US) had signed a memorandum of understanding in 1998 to work together to protect binational natural areas. One result of this memorandum was a beneficial attitudinal change in NCC. It involved a diversion from a previous focus on conserving a portfolio of sites that are important to conservation but were often identified opportunistically to a much greater reliance on ecoregional planning to strategically identify areas and places where private-sector action would produce the greatest benefits for Canadian biodiversity. The new approach is based on the geographical boundaries of natural ecosystems and their defining environmental conditions and biota, including longer-term dynamics that operate at a large scale. Consequently, it is a more ecologically based methodology of conservation planning than one based on political boundaries, such as those of countries, provinces, or states. TNC had developed and been using ecoregional conservation planning for some years, and its insistence that the methodology be a basis of collaborative work with NCC was of benefit to both organizations.

The memorandum had a focus on binational ecoregions that occur in the south of Canada and also in the contiguous north of the US, so their ecological values are a natural legacy of both countries and are sensible regions for collaboration. For example, any conservation projects in the tall-grass prairie regions of Canada, which occur in southeastern Manitoba and southwestern Ontario, also help to conserve many of the same tall-grass biodiversity targets of the nearby US states, and vice versa. This is an ecologically appropriate way to do conservation planning and to undertake on-the-ground projects of securement and stewardship, which are ultimately intended to ensure the viability of indigenous biodiversity regardless of political jurisdictions. Nevertheless, this large-scale ecoregional context does not obviate the need to do what is possible to conserve biodiversity on a jurisdictional basis, such as with the natural heritage of Canada and its provinces. In addition to the benefit to NCC of a greater impetus for science-based ecoregional planning, the agreement with TNC stimulated a helpful northward flow of financial support from some state chapters for conservation projects in shared eco-regions in adjoining provinces.

In December 1998, John Lounds and Larry Simpson made a presenta-tion to the House of Commons Standing Committee on Finance about the severe constraints that were being posed by capital-gains taxes on donations of ecologically important property. Afterwards, they met with Paul Martin, then–minister of finance of the Government of Canada, to deliver the same message. Their story made a great deal of sense: The appraised value of natural lands held by a private interest typically increased over time, and the accrued capital gains were subject to a tax. Although capital-gains tax is appropriate in the context of property that is sold for profit, it is a large financial disincentive to landowners who would like to donate an ecologically important property to a land trust. At the time, this represented a disbenefit to the public good because it interfered with worthwhile conservation actions. The only alternative was for a land trust to purchase the property, rather than receive it as a donation, but of course environmental charities suffer from a chronic lack of funds to undertake these sorts of actions. Moreover, at the time, capital-gains taxes were not paid for other kinds of appraisable donations to charities, such as art.

Clearly, additional progress in conserving the biodiversity of Canada would be made if the existing tax legislation were changed to favour relief from the capital-gains costs of donations of ecologically important property, and that was the message of the quiet NCC advocacy. This meaning was well received by the various politicians who heard it, and some months later the federal government moved to provide a measure of relief. Initially, it took the form of a Paul Martin–initiative in February 2000 to reduce the capital gains owing on donations of ecologically sensitive lands by 50 percent, followed by a second reduction to 75 percent in October 2000.[2] Finally, in 2006, complete relief against capital gains for such donations was provided by then–minister of finance Jim Flaherty. Moreover, Flaherty went considerably further by also providing a full exemption from capital-gains taxes on donations to charities of publicly listed securities, an action that was also highly beneficial to land trusts. These changes to Canadian tax law, as well as comparable ones in most provinces, were reasonable political responses to quiet but compelling advocacy by NCC and other like-minded organizations.

During a meeting of the Executive Committee in February 1998, the directors discussed the emerging situation in which the "demand" for new conservation easements on properties with high-quality habitat was exceeding the capacity of NCC to purchase them, or even to receive them as donations, and to then steward the natural values. The directors resolved to quickly build the capacity of NCC to deal with these pressing issues, which was done by ramping up the fundraising for conservation projects and to support employees whose responsibility is stewardship. Nevertheless, this has become a familiar and recurring problem for NCC and other land trusts. There are many more opportunities to conserve habitat for biodiversity on private lands than funds to achieve those actions, which are so necessary for conserving the natural heritage of Canada.

In April 1998, Robin Fraser was appointed the first honourary life member of NCC. This was awarded in recognition of his long service to NCC and its Board of Directors, which had extended from 1969 to his retirement in 1997 and included a term as the chair from 1987 to 1988. Fraser continued to regularly attend those meetings for several additional years, and still attends when the agenda has items that fall within his expertise as a lawyer or his personal interest as a conservationist. He also sits on the Board of the Friends of the Nature Conservancy of Canada (a US corporate entity that is described in the next chapter). In 2009, two additional honourary life member titles were awarded, one to Robert Carswell, who served as a director from 1981 to 2008 and as the chair from 1995 to 1996, and to Sherrold Moore, who served as a director from 1994 to 2005.

At the spring meeting of the Board in April 1998, John Lounds presented NCC's strategic plan for the next five years, to 2002. The plan was widely discussed and then adopted by a motion. The plan had six primary goals: (1) a stronger securement program, which was to be firmly advised by ecoregional planning; (2) an aggressive development and communications program, intended to double the revenue stream and build the National Land Conservation Fund to $10 million; (3) the attainment of fully enfranchised regional operations, each with its own board and at least two full-time employees; (4) the establishment of an in-house capability for conservation science, founded on ecoregional planning and enabling an improved screening of projects; (5) an increased emphasis on the stewardship of retained properties, and better monitoring of any that have been passed on to other organizations; and (6) excellence in all aspects of business operations.

Also at that meeting, director Robin Fraser presented a report on *Regional Board Guidelines* to direct the implementation and governance of those entities across the country. Essentially, the regional boards were to function as committees of the national board, with the latter holding fiduciary responsibility for business matters, but the regional directors expected to have a strong moral commitment to advancing NCC's goals within their domain. The chair of each regional board was to also sit as a director on the national board, so as to provide a necessary linkage. Those guidelines were adopted by the Board, as were a set of rules for the use of the National Land Conservation Fund (NLCF) for internal loans to the regions, in order to provide bridge financing for rapidly developing projects for which external fundraising was not complete at the time of closing. The loans from the NLCF were to be charged interest at a rate of 5 to 7 percent, with the lower being applicable to projects deemed to be of particularly high priority from a conservation perspective, and the funds to be repaid within two years. The first approved loan was one of $80,000 to the Ontario Region to bridge the purchase of McMaster Island off the western shore of the Bruce Peninsula.

In October 1998, Linda Stephenson was hired as the first full-time NCC employee in Atlantic Canada. She came to NCC with considerable experience in not-for-profit management and fundraising, along with a love for nature that had been instilled from an early age by her parents. She started out as the Atlantic director for the Conservancy, a position now referred to as vice-president Atlantic region, and continues to hold that position. Substantially through Stephenson's ongoing efforts, NCC Atlantic now has about twenty employees, swelling to thirty during the field season, working on various conservation projects out of offices in all four Atlantic provinces.

Also in 1998, NCC entered into a new arrangement with the Government of Ontario that offered programmatic funding for conservation projects. The program had actually started in 1996 under the name Ontario Parks Legacy 2000, in which the provincial government had committed four years of funding at $150,000 per annum, with NCC to deliver $1 million of land value toward the enlargement of provincial parks or the establishment of new ones.[3] However, after two years of this original agreement, Ontario Parks was so impressed with NCC's progress that it increased its contribution to $1.5 million for the next two years, with NCC now committed to securing $10 million of land value toward enhancing the parks system.

In February 1999, NCC hired its first full-time employee whose responsibility was to deal with science-related aspects of the organization's work. This initial step to develop an in-house capacity for conservation planning and stewardship ecology was an important move forward. Previously, NCC had relied on volunteer scientists on its boards and advisory groups, or in other organizations, to deliver those key functions. This first scientist to be hired was John Riley, an ecologist who came to NCC from an executive position with the Federation of Ontario Naturalists, and who had spent much field time studying boreal wetlands, especially in lowlands near James and Hudson Bays in northern Ontario. His new position with NCC was the director of conservation science and stewardship. At the fall meeting of the national board in September 1999, Riley described the following theme areas for his new program in ecoregional planning: the Northern Appalachians of eastern Canada, the Great Lakes Basin, the Superior Mixed Forest, the Prairies, and the Georgia Strait Lowlands of the southwestern mainland of British Columbia. At the following meeting of the Executive Committee, in December 1999, Riley made a presentation on the conservation blueprint[4] as a model for ecoregional planning, and the directors passed a motion to adopt this important tool for routine use in the organization.

Also at its fall meeting in September 1999, the Board engaged in a wide-ranging discussion of a proposed national Campaign for Conservation: Saving Canada's Natural Masterpieces. This five-year drive would ramp up the fundraising by NCC to secure more and larger properties while also building the organization's capacity for conservation planning and stewardship.

At this same time, Jim Coutts was approached to become a director. In addition to being a successful businessman and having held senior political posts including Principal Secretary to the Right Honourable Pierre Trudeau, Coutts was a keen birder and had a passionate interest in native prairie conservation. He agreed to join the board and to assist NCC in its fundraising efforts, and was instrumental in helping to develop the campaign approach and conservation directions that ensued.

By April 2000, the Campaign for Conservation had adopted a target of $200 million, with projects to be undertaken at fifty hot-spot locations labelled as "natural masterpiece sites," whose locations would be determined from the results of ecoregional planning. A year later, in September 2000, after considerable deliberations and planning about the proposed campaign, the national board gave approval for this national initiative. It would consist of a campaign running at a national level plus a confederation of regional drives, and would extend from 2001 to the end of 2004.

The new campaign took an important step forward in February 2000, when NCC hired Lynn Gran as its new director of development. She came to NCC from the World Wildlife Fund, where she had played a core role in recruiting major donors and in other areas, including the WWF Cuba program. Gran was to be a key person responsible for organizing and implementing the ambitious Campaign for Conservation. Her initial work involved boosting the direct-marketing program, and soon also the development of new initiatives to recognize higher levels of donation. These included the Leaders in Conservation category for annual donors of more than $1,000, as well as the Protectors designation that recognizes long-term monthly giving, which helps to provide a predictable flow of undesignated gifts. Lynn also developed NCC's direct-response television program (DRTV), for which she recruited celebrities as volunteer spokespeople and was the producer of the initial video products. Because the DRTV shows are seen by large numbers of people, they have greatly helped to build the supporter base of NCC, including the Protectors that provide core funding for operations. Gran is still with the Conservancy and is achieving ongoing successes in attracting national-scale business partners, including companies in the banking, retail, and resource sectors.

Also in 2000, NCC assembled its first truly functional regional board in Manitoba. Mike Moore was hired as the regional director for that province, and volunteer Jim Richardson came aboard as a highly engaged chair of the regional board and member of the national board. The first Regional Scientific Advisory Committee was also established in Manitoba in that same year.

At the fall meeting in September 2000, the Board considered the establishment of a new Stewardship Endowment Fund (SEF), initially to be capitalized using undesignated bequests that came to the organization. When this policy was formally implemented by a motion of the Executive Committee in February 2001, the target level of the new endowment was set at $15 million. It was to be managed as a single fund but with separate accounts for the national and seven regional offices, depending on their flows of contributions. The SEF was intended to provide an annual payout of 4.5 percent, with any excess of investment revenues to be recapitalized to grow the fund. The original intent of the SEF was to provide a predictable flow of revenues that could pay for some of the routinely predictable stewardship costs, such as property taxes and signage. Later on, when the fund grew much larger, it was further intended to pay the costs of at least one stewardship officer per region. However, the SEF was never intended to pay for all the costs of stewardship actions by the Conservancy. Instead, many of the stewardship costs, such as those for monitoring and management activities to maintain habitats in a suitable condition, were still be paid for by annual fundraising. The SEF was established because it is typically difficult to raise monies to pay for operational stewardship needs, as most donors prefer to contribute to acquisitions rather than the care of properties. By April 2002, only six months after it had been created, the new SEF already held $1.8 million from undesignated bequests. At that same time, the National Land Conservation Fund had a value of about $5.5 million; but, as it had previously been the repository for undesignated bequests, it would not grow much beyond that level.

In December 2000, John Lounds was appointed as the president of NCC, in addition to serving as its chief executive officer. This new appointment did not change his duties or responsibilities in any substantive way. Rather, it was viewed as being more appropriate to the governance structure of an organization as large as NCC had become.

Also in December 2000, the Executive Committee considered a discussion paper that had been prepared by several directors and was titled *The Nature Conservancy of Canada as One Conservancy: An Understanding Regarding the Balance of Resources.* This document examined several key principles of NCC's operations, including those related to conservation planning as well as a commitment to sharing resources among the operational regions across Canada. The document was accepted in principle and was then circulated to other members of the national and regional boards for their comments. At the next meeting of the Executive Committee, in April 2001, the modified *One Conservancy* document became enabled as policy by a motion of the directors.

Its principles were stated as follows:

The Nature Conservancy of Canada will undertake its program and projects with priority based on the biological importance from a national science perspective and the degree of threat that exists for the

This image from 1961 shows a number of people on a field trip after a meeting in Toronto to plan the mission and founding of NCC. From left to right they are Bruce Falls, Richard Pough, Aird Lewis, and David Fowle. Pough was the president of The Nature Conservancy (US), who was visiting to provide advice about the new land trust. The others are all inaugural trustees of NCC, which was founded in November 1962. Source: NCC

Left: Charles Sauriol began to work with NCC in 1966, when he served both as an employee and trustee. He worked in those capacities until 1983, including a stint as executive director from 1981 to 1983. After stepping down from that position he continued to assist NCC with its work in Southern Ontario for several years. In this image, Sauriol has just received a certificate of appreciation from NCC at a gala dinner held in his honour in 1985. Source: NCC **Right:** John Lounds has been the president and chief executive officer of NCC since 1997. During his tenure the operations of NCC have grown enormously. In this image Lounds is speaking at a public event in 2012 to announce the acquisition of a project in Norfolk County, Ontario. Source: Simon Wilson

Above: The Happy Valley Forest in the Oak Ridges Moraine supports mature stands of tolerant hardwoods, with spectacular displays of vernal wildflowers in the springtime understorey, such as the white trilliums (*Trillium grandiflorum*) in this image. Source: NCC **Right:** Dr. Henry Barnett and his spouse Kathleen were key early supporters of NCC's assembly of forested properties in the Happy Valley Forest. Source: Hope Rogers

Left: The extended Weston family and The W. Garfield Weston Foundation have been extremely generous and long-term supporters of the work of NCC. As of 2012, they had provided NCC with more than $95 million to support conservation science and the acquisition and stewardship of properties across Canada. This group photo of members of the Weston family was taken at a NCC event in May 2010 to celebrate an assembly of properties supporting Carolinian forest in Norfolk County in southwestern Ontario. Source: NCC

Above: Beryl and Richard Ivey have been long-term supporters of NCC projects to conserve southern forests in Ontario. Here they are shown at a dedication of a new protected area of a Carolinian tract at the Clear Creek Forest near Chatham in southwestern Ontario. Source: Tessa Buchan

Above: Peter Butala had a conservation vision for an extensive tract of prairie that his family had ranched for more than a century near Eastend in southwestern Saskatchewan, and he was able to achieve that goal by working with NCC. In 1996, the Old Man on His Back Prairie and Heritage Conservation Area (OMB) was dedicated, covering an impressive 5,300 hectares (13,100 acres). This image shows Peter and his spouse Sharon on that conserved site. Source: Todd Korol **Below:** One of the key stewardship actions at the OMB is the reintroduction of a small population of plains bison, which were the dominant large herbivore of the natural prairie in the ecoregion. Source: Bill Caulfeild-Browne

Daryl "Doc" Seaman and his family had a vision of conserving their extensive OH Ranch, located west of Calgary in southern Alberta. In 2009, NCC signed an agreement with the family for the donation of a conservation easement that covers about 4,050 hectares (10,000 acres) and is among the largest ever such agreements in Canada. This image shows a ceremony for the announcement of the OH Ranch project, with Doc Seaman standing at the far left. Source: NCC

Above: NCC is engaged in a large-scale assembly of conservation properties in the Crowsnest Pass area of southwestern Alberta, with one of the major objectives being to provide viable habitat links for wide-ranging carnivores such as the grizzly bear. Source: Don Dabbs **Below:** The Jean-Paul-Riopelle Nature Reserve conserves a forested tract on Isle-aux-Grues, located on the St. Lawrence downriver of the city of Quebec. This nature preserve was named after the acclaimed artist who maintained a home on the island and spent much time in the forested tract, whose natural elements inspired aspects of some of his painting and sculptural work. Source: Claude Duchaîne

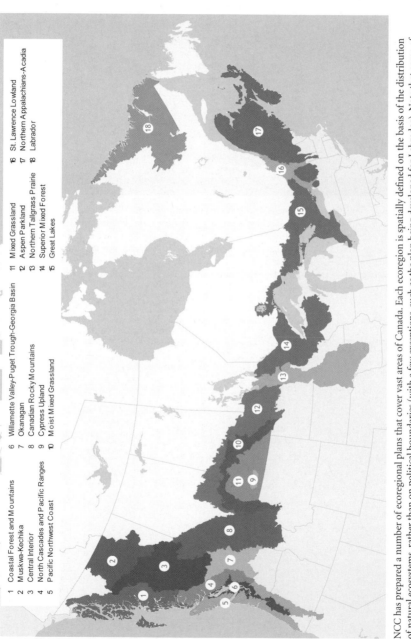

1	Coastal Forest and Mountains	6 Willamette Valley-Puget Trough-Georgia Basin
2	Muskwa-Kechika	7 Okanagan
3	Central Interior	8 Canadian Rocky Mountains
4	North Cascades and Pacific Ranges	9 Cypress Upland
5	Pacific Northwest Coast	10 Moist Mixed Grassland

11	Mixed Grassland
12	Aspen Parkland
13	Northern Tallgrass Prairie
14	Superior Mixed Forest
15	Great Lakes

16	St. Lawrence Lowland
17	Northern Appalachians-Acadia
18	Labrador

NCC has prepared a number of ecoregional plans that cover vast areas of Canada. Each ecoregion is spatially defined on the basis of the distribution of natural ecosystems, rather than on political boundaries (with a few exceptions, such as the plan being developed for Labrador). Note that some of the southern ecoregions extend into the United States, and in those cases the conservation planning and property acquisitions have involved binational collaborations. The focus of NCC's ecoregional planning has mostly been on southern regions of Canada, where biodiversity is most severely threatened and there are also opportunities to acquire tracts of private property (in northern Canada, most land is owned by governments). Source: NCC

Embedded within the various ecoregions are a series of more local "natural areas" that are focal places where land assemblies can result in the conservation of critical habitats and extensive representative ecosystems. As of 2012, NCC had prepared natural area conservation plans (NACPs) for about ninety of these land assemblies, which are the focus of the work of the organization. Each of the NACPs is a science-based blueprint of the most vital properties to acquire, including descriptions of the conservation targets, the anticipated stewardship actions, the operational partnerships needed for successful implementation, and anticipated sources of funding. Progress made in each NACP is annually reviewed by staff, volunteer conservation specialists, and both the regional and national boards of NCC. Updated NACPs are prepared on a five-year rotation. Source: NCC

NCC has been accumulating coastal properties at Johnson's Mills, New Brunswick, since 1994 and as of 2012 had conserved about 191 hectares (472 acres). Immense numbers of shorebirds flock to use mud flats near these properties in a region of the Upper Bay of Fundy known as Shepody Bay. They feed on abundant invertebrates in the extensive mud flats, approximately doubling their body weight over a period of several weeks. Their laid-down fat reserves fuel the birds during the next stage of their southward migration—an arduous non-stop flight to northern South America. NCC properties are conserving a critical habitat that the shorebirds use for roosting at high tide, when the mud flats are flooded. Source: NCC

conservation values at a site. It is recognized that there will always be more programs and projects than available dollars, both nationally and regionally. Therefore, all National and Regional Board members and all staff of The Nature Conservancy of Canada commit to focus their energies on and support NCC's conservation work at priority programs and projects, through Canada and in every region.

With respect to the sharing of resources among regions, the *One Conservancy* principle was "to ensure that NCC is committed to assisting financially those regions with a lesser ability to raise the necessary revenues locally to achieve the Conservancy's mandate."

Also at the executive meeting of April 2001, John Riley, the director of conservation science and stewardship, reported on further progress in the development of NCC's science program. The four pillars of the program were to be the development and implementation of (1) ecoregional planning, (2) the regional science advisory networks, (3) conservation data centres, and (4) stewardship capacity. He also noted that the first ecoregional planners to work for NCC had been hired in British Columbia and the Atlantic region.

In December 2001, director Ted Boswell presented the Executive Committee with a document titled *Expectations of National and Regional Board Members*. It was intended to further clarify the responsibilities of those key volunteer positions, including the need for regular attendance at meetings and diligent oversight of the business practices and financial and science aspects of NCC operations. The document also noted that directors were expected to be annual donors to the organization, at a level appropriate to their personal circumstances.

At the spring meeting of the national board in April 2002, Ted Boswell led a discussion of problems that had arisen with the stewardship of a number of properties that the Conservancy had transferred to partner organizations.

As a consequence of this and related discussions among directors and staff about the mounting needs for stewardship, NCC went on to enact a series of initiatives to improve the management of acquired properties. One of the changes was to use more specific language in the contractual arrangements when properties were transferred to third parties. This included a requirement that NCC would routinely negotiate a landholding agreement that specified stewardship actions that the partner had to undertake. Another major change was for the Conservancy to retain ownership of many more of its acquired properties and to grow its own in-house capacity to perform the stewardship necessary to maintain or enhance their ecological integrity.

In May 2002, the Board gave NCC staff in the Alberta region permission to move forward with an interest-free loan, offered by a generous supporter who wishes to remain anonymous, that supported conservation initiatives in western North America.[5] The initial $2-million loan was directed to acquisition projects in the Crowsnest Pass focal area of Western Alberta, and eventually the foundation provided about $3 million to NCC for work in that area. That property assembly in the Crowsnest Pass is a component of the Yellowstone to Yukon Conservation Initiative (Y2Y) that is intended to maintain a corridor of natural habitats extending from Yellowstone National Park all the way north to the coastal plain of the Yukon.[6] As was previously noted, a key aspect of the Y2Y vision is to maintain viable populations of large carnivores, particularly grizzly bear, timber wolf, and wolverine.

In the Crowsnest Pass assembly area, NCC focuses on maintaining the connectivity of habitats for grizzly bear, and a loan from a generous supporter was potentially forgivable if that conservation result could actually be demonstrated. To do the specialized field research, Y2Y commissioned several big-mammal ecologists to study large-scale movement of the bears. This research is done by capturing some of the animals, fitting them with a collared device that transmits radio signals to a satellite, and then monitoring their movements for up to several years. The research eventually showed that properties in the Crowsnest Pass are being used by bears in their long-distance movements, although habitats in nearby British Columbia are even more important to the animals. So far, the foundation has forgiven half of a $1.5-million loan on a property known as Swann, partly based on an expressed commitment from NCC to invest an even larger amount on other conservation properties in the Crowsnest Pass focal area.

In late June 2002, NCC hosted a series of public events during the run-up to that year's Canada Day. Ten such events, one per province, profiled a noteworthy project that NCC had undertaken in the past year. These events were called Gifts to Canadians and they became an annual celebration of NCC's work across the country. From the outset, these public events attracted considerable media attention, including consistent national-scale profiling by the *Globe and Mail*, and they have helped to raise the profile of the Conservancy and its work throughout Canada. In 2011, the program morphed into Gifts from Canadians, which featured an inspiring story of a particular donor in each province, more so than being about the actual properties they had helped to conserve. This was done as a way of showing appreciation for the generosity of the people who had been donors to NCC, while also profiling their personal satisfaction with the on-the-ground conservation that each of the stories represent.

During the annual meeting of the NCC Board in September 2002, John Lounds was authorized to sign a new memorandum of understanding with The Nature Conservancy (US). He described the memorandum as a non-binding, good-faith agreement that committed NCC to work with TNC in five priority areas: science and ecoregional planning, the boreal and tundra regions of the Canadian Arctic, the acquisition of properties of binational interest, fundraising, and organizational relationships and capacity. This NCC annual meeting was attended by Anthony Grassi, the chair of the TNC board of governors, and the minutes state that he "noted that TNC faces the same issues that NCC is dealing with . . . and that their $1 billion plus campaign is struggling due to the global economic climate. He also noted that the Memorandum of Understanding between the two organizations is a great partnership and he was looking forward to signing it at TNC's Board meeting in October."

Also in 2002, NCC and Shell Canada created the Shell Conservation Internship Program, which ran until 2012.[7] The program is open to current or recently graduated students of ecology, environmental science, or related fields, who apply for paid four-month summer jobs. The varied tasks might involve the preparation of management plans for NCC properties, collecting data on the plants and animals present, or stewardship work to reduce the abundance of invasive species. These opportunities for real-world conservation experience provide a genuine boost to the career development of the interns, more than 175 of whom have participated since the inception of the program. According to Adrian Loader, president of Shell at the time (in 2011): "The hard work, enthusiasm and ingenuity of NCC and the Shell Conservation Interns will be critical to ensuring Canada's biodiversity remains as spectacular tomorrow as it is today."[8]

Another successful collaboration that began in 2002 was with the *Globe and Mail* as NCC's national print media partner. This involved the national newspaper placing an annual four- to eight-page insert about the Conservancy, plus a number of smaller adverts at times chosen by the Conservancy. The annual insert typically includes articles about the mission of NCC, its projects, and its supporters, as well as a number of paid advertisements by corporate patrons. In 2008 and onward, the insert was a full-colour edition, which further heightened the visual appeal of the featured projects.

Also in 2002, The W. Garfield Weston Foundation provided a grant to further its work in conservation planning and to establish a new endowment whose yield would be used to perpetually fund core science positions in NCC. It now pays for the salaries and program costs of positions known as Weston Scientists, whose responsibilities include the development of standards and methodologies for conservation planning and stewardship. The fund also provides seed funding to the regions to help with their implementation of new protocols or to undertake special projects related to conservation science. This new Weston Family Science Fund proved to be catalytic in moving NCC rapidly forward in its development and implementation of protocols for conservation planning and stewardship.

Because NCC was now holding large and increasing sums of money in its science and stewardship endowments and the existing National Land Conservation Fund, the Board moved in 2002 to create an Investment Subcommittee of the Finance Committee. Its mandate was to recommend policy and monitor the performance of the endowments and other invested funds of the Conservancy. One of the first priorities was to hire an external investment manager and, after interviewing various potential firms, the Board retained one to perform this function. According to the minutes of an executive meeting in February 2003, when the decision was made to hire an investment manager, the directors felt that "deep value management rather than growth management was prudent, conservative, and most fitting to NCC" and for the management of its hard-won and treasured endowment and other invested funds.

In early 2003, the Canada Revenue Agency (CRA) had initiated a review of conservation easements held by the Conservancy in Alberta. The CRA commissioned its own appraisals of several easements and valued them at lower amounts than the appraisers working for NCC did. The differences largely reflected variations in the ways that the CRA and NCC appraisers had determined the change of property value when subdivision rights were removed by a conservation easement. Such differences were not unexpected, in view of conservation easements being a relatively new instrument in the toolkit of land trusts.

At a meeting of the Executive Committee in May 2003, a major item of discussion was the progress of the Campaign for Conservation. The fundraising was going well, but the timing of cash flow was an issue. Large upfront investments were being made in fundraising and other development activities in anticipation of substantial increases in donations during the next several years of the campaign. With such large front-loaded expenses for the campaign, unrestricted funds were urgently needed if a substantial operating deficit was to be avoided in the present fiscal year. To deal with the situation, the directors authorized staff to borrow as much as $1.4 million from the Stewardship Endowment Fund, in order to bridge-fund the shortfall in funding early campaign expenses, while also avoiding the poor optics of an operating deficit for that year.

In July 2003, Kamal Rajani began to work at NCC as a project accountant, initially to clear up a persistent reporting backlog with the North American Waterfowl Conservation Plan program. He was soon promoted to controller, at which time he took responsibility for the implementation of a new accounting system, and he is now the chief financial officer of the Conservancy. At the time Rajani was hired, NCC was experiencing some difficulties with its system for financial reporting, which needed to both serve the requirements of the Board for its oversight of operations and report to the US Fish and Wildlife Service on the use of grants under the NAWCA program. Rajani and others worked hard to replace the underperforming accounting system with a much better one, while also improving the procedures for tracking vital aspects of financial review and control. These were particularly related to the planning of projects, approval of transactions, accounting of revenues and disbursements, the use of restricted funds, and charging of operational costs and staff time against projects. The new policies and processes were communicated across the organization so as to become routinely used, which greatly improved the business operations of NCC. Meanwhile, additional financial personnel were recruited, including at the regional level, which further helped to improve the business and reporting systems across the organization.

At the annual meeting of the Board in September 2003, a decision was made to establish two new committees of the Board of Directors: one for governance and another for stewardship. Ted Boswell was asked to chair the Stewardship Committee and to determine its terms of reference.

In April 2004, Michael Bradstreet was hired as the new regional director for Ontario. He came to NCC from a position as president of Bird Studies Canada, where he had been involved in research and cross-Canada initiatives related to avian studies and to conservation more generally. This appointment turned out to be an extremely important one for the Conservancy, initially because Bradstreet implemented a high degree of scientific and business rigour to conservation planning and stewardship activities in Ontario, which helped to attract high-end support for several large projects in the province. Especially important was the design and use of a new conservation-planning model that was based on ecoregional planning but executed at a smaller scale of focal assemblies of properties. These became known as natural area conservation plans (NACPs), and the first of them were undertaken for wetlands at Long Point, stands of Carolinian forest in Norfolk County, and various habitats on Pelee Island.

In 2007, Bradstreet became the vice-president of conservation, in which he was influential in persuading the Board to implement a policy requiring all securement projects to have a contribution to a stewardship endowment in place at the time of closing. Also important was Bradstreet's push to ensure that the NACP model became the basis of almost all conservation planning in NCC. This resulted in a great improvement of the already good planning standards that the organization was using, and the NACP model has become a gold standard for private-sector conservation work in Canada. As we will see in the following chapter, the use of NACPs was a key aspect of how NCC was able to elevate its conservation science to a plateau high enough to satisfy judicious scrutiny of its planning processes. This vital characteristic enabled the organization to attract unprecedented levels of support for its next fundraising campaign, including from the federal government.

In March 2004, the NCC family suffered a sad loss when Ted Boswell passed away after a struggle with an aggressive cancer. Boswell had been an extremely influential member of the Board since 1995 and its chair from 1999 to 2001. He had started his work life as a forester and had become the president of E.B. Eddy Forest Products. This circumstance was noted in a profile about him in *Report on Business* magazine that was titled "He's a Lumberjack and He's OK." His enduring contributions to NCC involved a relentless pushing for greater rigour in conservation planning and stewardship, in establishing an internal revolving-loan fund for the bridge financing of projects, and in pushing for regionalization of much of the conservation work. As a memoriam to Boswell, the National Land Conservation Fund was renamed the Ted Boswell Land Conservation Fund, now affectionately referred to as the Boswell Fund.

In May 2004, the Campaign for Conservation held its public launch in the historic Distillery District of Toronto. Typically, a large fundraising campaign stays in a "quiet" phase until more than half of its target is raised or pledged. During that period, NCC employees approach potential donors of larger gifts, such as corporations, foundations, governments, and high-capacity individuals. At the time of the campaign's public launch, the donation tally stood at about 87 percent of the $200-million goal. The event was attended by several hundred supporters of NCC, who heard brief but inspiring speeches by NCC leaders, including its president, John Lounds; the chair of the national board, Jon Grant; the chair of the campaign, Charles Baillie; and celebrity spokesman Dan Aykroyd. Staff and volunteers were then energized to push the Campaign for Conservation over the top, which happened about a year later.

At the annual meeting of the Board in October 2004, the following governance documents were ratified: *Expectations of National and Regional Board Members*, *Code of Ethics for National and Regional Board Members*, *Policy on Conflicts of Interest*, and *Terms of Reference for the Board of Directors*. These policies are still in place, in some cases with subsequent minor improvements, and they are important elements of the *Board Manual* that is now a key resource for all NCC directors.

In early 2004, NCC's new half-hour direct-response television program began to air. In the world of philanthropy, DRTV refers to programming that is aimed at directly influencing the attitudes of large numbers of people, and ideally to attract them to become interested in learning about and supporting the organization. An effective DRTV program must be professionally developed and produced, and commercial airtime is purchased to ensure that the show runs at effective times of the day. This first NCC show was titled *Fighting for Canada*, and its considerable production costs were underwritten by Jennifer Ivey Bannock, a Board member. The video featured evocative and hard-hitting testimonials by NCC donors, staff, directors, and celebrity spokespersons, the latter including Dan Aykroyd, Mike Farrell, Cathy Jones, Rick Moranis, Albert Schultz, William Shatner, and Justin Trudeau. Joni Mitchell donated the use of her song "Big Yellow Taxi" for inclusion in the DRTV shows until 2015.

One of the key intents of *Fighting for Canada* was to encourage people to visit the recently developed NCC website, where they could easily commit to being a monthly donor to the organization—a Protector. The beauty of monthly donations is that they provide a charity with a predictable flow of undesignated funds, which are vital to sustaining the organization. Over the next several years the *Fighting for Canada* show was broadcast widely in Canada and was instrumental in building the supporter base of NCC, and in particular the numbers of monthly donors. In December 2005, the directors approved the spending of up to $500,000 of undesignated bequest funds to pay for additional media buys for the *Fighting for Canada* show, which continued to be used until 2009.

At the same time that *Fighting for Canada* was airing, NCC placed advertising panels in various prominent locations, such as bus shelters, magazines, and newspapers. Several themes were used in those adverts. In one of them, the maple leaf was seen to be falling out of the Canadian flag, implying the loss of an inherent value if natural lands were not conserved. Another panel featured a vending machine for bubblegum, but instead of candy monarch butterfly larvae were inside; if you put money into the machine, a mature butterfly emerged. The advertisement conveyed the idea that money must be spent to conserve the nature we love. A third advert featured a grizzly bear trundling across a meadow, and it was titled "Ranching with the Grizzlies" to illustrate how conservation easements help to conserve habitats for these and other wild creatures. The *Fighting for Canada* show, along with the advertising panels and other media that NCC was using to reach out to Canadians, were instrumental in helping to build the numbers of supporters during the Campaign for Conservation, as well as the brand of the organization.

In December 2004, the directors passed a motion that would allow staff to establish a line of credit for the purpose of providing bridge financing for fast-breaking land purchases for which there was insufficient time to engage in campaign-type fundraising. The Conservancy already had the Ted Boswell Land Conservation Fund for this purpose, but that facility was not large and was often heavily committed, so it was not in itself sufficient to provide for all the bridge-financing needs of the organization. According to the proposal, the new line of credit would be called the Land Conservation Finance Project and its capacity was not to exceed the approximately $5.5 million value of the Boswell Fund. Having a facility to access external loans was an important step forward in terms of the developing maturity of NCC. It also represented a high level of confidence of both staff and directors in the ability of the organization to raise large sums of money to repay external loans, especially for projects in which the property was already secured (even if not fully paid for), so that for many potential donors the sense of emergency might have become dissipated. As we will see, however, it can be rather complicated for an environmental charity to obtain a large-capacity line of credit, and it took several years for the facility to be implemented.

A related motion in December 2004 was designed to transform the Boswell Fund from a revolving-loan fund into an internally endowed fund, with an initial base capital of $5.5 million. Any investment income from the new fund was to be used for administration of the bridge-financing facility, easement and legal defences, and national and regional operations in support of land conservation. Of course, the capital of the Boswell Fund still remained available to provide internal bridge-financing loans, with interest charged.

Late in 2004, the Conservancy received a pleasant surprise when it was learned that Roberta Langtry, a retired school teacher in Toronto, had left NCC an unexpected bequest of what turned out to be about $4.4 million.[9] Langtry was an elementary school teacher and speech therapist who had lived a modest lifestyle, invested well in blue-chip stocks and bonds, and amassed considerable wealth. She had been a regular but modest supporter of the Conservancy since 1999, but her large bequest, the biggest ever received by a conservation charity in Canada, was quite unanticipated. The Langtry funds were essentially undesignated, meaning they could be used for the best purposes of the time, rather than only for a designated use such as the acquisition of a particular property. Undesignated monies are the toughest kinds of funds for a charity to raise, but they are always urgently needed to pay salaries, rent, light and heat, and for other essential purposes. NCC worked with the executor of the Langtry estate to develop a use for the bequest that would be sympathetic to Langtry's interests. Most of the funds were spent to help conserve wetlands across Canada, to communicate NCC's science work, to support activities that would raise awareness and enhance fundraising, and to assist with projects in the Oak Ridges Moraine. In addition, $1 million of the bequest was set aside to help fund communications work by NCC.

At the national meeting of the Board in September 2005, a motion was passed relevant to important changes in the governance of NCC. The result was that the Board of Directors would have the following committees: an Executive Committee, an integrated Finance and Audit Committee (with an Investments Subcommittee), a Governance and Nominating Committee, and a Conservation and Stewardship Committee. The latter was charged with determining how the regional science advisory networks should function within NCC, with creating an ad hoc group to provide advice on science-related matters for the next fundraising campaign, and with developing a process for review of high-level assembly projects.

At that same meeting, there was discussion of the policy of all projects having a routine levy that would be used to capitalize a Stewardship Endowment Fund. Various funding models were considered in that and other meetings. Eventually it was decided that all securement projects would be required to have a contribution to a stewardship endowment that was equivalent to 15 percent of the appraised value of the property, with that sum being in place at the time of closing. The stewardship levy was to be applied to all property-related transactions, whether fee-simple purchases or donations, and including real estate as well as conservation agreements (such as easements). In cases where the contribution to the endowment had not yet been entirely raised, a loan would have to be obtained from a bridge-funding facility, such as the Boswell Fund or an external line of credit. The intent of the 15-percent levy was to provide perpetual funding for routine stewardship costs, such as property taxes, signage, insurance, and security. Another goal was to help ensure that salary was in place in each NCC region for at least one full-time steward-ship position. These expenses typically account for 30 to 40 percent of the total stewardship costs, so the rest would still have to be raised on an annual basis.

This new policy caused a bit of consternation for some NCC staff and directors, who felt that the additional fundraising needed for the stewardship levy would slow the rate of completion of securement projects, particularly since many donors would specifically not provide funds for endowment purposes. Nevertheless, all were in agreement that NCC had to ramp up its stewardship program and that it would be helpful to have a source of core funding for a significant portion of that necessary work. The key change in mindset that allowed everyone to become comfortable with the new requirement for a stewardship endowment was for staff and directors to stop thinking about securing properties and to switch to the more appropriate concept of undertaking projects. In that sense, a conservation project involves good planning, the acquisition of property, the establishment of an endowment to help provide funds for its necessary management, and the long-term execution of an appropriate stewardship program.

In July 2005, NCC publicly announced the successful completion of the Campaign for Conservation: Saving Canada's Natural Masterpieces. This was the first national campaign that NCC had undertaken and the largest private fundraising drive ever to have been completed in support of conservation in Canada. The campaign goal of $200 million was surpassed thanks to generous support from many individual Canadians, foundations, corporations, and governments. The funding was used to secure 96,800 hectares (239,000 acres) of vital natural areas across Canada and to build NCC's capacity to perform in-house science in support of conservation planning and stewardship.

The campaign was a success despite the fact that the original hope to raise a contribution of $100 million of programmatic funding from the federal government was not achieved and even though some provincial governments did not participate. The failure of those political aspects of the campaign goals was mystifying to NCC staff and volunteers in view of the relatively strong profile of conservation issues at the time and of the supportive views that many senior politicians and governmental bureaucrats had expressed. Nevertheless, the campaign was over the top in terms of meeting its financial goals, coming in at about $207 million. NCC was now raising more money in Canada for conservation than any other non-governmental organization.

In a joint statement, Jon Grant, the chair of the Board, and John Lounds, the president of NCC, said the following about the success of the Campaign for Conservation[10]: "We Canadians aren't known for our tendency to blow our own horns. As a nation we are often described as 'unassuming.' And for the most part this is true—except when it comes to our nature. We are passionate about our natural heritage and the strong connection we have to it and we are a country that is determined to leave a natural legacy like no other. This past year was one we can be proud of, but nowhere is the job finished. Protecting the best of natural Canada is an ongoing challenge—one that requires a continued commitment."

Overall, the NCC family was in a buoyant mood at the end of 2005, and planning soon began for the next national campaign, which would have substantially larger fundraising and conservation goals.

The Conservation Program, 1998–2005

In 1998, NCC accepted the donation of a 42-hectare (104-acre) property in an area known as the Carden Alvar, located northeast of Lake Simcoe, Ontario.[11] This land donation took place through the federal Ecological Gifts Program, and it resulted in the designation of the Katherine McCuaig McDonald Nature Reserve.[12] An alvar is an uncommon habitat where a flat plane of limestone bedrock occurs at or near the surface. Such areas typically support a mosaic of habitats depending on the soil depth, including grassland, shrubland, and forest, and there may be shallow wetlands in bowl-shaped depressions in the bedrock. Because the limestone substrate is calcium-rich, the habitat supports otherwise uncommon or rare plants that can tolerate the alkaline conditions. Alvars are an uncommon geographical feature, and so they have high conservation value because they support unusual ecological communities and species-at-risk, such as in Ontario, the endangered eastern loggerhead shrike (*Lanius ludovicianus*).

The Carden Alvar is one of the most important such habitats in Canada and it is still an ongoing assembly area for NCC.[13] In 2002, NCC acquired the Cameron Ranch on this alvar, an outstanding property of 1,162 hectares (2,869 acres) that was obtained at a project cost of $1.66 million, including a stewardship endowment of $250,000. On some of the NCC properties, grazing by cows at an appropriate density is used to prevent excessive incursions of shrubs and trees, thereby maintaining the open grassland needed by many of the rare species of the alvar. NCC's Carden Alvar Natural Area contains a provincially designated Life Science Area of Natural and Scientific Interest and is part of the Carden Plain Important Bird Area. Partners in NCC's work in the Carden Alvar include the Couchiching Conservancy, the Ontario Ministry of Natural Resources, the Carden and Orillia Field Naturalists, the Toronto Ornithological Club, and the Ontario Field Ornithologists. As of 2011, NCC had contributed to the protection of about 3,380 hectares (8,348 acres) in the Carden Alvar.

In 1999, NCC acquired the eleven-hectare (twenty-seven-acre) Elkington property, located in the Cowichan Valley near Duncan on southern Vancouver Island, in a project valued at about $1 million. The property was purchased from Gerald Elkington, a ninety-nine-year-old who had been born in the house on the property. NCC granted him a life estate, and six years later he passed away in his home at age 105.[14] Now known as the Cowichan Garry Oak Preserve (CGOP), this property supports the best remaining stand in Canada of a rare woodland and meadow community dominated by Garry oak (*Quercus garryana*), which occurs only in a region of drier Mediterranean climate on southeastern Vancouver Island.[15] It is estimated that less than 10 percent of the original extent of this community still survives in Canada and

globally. The community supports many species-at-risk, including the del-
toid balsamroot (*Balsamorhiza deltoidea*), Howell's triteleia (*Triteleia howel-
lii*), and yellow prairie violet (*Viola praemorsa praemorsa*). Historically, some
of the property had been seeded with alien agronomic grasses to develop
a pasture, and additional non-native plants had invaded the site, and that
degraded habitat needed to be restored to a better condition.

In addition, in 2001, NCC purchased a piece of agricultural land of eleven
hectares (twenty-seven acres) adjacent to the CGOP that extends to the shore
of Quamichan Lake and is now called the Quamichan Garry Oak Preserve.
That property had no intact natural habitat, although it did have some persistent rare plant species, and the largest Garry oak tree in Canada grows there.
NCC has undertaken an innovative program of ecological restoration on that
property and the degraded part of the Elkington tract to enhance the habitat
for species-at-risk of the Garry oak community, as well as that of several wetlands closer to the lake.[16] This work included the propagating and planting of
native-plants-at-risk by using seed collected from the property, along with the
planting of more widespread native species appropriate to the community. In
addition, invasive alien plants are being manually removed from both of the
Garry oak properties and prescribed burns are used to control non-native
grasses. These measures have helped to improve the habitat for the Garry
oak–associated biodiversity-at-risk. Andrew MacDougall of the University of
Guelph, researchers at other universities, and Environment Canada's Habitat
Stewardship Program have been key partners in NCC's ongoing management
activities in this focal area.

At a meeting of the Executive Committee in February 1999, the directors
approved a proposal to begin an extensive land assembly in the Crowsnest
Pass region of west central Alberta. As was previously noted, this project
is related to a large-scale conservation initiative known as Yellowstone to
Yukon, which has a vision of maintaining the landscape-scale connections
needed by wide-ranging species, particularly large carnivores. In the original
ecoregional plan and proposal for the Crowsnest Pass, NCC hoped to acquire
about 3,240 hectares (8,000 acres) at a cost of $4 million, and in 2002 the pro-
ject got a considerable boost from potentially forgivable loans of $3 million
from a generous (but anonymous) supporter.

In 1999, the Conservancy began to develop an interesting project in the
Campbell River estuary, in the town of Campbell River on the east coast of
Vancouver Island.[17] NCC acquired from a timber company twenty hectares

(fifty acres) of land that included a former industrial sawmill site. The degraded areas were then restored to their original condition of intertidal salt-marsh and forested riparian habitat. This project involved NCC purchasing Baikie Island in the estuary plus a nearby area of foreshore. The restoration was done by ripping up concrete pads, excavating large amounts of industrial fill, grading the shoreline to natural intertidal contours, digging a new channel for river flow and to enhance the aeration of previously dredged log-booming areas, and planting native vegetation to develop salt-marsh and riparian habitats. Remarkably quickly, native animals began to utilize the new terrestrial and aquatic habitats, including various birds and young stages of salmon. The cost of the initial project was $1.8 million, most of which was spent on the ecological restoration. In 2008, an adjacent sawmill site was purchased and the next year similar restoration work began. Key partners in these projects were the City of Campbell River, The W. Garfield Weston Foundation, BC Hydro, the Department of Fisheries and Oceans, and the Tula Foundation. The project is ongoing, and NCC and its partners are examining additional sites in the Campbell River estuary for ecological restoration.

Also in 1999, NCC and its partners announced the Whaleback project in southwestern Alberta. The region known as the Whaleback is considered to be the last foothill and montane landscape in the province to be in a true wilderness condition. The region has considerable habitat diversity, and about 150 species of birds and 57 of mammals occur there, including uncommon larger ones such as grizzly bear, mountain caribou (*Rangifer tarandus*), and mountain goat (*Oreamnos americanus*). The area also has rare old-growth stands of timber, with trees of limber pine (*Pinus flexilis*) aged up to 575 years and Douglas-fir (*Pseudotsuga menziesii*) to 400 years. Some years earlier, Amoco Petroleum Canada had considered exploratory drilling for hydrocarbons in this area, but its proposal became highly controversial and it decided not to proceed. Moreover, to further protect the Whaleback from drilling, Amoco donated its 11,745 hectares (29,000 acres) of subsurface mineral leases in the Black Creek Heritage Rangeland to NCC.

With those rights in conservation ownership by the Conservancy, Premier Ralph Klein then announced that two protected areas would be designated in the Whaleback. The Bob Creek Wildland and Black Creek Heritage Rangeland together amounted to about 28,633 hectares (70,700 acres). These are now multi-use areas that allow hunting, fishing, cattle grazing, hiking, and natural history activities such as bird watching.

In July 1999, NCC's efforts to acquire Middle Island gathered a great deal of public attention.[18] This small limestone island of about eighteen hectares (forty-six acres) in Lake Erie is literally the southernmost place in Canada, being located at a latitude of 41°41' N (or 41.7° N). The island has a rather complicated history, which has included the cultivation of wine grapes over part of its area and, more colourfully, serving as a frequent way station for the illegal transport of alcoholic products from Canada to the US during the Prohibition era of 1920 to 1933. At one time the island had a modestly sized hotel and fishing lodge that catered mostly to Americans, particularly during Prohibition but also into the 1940s. However, those facilities were run down and Middle Island was uninhabited when it came onto the market in 1999.

More importantly, the island sustains excellent natural values, including the presence of a number of plants and animals that, in a Canadian context, are rare and at risk. These include southern trees such as blue ash (*Fraxinus quadrangulata*), common hoptree (*Ptelea trifoliata*), and Kentucky coffee-tree (*Gymnocladus dioica*), as well as low-growing plants such as creeping chervil (*Chaerophyllum procumbens*), Lake Erie pinkweed (*Polygonum pensylvanicum eglandulosum*), Miami mist (*Phacelia purshii*), and wild hyacinth (*Camassia scilloides*). The island also supports the endangered Lake Erie water snake (*Nerodia sipedon insularum*) and once had the extirpated timber rattle-snake (*Crotalus horridus*). There are many southern breeding songbirds, such as the Carolina wren (*Thryothorus ludovicianus*) and yellow-billed cuckoo (*Coccyzus americanus*). Large numbers of colonially nesting birds breed on Middle Island, including several species of gulls, herons, terns, and beginning in the 1980s and now the most abundant breeders, the double-crested cormorant (*Phalacrocorax auritus*).

In 1999, Middle Island was privately owned by a US interest, which NCC approached about a conservation purchase. The owner decided that it might be more profitable to put the property up for public auction. That sale happened in Cleveland, and the Conservancy was represented there by James Duncan (he is still with NCC as the regional vice-president in Ontario). Duncan had been given a spending limit of $1.5 million, but after some furious auction action managed to secure the property for $1.3 million (the total project cost was $1.48 million). According to Duncan, "a Board member from TNC Ohio was sitting beside me at the auction in support, and just as the auction was about to start he leaned over and said: 'Now, son, if you hit that upper limit just keep going, we're good for the rest.' ... I nearly fell over then and there!"[19]

The major donors for the acquisition of Middle Island were Parks Canada ($700,000), Canadian Wildlife Service ($100,000), the International Fund for Animal Welfare ($365,000), Suncor ($200,000), Donner Canadian Foundation ($57,500), and Richard Ivey ($25,000). Smaller donations were also made by many individual donors, all of whom wanted to see Middle Island and its natural values repatriated to Canadian ownership. On the day that the deal was done for the island, NCC's accomplishment received a great deal of attention from the Canadian media, including a segment on the evening newsmagazine *The Journal* of the Canadian Broadcasting Corporation. That news item featured a video segment of NCC personnel in Toronto excitedly cheering at the moment they received a phone call telling them that Middle Island was again in Canadian ownership. In September 2000, the property was passed to Parks Canada for incorporation into Point Pelee National Park.

Interestingly, Middle Island became contentious again, beginning in the middle years of the first decade of the twenty-first century and continuing to the present (to 2012, when this was written). This controversy ignited when Parks Canada announced that it would be taking measures to reduce the numbers of double-crested cormorants breeding on the island. This species had increased enormously from only three nests in 1987 to an extremely abundant 4,700 to 6,600 nests between 2002 and 2007.[20] The ecological problem was that the caustic excrement of the birds was killing trees and extensively damaging the habitat of rare plants. In the spring of 2008, Parks Canada began actions to reduce the number of cormorants, with the aim of decreasing them to six hundred to eleven hundred breeding pairs. The cull mostly involved shooting by marksmen working under the supervision of a veterinarian (more than 98 percent of their shots were deemed immediately lethal), and a total of 8,236 cormorants were killed during 2009–11. In addition, several hundred nests were knocked down in particularly sensitive places, such as the vicinity of endangered understorey plants such as the red mulberry (*Morus rubra*). These efforts have decreased the numbers of cormorants breeding on the island, but it is too soon to tell whether the affected vegetation is recovering. Having to kill hyper-abundant native birds in order to enhance the prospects of at-risk native plants is an awful exercise, but in this case it was deemed necessary to the appropriate management of Middle Island.

Another important initiative in 1999 was the acquisition of a large block of natural grassland, Palmer Ranch in the Waterton Front project area. This

2,025-hectare (5,000-acre) expanse of grassland borders the Waterton River and it was the largest contiguous area of privately owned natural grassland remaining in that project area. To acquire this important tract, NCC acquired bridge-financing loans of about $5.5 million, of which $5 million was generously provided by TNC.[21] This fee-simple acquisition was the largest that NCC had ever made and by far was the biggest loan it had ever taken on. The organization was unsure as to how to raise the funds to pay for that immense obligation and was seriously worried about this matter. One less-desirable option was to sell the property to a sympathetic buyer, subject to a conservation easement that would protect its core natural values. To that end NCC placed an advertisement in the *Globe and Mail* that stated, "Magnificent Ranch—5,000 acre Alberta Foothills property for sale. 3.5 miles of river frontage, lakes, and 180 degree view of the Rockies. The land offers a variety of wildlife including deer, elk, moose and waterfowl. A conservation oriented purchaser preferred. Please call . . ." That advert attracted the attention of John and Barbara Poole of Edmonton, who had previously supported an NCC acquisition in the foothills. He called Larry Simpson, the NCC program director for Alberta, to alert him about the property and to find out if NCC might be interested in purchasing it! Larry explained, to Poole's surprise, that NCC already owned the Palmer Ranch but was exploring the possibility of selling it to a conservation-minded buyer because of the tough prospects of raising funds to pay off the big loan that had been taken on. Poole carefully listened to Simpson's explanation of this circumstance, thought about it for several days, and then decided that conservation of the natural heritage of the foothills would be better served if NCC continued to own the real property of the ranch. Within a few days, John Poole called Simpson to tell him that he and Barbara would provide a gift to NCC to pay out the entire loan on this magnificent property. They viewed this donation as a millennium gift to Canada and Alberta, as the year 2000 was fast approaching.

John and Barbara subsequently became more engaged in the work of NCC and arranged for financial support to help conserve additional conservation treasures in Alberta. In the process, they helped to develop one of the largest conservation legacies by a couple in Canada, amounting to an area larger than 17,000 hectares (41,000 acres).[22] That money has been synergetic in the purchase of a number of important properties and in helping to fund their stewardship. Simpson worked closely with the Pooles and has written that "their gift [for the Palmer Ranch] changed our thinking as an organization so that we began to believe that we could do bigger projects. I do not believe Darkwoods would have happened and so many other large and significant projects if not for this turning point."[23] In a comparable vein, John Lounds said that "their gift made us believe we could think bigger." The remarkable increase in the scale of NCC's activities at this time encouraged other key donors to believe that private-sector conservation could and should be done on a big scale. Most notably, the escalation of NCC's activities had a favourable impact on the thinking of The W. Garfield Weston Foundation, which has been NCC's largest private supporter.[24]

In 2000, the Conservancy began an assembly known as the Clear Creek Forest by purchasing a 232-hectare (572-acre) property of rare Carolinian woodland on the north shore of Lake Erie in Ontario.[25] This older-growth tract of southern hardwood forest supports a number of rare animals that are at risk in Canada, including the Acadian flycatcher (*Empidonax virescens*), eastern foxsnake (*Pantherophis gloydi*), southern flying squirrel (*Glaucomys volans*), and giant swallowtail butterfly (*Papilio cresphontes*). There are also many plants-at-risk in the tract, including the Shumard oak (*Quercus shumardii*), American chestnut (*Castanea dentata*), lily-leaved twayblade (*Liparis liliifolia*), green dragon (*Arisaema dracontium*), and tall ironweed (*Vernonia gigantea*). The project cost to secure that initial woodland was $1.5 million. Adjacent properties have since been acquired, including a 92-hectare (227-acre) property in 2001 and a 61-hectare (150-acre) tract in 2005, so the assembled area is about 385 hectares (950 acres). The total cost of this project to NCC has been more than $3.1 million. Richard and Beryl Ivey were key donors, but more than one thousand people contributed to the project, along with various corporations.

The acquisitions at Clear Creek Forest included areas that had been used for agriculture and also an abandoned gravel pit. These degraded habitats are being ecologically restored. The key tactic is the planting of an appropriate mixture of Carolinian tree species. However, natural old-growth hardwood forest typically has a pit-and-mound surface topography caused by large trees being blown over during windstorms, so that a crater is formed where the root mass was lifted out and a mound where the dirt was eventually deposited.[26] This surface characteristic provides microhabitat for the many plants and animals that require ephemeral pools and other wet habitats in the Carolinian forest. To roughly simulate that topography in the level farmland that was being afforested, sporadic pits of an appropriate depth and area were excavated, and the removed soil piled beside them. NCC stewardship officers are monitoring these microhabitats to determine whether the surface excavations are an effective way to create new habitat for dependent species.

The properties in the Clear Creek Forest were acquired under the Ontario Parks Legacy Program, which was a partnership between NCC and the Government of Ontario.[27] In 2001, those parties agreed to a ninety-nine-year lease for the NCC-held lands, with Ontario Parks taking on the responsibility of stewarding the Clear Creek Forest as a nature reserve under the Provincial Parks Act. The agreement specified the various management actions that are necessary to maintain and improve ecological integrity in the tract, with the Government of Ontario having the responsibility of undertaking the stewardship and NCC that of monitoring that it is done.

Another important project in 2000 in Ontario was the acquisition of a huge tract at the western end of Manitoulin Island that conserves extensive alvar habitats. This purchase of 6,680 hectares (16,500 acres) was the largest that NCC had yet undertaken. The deal involved the purchase of 6,450 hectares (15,925 acres) for $4.3 million from Donohue Inc., with the rest of the property being donated to NCC by that forestry company. Coastal reaches of the tract provide habitat for rare wetland plants, including the dwarf lake iris (*Iris lacustris*). This property was considered the best opportunity in North America to conserve an extensive alvar in natural condition, and so The Nature Conservancy (US) contributed to the acquisition, as did The W. Garfield Weston Foundation and the provincial government under the Ontario Parks Legacy 2000 partnership.[28] In 2011, the tract was proposed for registration as the Queen Elizabeth The Queen Mother Provincial Park (M'Nidoo M'Nissing Provincial Park), to be managed as a "natural environment" class park.[29] Several members of Canadian royal societies had supported the project with gifts as a means of recognizing the one-hundredth birthday of the Queen Mother, and that was the reason for one of the names of the new park.

Also in 2000, the Conservancy began an assembly of islands in the estuary of the Musquodoboit River, located near the village of Musquodoboit Harbour, east of Halifax on the Atlantic coast of Nova Scotia. This estuary provides habitat for large numbers of migrating waterfowl and shorebirds, and its islands are anchors of a provincial sanctuary for migratory waterfowl during the hunting season.[30] The estuary supports as many as eight thousand Canada goose (*Branta canadensis*) during the spring migration, up to three thousand green-winged teal (*Anas carolinensis*) during the fall migration, and more than two thousand American black duck (*Anas rubripes*) during the winter. In addition, the endangered piping plover (*Charadrius melodus*) breeds on Martinique Beach, which encloses the estuary and is one of the longest sandy beaches in Nova Scotia. The estuary is also well used by other migratory birds, especially sandpipers and plovers. The importance of the area was recognized when the Musquodoboit Harbour Outer Estuary, an area of 1,926 hectares (4,756 acres), was designated as a Ramsar site and as an Important Bird Area. NCC had first worked in the estuary in 1991, when it helped to acquire the twenty-seven-hectare (sixty-six-acre) Cheticumchek Island. However, the initial NCC proposal in the new assembly project was to acquire Francis Nose (341 hectares; 842 acres), Gunners (77 hectares; 189 acres), and Bayers Islands (32 hectares; 79 acres), which was done. Subsequently, the Conservancy also secured Goose Point (55 hectares; 135 acres) and Mike's Islands (16 hectares; 40 acres). The total project cost for all of this work, which was done in collaboration with the Nova Scotia Department of Natural Resources, was about $1.7 million, with major sources of funding coming from the Province of Nova Scotia, the Nova Scotia Crown Share Land Legacy Trust, and Ducks Unlimited Canada.[31]

Several other longer-term assemblies were also begun in 2000 in coastal areas of the Bay of Fundy of New Brunswick. The first involved the acquisition of Pendleton Island, a 121-hectare (299-acre) island in Passamaquoddy Bay of the lower Bay of Fundy. The island was to be donated to NCC by the Pendleton family, but the deal turned out to be one of the most complex that NCC had ever undertaken. This was because Pendleton Island was owned in common by what was initially thought to be about 125 scattered descendants of Ward Pendleton, the original owner. A diligent attempt had to be made to contact all of them to determine whether they were in favour of the donation. It took several years for the various legal machinations to play themselves out. Eventually, almost all of the 143 owners-in-common—many of whom did not even know of their communal property—signed off on the donation to NCC. Interestingly, the process of contacting the many dispersed members of the Pendleton kinfolk resulted in the re-establishment of a family network, one outcome of which has been several reunion picnics on Pendleton Island, which although now protected from development, still invites visitation.

A second assembly in New Brunswick is a long-term aggregation of coastal properties around the Musquash Estuary, located south of Saint John. This embayment is considered the healthiest large estuary on the Fundy coast, in terms of its ability to support the biodiversity and ecological functions of this sort of semi-enclosed tidal ecosystem.[32] The intent of the NCC assembly is to conserve the fringing lands of the estuary, in large part to provide a buffer zone to help protect its marine values. The first coastal property to be acquired was a 45-hectare (112-acre) tract in 2001, and since then a total of 1,587 hectares (3,919 acres) has been accumulated. The total project cost of the habitat assembly at Musquash has so far been about $4.2 million, with the largest donors of cash being The W. Garfield Weston Foundation, the governments of New Brunswick and of Canada, and the US Fish and Wildlife Service through the NAWCA program. The largest acquisitions have been a donation of 729 hectares (1,801 acres) in 2007 by Business New Brunswick, another of 163 hectares (403 acres) in 2005 by J.D. Irving Ltd., and a split-receipt donation of the 292-hectare (722-acre) Fitz-Randolph property.

The latter deal was one in which the price of purchase was considerably less than the appraised value of the property. In this case, the generous landowner was Mabel Fitz-Randolph, who did not want to receive the full appraised cash value of her property because she was so pleased that NCC was conserving land around the Musquash Estuary, where she had spent her entire life.

In March, 2007, the marine portion of the Musquash Estuary was designated as the sixth Marine Protected Area (MPA) in Canada, and the first in New Brunswick. An MPA is designated by the federal Department of Fisheries and Oceans under Canada's Oceans Act. However, the designation of an MPA protects only intertidal, subtidal, and deepwater habitats, in this case of an estuary. The surrounding terrestrial habitats are also vital to the health of the contained marine habitats, and these are being protected by NCC's ongoing assembly of salt-marsh, coastal islands, upland forest, and other buffer habitats around the Musquash Estuary.

In June 2000, the Board approved a project to acquire the Tatlayoko Ranch in the southern interior of British Columbia, for a project cost of $1.5 million. This property supports a range of habitat types, including productive wetlands at the foot of Tatlayoko Lake that are well used by migratory waterfowl.[33] The larger vision is to assemble additional properties in this spectacular valley to help conserve an important link between rainforests of the Pacific Coast ecoregion and drier habitats of the Central Interior. Such linkages are vital to wide-ranging carnivores such as grizzly bear, cougar, and timber wolf, as well as to migratory waterfowl such as trumpeter swan (*Cygnus buccinator*) and many songbirds. The Conservancy is trying to conserve this natural corridor by protecting key ecological communities and the natural processes that sustain them, while also respecting the interests of human residents of the area. To accomplish this goal, site-level planning has identified seven conservation targets: interior Douglas-fir forest, grizzly bear, riparian woodland, migratory waterfowl, drier sage south slopes, wet meadows, and the Upper Homathko River aquatic system. In addition, the Tatlayoko Lake Bird Observatory has been established to study migratory birds that are using the valley as a corridor. The observatory is headed by ornithologist Steve Ogle and involves volunteers who are collecting data needed to monitor population trends in a large region to the north of Tatlayoko Lake.

To conserve the full array of ecosystems and biodiversity in the Tatlayoko Lake Valley, NCC is pursuing a community-based approach that energizes a wide variety of public and private partners. The direct action by NCC is anchored by its 380-hectare (939-acre) Tatlayoko Lake Ranch, which was secured using an interest-free loan provided by a Swiss businessman and conservationist and then repaid by grants from the Paul G. Allen Forest Protection Foundation of Seattle and the US Fish and Wildlife Service through the NAWCA program. In addition, NCC is securing other properties adjacent to the ranch. As of 2011, it had helped to protect a total of 1,411 hectares (3,485 acres) in the valley. However, the reach of NCC conservation activities in the area is somewhat broader than that, because it extends to working with sympathetic landowners in the area to manage their properties in ways that are friendly to biodiversity.

In 2002, the Conservancy began to acquire properties in an area known as the Happy Valley Forest in Southern Ontario.[34] One transaction was a donation by Henry and Kathleen Barnett of a conservation easement on their thirty-two-hectare (seventy-nine-acre) forested property, another a land donation by Dorothy Izzard of nine hectares (twenty-one acres), and the third a purchase of eight hectares (twenty acres). Like so many people who pass on natural properties to NCC, these landowners were pleased to know that the habitats they had carefully stewarded would be taken care of beyond their own lives. At the time of his donation, Henry Barnett said, "People will be able to walk through this forest nine hundred years from now, and it will be the same, the scarlet tanagers will still be in the trees, the rose-breasted grosbeaks will still be singing here. The wood thrush will be there in the morning."[35]

The Happy Valley Forest covers about 631 hectares (1,560 acres) and is the largest tract of intact upland forest in the Oak Ridges Moraine, an area of hilly terrain characterized by drumlins and other glacial features north of Toronto. The moraine is ecologically important because it is still mostly forested and so provides an opportunity to maintain a natural greenbelt north of the city, both to support sylvan biodiversity and because the area provides a source of clean groundwater for people in the region. The dominant stand type in the Happy Valley Forest is older-growth dominated by sugar maple (*Acer saccharum*) and beech (*Fagus grandifolia*), but younger forests, wetlands, and other habitats are also present. The area supports more than 110 species of breeding birds and additional migratory ones, including uncommon and at-risk southern birds such as the Acadian flycatcher (*Empidonax virescens*), cerulean warbler (*Dendroica cerulea*), hooded warbler (*Wilsonia citrina*), and red-shouldered hawk (*Buteo lineatus*). The Happy Valley Forest is designated as an Area of Natural and Scientific Interest by the Ontario Ministry of Natural Resources. Being close to Toronto, the area is greatly threatened by residential development.

The donations and purchase in 2002 were a catalyst for additional acquisitions of forested properties in the Happy Valley Forest, where NCC now has 221 hectares (547 acres) under conservation stewardship, 83 percent of which are owned fee simple and the other 17 percent are conservation easements. The long-term goal is to have a two-hundred-hectare (five-hundred-acre) tract of core heritage forest of older tolerant hardwoods under management, plus an additional eighty-one hectares (two hundred acres) of younger buffer lands. More broadly on the Oak Ridges Moraine, NCC has contributed to the protection of about 1,012 hectares (2,500 acres).

Also in 2002, Hydro-Québec donated three other islands to NCC in the Lachine Rapids near Montreal: Île aux Hérons, Île aux Chèvres, and Îles Sept-Sœurs had an aggregate value of about $1 million. The latter "seven sisters" are actually an archipelago of eleven small islands, some of which are just islets. These islands contributed to the long-running Un Fleuve, Un Parc assembly. The jewel of the lot is Île aux Hérons, which has a mixed rookery that includes the largest breeding colony of black-crowned night heron (*Nycticorax nycticorax*) in the province, the second-largest of great blue heron (*Ardea herodias*), as well as a number of great egret (*Ardea alba*).[36]

At the spring meeting of the Board in June 2002, the directors approved the purchase of an important tract of Carolinian forest located on the north shore of eastern Lake Erie near the town of Fort Erie. This property was Marcy's Woods, having an area of 113 hectares (280 acres) and an estimated land value of $1.8 million. The property had come on the market when its owner died, but the heirs disagreed with respect to selling the property to either a conservation buyer or a different private interest. Regrettably, this problem proved to be insurmountable, and despite NCC raising its offer for Marcy's Woods to $2.6 million, the property was sold to a competing bidder representing a local family. The failure to acquire Marcy's Woods was a major disappointment to NCC staff and volunteers, and in a larger sense it was a poignant reminder of the always-present financial constraints on conservation actions by an environmental charity. For several years following the sale of the property, a Minister's Order placed on the tract by the Government of Ontario protected it from development. That action has since expired, but the land is now subject to municipal and provincial zoning restrictions that prohibit the development of the property (the site has been designated an Area of Natural and Scientific Interest).[37] In any event, the present owners are maintaining the natural values of the forest as a private nature preserve, allowing only low-intensity public access.[38]

In 2002, the Conservancy began to work on several new projects with forestry companies in the Atlantic provinces. In Nova Scotia, Bowater Mersey Ltd. agreed to sell two properties and donate two easements to NCC, all of which were inholdings in large tracts already designated by the province as wilderness areas. The acquisition of inholdings is an important way of managing protected areas, and at the time these were among the most important such targets in the province. The four properties had a cumulative area of 1,599 hectares (3,947 acres) and an appraised value of $2.88 million, of which $1.84 million consisted of timber rights on the easements donated to NCC. These properties were eventually transferred to the Province of Nova Scotia for incorporation into their surrounding wilderness areas. The Conservancy has gone on to acquire other inholdings and properties adjacent to wilderness areas in the province. As of 2011, there were fourteen such projects (including the original four) with a cumulative area of 3,040 hectares (7,508 acres) and a project value of $1.89 million of fee-simple acquisitions and $1.84 million of easements.[39]

Meanwhile, in 2003 on the island of Newfoundland, Abitibi Consolidated donated a tract of 880 hectares (2,174 acres) known as the Lloyd's River Escarpment. This extensive area of wilderness consists of remote forest, shrubby habitats locally known as "barrens," and wetlands. Its wilderness provides habitat for the endangered Newfoundland marten (*Martes americana atrata*), as well as increasingly rare lynx (*Lynx canadensis*) and white pine (*Pinus strobus*), all of which are much less abundant on the island than in former times. The cost to NCC of this project was only $117,000, even though the tract had an appraised value exceeding $1 million. This was the largest land donation to a conservation interest that had ever been made in Newfoundland and Labrador, rivalled only by a gift to NCC by the same company in 1995 of 1,899 hectares (4,693 acres) of timber and mineral rights that resulted in the designation of the King George IV Ecological Reserve.

Also in 2003, NCC received a donation of a rather unusual property from Hydro-Québec, which consists of all rights of use to the bed of the Richelieu River. The donation involved a length of riverbed of about 15 kilometres at an average width of 1.8 kilometres, or an area of 271 hectares (670 acres). The Conservancy has also gone on to acquire several forested islands in the Richelieu River: l'Île Jeannotte and l'Île aux Cerfs in St-Charles-sur-Richelieu. These islands have an area of about thirty-one hectares (seventy-six acres) and were acquired at a project cost of about $486,000.

A major conservation target in the Richelieu River is an endangered fish known as the copper redhorse (*Moxostoma hubbsi*).[40] This rare fish is endemic to Quebec, meaning it occurs nowhere else in the world but the Richelieu River, where its only known spawning sites are located, and in nearby portions of the St. Lawrence River. The Conservancy has been helping to conserve the riverine habitat of the copper redhorse, including the restoration of about two kilometres of riparian vegetation important to the fish on the Richelieu River. NCC has also developed an outreach program to inform local people about the conservation needs of the rare fish. The Conservancy is also participating in the recovery plan for the endangered redhorse by assisting with a program of captive-breeding and release of young fish. Partners in the recovery work are the Ministère des Ressources naturelles et de la Faune, the Fondation de la faune du Québec, and the Fondation Hydro-Québec pour l'environnement. The Pierre-Étienne-Fortin Wildlife Refuge, created especially to conserve the largest of the two known breeding habitats of the endangered copper redhorse, includes some of the NCC properties.[41]

At a meeting of the Executive Committee in December 2004, Michael Bradstreet presented an innovative proposal for a long-term property assembly in the Norfolk Forest and Long Point Wetlands area in Southern Ontario. The area sustains a great deal of Canadian biodiversity-at-risk, much of which is of a southern distribution. The natural area supports 60 species that are listed by COSEWIC as being at risk nationally, and 221 at the provincial level.[42] Among the many species-at-risk are southern trees such as the American chestnut (*Castanea dentata*), black gum (*Nyssa sylvatica*), cucumber magnolia (*Magnolia acuminata*), eastern flowering dogwood (*Cornus florida*), sassafras (*Sassafras albidum*), and tulip tree (*Liriodendron tulipifera*). The assembly is intended to conserve the best remaining stands of Carolinian forest and other natural communities, and there are also actions to enlarge and connect the remnant tracts by restoring forest, savannah, and prairie on intervening agricultural land. By restoring functional corridors for biodiversity, species that would otherwise be ecologically isolated will be able to move among stands of appropriate habitat.

A conservation plan had been developed by NCC to identify a portfolio of important properties to be assembled in the Norfolk project area. The Board moved to approve this large-scale project, with a total budget of $9.4 million in its initial three-year phase, subject to annual reporting on its progress. The W. Garfield Weston Foundation became the major supporter of the project.

The most vital acquisitions in the Norfolk assembly have been woodlots supporting stands of Carolinian forest, including Backus Woods, by all accounts the best and oldest remaining stand of Carolinian forest in Canada. However, in some places NCC has also acquired adjacent agricultural land, which it has been restoring to natural habitats by planting appropriate mixtures of native trees and other plants. So far, NCC has done this on about 275 hectares (680 acres) assembled to date, with additional restoration planned until at least 2014.

In 2004, NCC completed a project with Domtar, a forestry company, in the Sutton Mountain Range of southern Quebec.[43] This project involved a split-receipt donation of 4,050 hectares (10,000 acres). The property was appraised at $8.3 million but was purchased for $5 million, plus a tax receipt for the donated portion. In 2000, NCC had identified the Sutton Mountain Range as a focal area for conservation planning and securement, and its first purchase there was in 2001 when a 467-hectare (1,154-acre) property was acquired at a project cost of $600,000. The forest cover in the area is largely dominated by tolerant hardwoods in the low areas and middle slopes, while the upper tracts have stands of spruce and fir. Most of the forest is mature, with some older-growth stands that are up to 120 years old. The great diversity of habitats supports at least 460 species of vascular plants, including the regional endemic Green Mountain maidenhair fern (*Adiantum viridimontanum*). There are more than ninety species of birds, including the threatened Bicknell's thrush (*Catharus bicknelli*), and also a richness of mammals, reptiles, and amphibians, including the at-risk spring salamander (*Gyrinophilus porphyriticus*). As of 2011, NCC had assembled 8,012 hectares (19,785 acres) in the Sutton Mountain Range, representing the largest protected area owned by a private organization east of Alberta. The largest financial contributors to this project have been the Government of Quebec, Environment Canada, and the Sweet Water Trust, but many smaller contributors have also been vital to its success. The ecoregional plan for the Green Mountains natural area calls for the eventual securement of about ten thousand hectares (twenty-five thousand acres) of core wilderness habitat and a similar area of buffer zones.

12

A Force for Nature, 2006–11

In 2006, the Nature Conservancy of Canada had begun the advanced planning for its second national fundraising campaign, having just successfully finished its first one. All circumstances augured well for mission success during this campaign, which would extend through to the year 2012. There was a well-staffed national office and fully functional regional and even local ones whose dedicated employees were engaged in fundraising, communications, conservation planning, property acquisition, and stewardship. Teams of energized directors sat on the national and seven regional boards. All elements were in place for NCC to approximately double the scale of its conservation operations through its A Force for Nature campaign. The goals were to raise more than $500 million by 2012, while also securing at least two hundred thousand hectares (five hundred thousand acres) of ecologically important habitat.

Money raised during the campaign would be used to undertake much larger conservation projects throughout Canada. Just as importantly, it would help to build the capabilities of the Conservancy to much higher but sustainable levels with respect to fundraising and its science-driven conservation planning, project development, and stewardship activities. A defining aspect of this campaign was the establishment of the Natural Areas Conservation Program by the Government of Canada. The government invested $225 million in the program, to be led by NCC. This was by far the largest contribution ever made by a government in Canada to private land conservation. In addition, most provinces engaged in the campaign with programmatic funding that contributed to work in the respective province. That some provinces did not participate highlights the perennial difficulties in building consistent partnerships to further biological conservation.

To some degree, however, the fact that not all provinces engaged in A Force for Nature was offset by a remarkable success in attracting participation from many large businesses that had not previously been supporters of the Conservancy. Much of this progress was a result of effective networking by a team of highly influential businesspeople who agreed to work with NCC as members of a Campaign Cabinet. These prominent Canadians were instrumental in opening the doors of many people in the upper echelons of corporations and private wealth to solicitations by the Conservancy's development staff and directors, and many of those contacts resulted in sizeable donations. Another key to the success of the campaign was the enthusiastic support of several family and corporate foundations, most especially The W. Garfield Weston Foundation.

The A Force for Nature campaign also provided great impetus for building the stewardship endowment of the Conservancy, with almost all monies for that purpose being raised from the private sector rather than from governmental sources. This endowment will be vital to NCC meeting the perennial stewardship responsibilities that are inherent in its increasing portfolio of protected areas. The campaign also resulted in a beneficial shift of conservation planning to a new model of natural area conservation plans. This shift allowed NCC to undertake almost all of its securement projects in eighty-nine focal areas that had been objectively determined to be the best places where private-sector action would make the greatest difference to conserving the imperilled biodiversity of Canada.

Immense conservation projects of a historic scale were implemented during this period of rapid growth of NCC. The most impressive of these was the Darkwoods project in southeastern British Columbia, which at about 55,000 hectares (136,000 acres) is by far the largest acquisition ever made by a private conservation organization in Canada. The sale of a portion of the ecological carbon credits from this project was also a groundbreaking initiative, with a potential to uncork a valuable new source of funding for private-sector conservation actions. There were also impressively large projects at other places, including the Green Mountains Nature Reserve in Quebec (6,750 hectares; 16,667 acres), the Frolek Ranch in British Columbia (3,170 hectares; 7,828 acres), the Canyon Ranch (5,178 hectares; 12,786 acres) and OH Ranch (4,050 hectares; 10,000 acres) in Alberta, the Wilson Archipelago (1,900 hectares; 4,700 acres) in Ontario, a coastal-plain acquisition (1,580 hectares; 3,900 acres) in Nova Scotia, and the Grassy Place (1,575 hectares; 3,890 acre) in Newfoundland and Labrador.

In addition, the Conservancy provided funds to the Province of British Columbia to offset the cost of implementing a memorandum of understanding with the state of Montana. The result was the Flathead Watershed Area

Conservation Act, which removes mining, oil and gas exploration, and other development threats from the Flathead Watershed, a great tract of 162,000 hectares (400,000 acres) in southeastern British Columbia. This action will help to maintain natural values in that vast wilderness, including habitat for wideranging species and large carnivores.

These and other extraordinary conservation actions are among the crown jewels of the many actions undertaken by the Nature Conservancy of Canada during its first half-century of direct-action conservation work in the private sector of Canada. The projects foretell a successful future for the organization and its vital work, notwithstanding the fact that much more natural habitat must be conserved if the indigenous biodiversity of Canada is to be sustained.

The Organization, 2006–11

In 2006, the NCC Board had thirty-two directors representing all regions of southern Canada, and there was also a full slate of well-stocked regional boards.[1] The Atlantic regional board, responsible for the four eastern provinces, had eighteen regional directors, while Quebec had fourteen, Ontario eleven, Manitoba eleven, Saskatchewan eleven, Alberta seventeen, and British Columbia eleven. Fifty-three NCC employees worked out of the national office in Toronto, and 146 staff worked in other parts of Canada from offices located (from west to east) in Victoria, Vancouver, Invermere, Waterton, Calgary, Red Deer, Lethbridge, Rimbey, Regina, Brandon, Winnipeg, Vita, Thunder Bay, London, Guelph, Port Rowan, Utopia, Ottawa, Montreal, Fredericton, Halifax, and St. John's.

NCC's total revenue in 2006 was $60.1 million,[2] including $40.8 million of donated cash and grants, $15.4 million of donated conservation lands and easements, $2.8 million raised from property sales for conservation reinvestment,[3] and $1.1 million of other income such as interest on endowment funds. Of the cash and grant income, 31 percent was from governments, 28 percent from foundations, 26 percent from about 26,800 individuals, 8 percent from other organizations, and 7 percent from corporations. NCC's capital assets in land and easements had a value of $201 million in 2006, and the several endowment funds totalled $18.3 million. The total program support expenses in 1996, used to pay for general and administrative costs, including fundraising, was about $10.0 million, or 17 percent of the total revenues.

At a meeting of the Executive Committee in February 2006, the directors discussed the Conservancy's progress in the establishment of an external line of credit. The intent of that facility was to provide bridge financing for projects that have an imminent closing but for which not all monies had been raised, and for which the Ted Boswell Natural Land Conservation Fund did not have sufficient resources to provide an internal loan. The Board had previously agreed in December 2004 that such a facility was needed, and in that original proposal any external loans would have been guaranteed using capital in the Boswell Fund. In the new proposal, however, the loans were to be guaranteed by assets of three charitable foundations that were long-term supporters of the Conservancy. In the end, however, this new policy was not acted upon because subsequent legal advice was equivocal regarding certain interpretations of the Income Tax Act, under whose provisions charitable foundations are not allowed to loan funds. In the unlikely event of a default by NCC on a loan from its line of credit, the guarantees by the foundations would be called upon and they would have to repay the lending bank, and NCC would then owe them the money. That circumstance might be construed as representing a loan to NCC from the foundations. Consequently, other means were sought to implement the line of credit, a development that took several additional years (see below).

Because NCC was beginning the "quiet" phase of its second national fundraising campaign, events were being arranged in various places as a way of attracting donors to the organization. At an executive meeting in February 2006, Lynn Gran, vice-president of development, reported on a dinner that NCC had hosted in the historic Distillery District of Toronto, with entertainment by the Soulpepper Theatre Company. A highlight of the evening was the awarding of inaugural Steward of the Land Awards to the Ivey, Poole, and Weston families, all of whom have been generous and long-term supporters of the work of the Conservancy. The presentation to each family included a working replica of a bronze astrolabe, which is an archaic device once used by navigators and astronomers for various surveying purposes, including determining longitude and locating and predicting the positions of celestial bodies.

The astrolabes were replica instruments that had been closely modelled after the most famous one in Canada: an astrolabe that Samuel de Champlain (1567–1635), the most important French explorer of North America during the early colonial period, had lost in 1613 during a portage along the

Ottawa River at Green Lake near Cobden, Ontario.[4] The misplaced relic was unearthed by a fourteen-year-old farm boy in 1867, sold to a collector, passed to the New-York Historical Society in 1942, and repatriated to Canada in 1989 when purchased for the Museum of Civilization at a cost of $250,000. The source of the NCC replica astrolabes involved Leonard Lee, a director from Ottawa. Lee had proposed that a high-end giving club be developed called the Company of Explorers, for whom a membership premium would include a gift of a replica of Champlain's astrolabe. To further this initiative he had his firm, Lee Valley Tools, fabricate a number of the astrolabes for NCC to use. In the end, the Conservancy did not move forward with the Company of Explorers. Instead, it has used the astrolabes as presentation pieces to supporters who have made important contributions to conservation as a "steward of the land." A few other generous supporters and long-term volunteers of the Conservancy have also received an astrolabe as a token of appreciation. I want one too, please.

At an executive meeting in May 2006, Michael Rea, the chief operating officer, reported that NCC had completed the transfer of copies of its property records from a system involving reams of catalogued paper in filing cabinets to a more technologically facilitated electronic database. He also noted that NCC was developing a framework for an advanced land information system (LIS) that would gather and store information about properties while allowing authorized users to query the system for the purposes of conservation planning, report preparation, and responding to inquiries from donors and other partners. The data in the new LIS would be organized on a regional basis but could also be rolled up to the national level. The implementation of the new LIS will be described later in this chapter.

At that same meeting, John Lounds made the first mention of a potentially immense project in the West Kootenay region of southeastern British Columbia. It was called the Darkwoods project and would involve about 55,000 hectares (136,000) of landscape owned by a German forestry company that had been harvesting timber on a relatively sustainable basis, so that most of the area was in a natural condition. The tract supports grizzly bear (*Ursus arctos*) and other large mammals, including a small population of mountain caribou (*Rangifer tarandus caribou*), which are critically endangered in the region. In fact, these are the only caribou whose seasonal movements include parts of the nearby lower forty-eight United States. We will return to this terrific project several times in this chapter.

At the spring meeting in June 2006, Jim Coutts, the chair of the Board, led a discussion of a new strategic plan for NCC, which had been developed by staff and senior volunteers during the previous nine months. After a wide-ranging discussion, the emergent directions were for NCC to continue to move forward on its "traditional" mandate of direct action to protect and steward natural lands across Canada, but with an even greater focus on larger landscapes whose high priority had been identified through rigorous conservation planning. However, if opportunities arose to conserve important properties outside of an identified priority landscape, NCC should maintain an adaptive capacity to potentially become involved in those as well. There was also a general feeling that NCC should do more in the realms of public education and awareness, and on an international front. Despite this, people believed that large amounts of existing resources should not be redirected to those sorts of initiatives, partly because other environmental charities were already working hard and well in those realms.

At that same meeting, Coutts reported on advanced planning for a fund-raising campaign that would subsequently be called A Force for Nature. This five-year drive, running from 2007 to 2012, was intended to raise at least $500 million, or about $60 million per year above NCC's base fundraising at the time of about $40 million per year. The vision of the campaign was to make great progress in securing large properties on priority landscapes all across Canada, while building NCC's capabilities in conservation planning and stewardship, and also in fundraising. The more-specific conservation goal was the securement of at least two hundred thousand hectares (five hundred thousand acres) of ecologically important habitat. The great hope was to engage the federal government in providing a large fraction of the campaign, perhaps as much as one-third of it, while also attracting the support of provincial governments, foundations, the corporate sector, and large numbers of individual Canadians. Coutts noted that two prominent businessmen, Paul Desmarais Jr. of Montreal and John Risley of Halifax, had agreed to serve as co-chairs of the campaign, a development that augured well for its success.

Also at that spring meeting, director Ray Woods presented a report on the work of the Conservation and Stewardship Committee. He noted that the activity of the committee had been ramped up to ensure that all science-related aspects of NCC operations were functioning on a scale and at a level of diligence appropriate for the campaign. The operational structure is for every NCC region to have an energized science advisory network that provides high-level oversight of natural area conservation plans (NACPs), but not necessarily an in-depth review of individual projects.

The NACPs were a major change in the paradigm used by the Conservancy for conservation planning and in the process for approving land-securement proposals. The intent is for NCC science employees to develop an NACP for each priority landscape that has been selected as important for sustaining species-at-risk and endangered ecological communities, while also being a region where private-sector action would make an enduring difference to conserving the biodiversity of Canada. Each NACP is a comprehensive assessment of both the need and feasibility of conservation work in a focal area, based on the best available science, and the capacity for fundraising. In cases where an approved NACP is in place, the national board needs to approve only particularly large or unusual acquisition projects. Otherwise, if full funding is in place for projects, the regional board can provide a "blanket" approval for transactions within an approved NACP within a particular year, as long as the plan undergoes an annual review during which the progress of its objectives is examined. Every five years, an updated NACP is to be prepared.

At the next meeting of the national board in September 2006, a Conservation Policy Framework based on these principles was approved. The framework had three major policy areas: the application of conservation science in support of NCC's mission, the approval and review process related to NACPs, and the implementation of projects and their long-term stewardship.

Also at that meeting in September 2006, John Lounds introduced three draft NACP "landscape plans" that science personnel were presently working on. These were intended to serve as case examples of how a priority landscape is chosen and an NACP developed and then implemented. The three model NACPs were as follows: (1) the Waterton Front of southwestern Alberta, where NCC had been working since 1997, (2) the South Selkirks in southeastern British Columbia, where the new Darkwoods project is located, and (3) the Norfolk Forests and Long Point Wetlands assembly in southwestern Ontario that had begun in 1994. These case studies were extremely helpful in terms of allowing the directors to understand the inherent logic and utility of the NACP approach, which has since become the foundation of NCC's conservation planning, securement, and stewardship across Canada.

Jane Lawton, the director of communications, also made a presentation at that meeting. She spoke about plans for the Conservancy to employ public outreach in order to build a wide engagement of Canadians in the national campaign and in the larger mission of conservation. The key messages would be the need for effective conservation action at well-chosen priority landscapes, while highlighting NCC's reputation as a leading science-based organization. A broader goal would be to foster a conservation ethic among Canadians, including younger generations who are not yet donors but like everyone have a stake in our natural heritage. The key strategy to achieving these objectives is to further societal-level awareness about NCC's programs. Key tactics would include the issuing of news releases to stimulate reporting by the mass media, advertising placements in national media such as the *Globe and Mail*, direct-response television programs, revamping and popularizing of the NCC website, and perhaps the use of the rapidly emerging phenomenon of social media networking. The Board was supportive of the strategy and its suggested tactics, but was wary of diverting large amounts of existing resources from the core NCC programs of conservation planning, acquisitions, and stewardship. Nevertheless, all the suggested broad-scale engagement tactics were implemented during the campaign, although to varying degrees depending on the available funding.

Another unusual fundraising tool was unveiled in September 2006 by Linda Stephenson, the Atlantic vice-president, at a public event associated with the annual meeting in St. John's, Newfoundland. This involved the Quidi Vidi Brewery working with NCC by selling cases of beer with specialty labels featuring six species-at-risk in the province. Species on the brightly illustrated labels included the Newfoundland red crossbill (*Loxia curvirostra percna*), northern right whale (*Eubalaena glacialis*), and Burnt Cape cinquefoil (*Potentilla usticapensis*). For every case of twelve beers branded and sold with these labels, NCC would receive a royalty of fifty cents.

In March 2007, private-sector conservation in Canada took a great and historic leap forward when Prime Minister Stephen Harper announced that the federal government would be supporting NCC and other conservation NGOs through the Natural Areas Conservation Program. The announcement was held at the Happy Valley Forest, just north of Toronto, and as part of his remarks the prime minister said, "This investment will result in the long-term protection of Canada's natural treasures. . . . We are taking concrete action to protect species at risk and their habitat."[5] During his own remarks, a proud John Lounds said, "This public-private partnership represents a major step forward for science-based habitat conservation in Canada. . . . In the context of our national conservation challenges, this is significant progress. We are delighted that the government has made a strong, brand new commitment to the protection of our natural heritage and that it has chosen to partner with us to undertake this critical work."[6]

The amount of federal support of this national initiative was $225 million, an unprecedented scale of investment in a non-governmental environmental sector in Canada. Of that total, $185 million was to support the direct work of NCC, while $25 million would assist securement projects by Ducks Unlimited Canada and $15 million would go to other land trusts through a grants program to be developed and administered by NCC. This impressive engagement of the Government of Canada in the Natural Areas Conservation Program was the culmination of several decades of persistent groundwork with senior federal politicians and bureaucrats. That networking had always found a sympathetic audience within agencies of the federal government and among many of the bureaucrats and politicians with whom discussions were had. NCC had several times come agonizingly close to achieving programmatic support. Now, however, the profound hopes had become a reality. NCC publically committed to match the federal investment in the Natural Areas Conservation Program at least dollar for dollar in the value of donated funds and property, as well as to secure at least two hundred thousand hectares (five hundred thousand acres) of ecologically important property across Canada.

The federal program would be implemented using funds provided to NCC on an annual basis, according to a budgeted request prepared in collaboration with Ducks Unlimited. The funds were to be held in deferred accounts and would be brought into revenue as projects were undertaken. The monies allocated to NCC would mostly be used to support securement projects, plus some funding to help to administer the overall program, including the one for other land trusts.

At a meeting of the Executive Committee in May 2007, John Lounds led a discussion about contractual requirements of the federal agreement and associated issues. The broader gist was that NCC's delivery of the program needed to be founded on two major considerations: (1) first-rate business practices and prudent expenditures on properties and related work, and (2) use of the best-available ecological and biological science as a foundation of the conservation planning that underlies securement and stewardship actions. Within that broader context, key actions and criteria would be the following:

- projects would receive funding through the program only if in a natural area with an approved Natural Area Conservation Plan;
- the dollar value of federal investments would be matched by at least a one-to-one basis;
- federal monies could not be used toward endowment;
- oversight of the Program would be provided by a committee with membership from senior levels of Environment Canada and NCC's Board of Directors, supported by senior NCC staff;
- an investment committee would oversee, using conservative investment criteria, the management of federal funds received under the Program;
- NCC would need to accelerate the development of Natural Area Conservation Plans and stewardship programming across the country;
- funding provided under the Program to support the work of other qualified land trusts at approved natural areas would be delivered under a similar formula as those funds being provided for NCC's own conservation efforts; and
- the conservation work of Ducks Unlimited Canada under the Program would utilize DUC's conservation planning methodology to identify, secure, and steward priority sites.

It was also announced at that meeting that the Friends of the Nature Conservancy of Canada (FNCC) had now become a functional organization. This meant that FNCC could operate as a US charity that works to support NCC's conservation work in Canada by raising funds and accepting donations of ecologically important properties from US residents. The FNCC has its own board of directors and is at arm's length from NCC, but when it receives donations they are used to support conservation actions in Canada based on the directions of the donors and often in support of the initiatives of the Conservancy. The formation of FNCC had begun in 1996 when that organization was incorporated in the state of New York. However, a protracted series of applications to the federal governments of the US and Canada then ensued before the FNCC was enabled to offer tax benefits for US-sourced donations. The first key hurdle was passed in 2005 when FNCC received its 501(c)3 status from the US Internal Revenue Service, allowing donors to receive a tax benefit in that country for donations to FNCC. The next one occurred in 2007, when FNCC was granted prescribed donee status by the Government of

Canada, allowing US residents to donate ecologically important lands owned in Canada without incurring tax on capital gains on the property.

At a teleconference in May 2007, the Executive Committee considered a novel proposal from the British Columbia region to acquire a commercial building that would serve as its main office in Victoria, with any residual space to be rented out. The intent of this project was to control and stabilize the occupancy costs of office space for the BC region. After considerable discussion, permission was given to acquire the Mellor Building, with financing from VanCity, the largest credit union in Canada. The total capital cost was about $2.5 million, to be financed by two mortgages, one for the building and a second for an extensive renovation.

In June 2007, Nathalie Zinger was hired as the regional vice-president for NCC in Quebec. Zinger came with considerable experience in the community of conservation NGOs, having worked as the executive director of Heritage Montreal and before that heading the provincial office of the World Wildlife Fund (Canada). Highlights of the Conservancy's work in Quebec since Zinger came on board include the conservation of extensive tracts in the Green and White Mountain ranges, the partnered establishment of the 6,750-hectare (16,667-acre) Réserve naturelle des Montagnes-Vertes east of Montreal, the protection in the Outaouais region of about 2,500 hectares (6,200 acres) of forest, wetland, and alvar communities, the protection of 90 percent of the Tea Fields (the largest bog south of Montreal), the acquisition of the 458-hectare (1,130-acre) Piedmont and Prévost Escarpments at the gateway of the Laurentian Mountains, and programs to enhance public awareness of conservation needs in various project areas.

In February 2008, the NCC Board held its first-ever winter meeting. This has become an annual event, so the full national board now had three meetings every year, thereby allowing the directors to be more fully informed about the diverse issues and projects of the rapidly growing organization. A new *Conservancy Manual* was distributed for that meeting, a helpful and comprehensive document that was prepared for directors and staff, and for which the hard work of Kyla Winchester and Bob Alexander was acknowledged at the meeting. A major topic of discussion was the Stewardship Endowment Fund (SEF), which then stood at about $15 million but was projected to be as large as $75 million by 2015. Although the SEF was expected to pay for about one-third of ongoing stewardship expenses, there would always be a need to raise the rest of the funds on an annual basis.

There was also a broad-reaching discussion of the A Force for Nature campaign, for which a planning workshop had been held the previous evening. Key results of that meeting were that the Conservancy should focus on communicating the importance of its conservation work on great Canadian landscapes and on finding ways to increase the numbers of people who understand the need to achieve large-scale results. It was recognized that middle-aged and older Canadians are the core supporters of NCC and that base had to be well stewarded, but there was also an emerging constituency of persons aged twenty to forty. It was also announced that A Force for Nature now had an impressive slate of high-profile businesspeople on its National Campaign Leadership Team. Those key volunteers were led by Paul Desmarais Jr. and John Risley and, as of 2011, included David Aisenstat, Ron Brenneman, Pat Daniel, David Dubé, Darren Entwistle, Kerry Hawkins, and Barbara Stymiest. Among other campaign-related duties, those influential Canadians were asked to headline campaign events intended to build support in the business and governmental communities.

At an executive meeting in May 2008, Julie Wood was introduced as the new vice-president of corporate, having moved to NCC from an executive position with the International Private Banking operation at the Royal Bank of Canada. She has been one of the key staff members involved in developing NCC's risk management framework. Review of risk management issues has now become a routine part of all meetings of the NCC Board and its Executive Committee. At the spring meeting in June 2008, the Finance and Investment Committee advised that, because of relatively unsatisfying investment performance, the endowment funds would be transferred to a different commercial manager. The process would involve a liquidation of the Conservancy's portfolio of securities in equal tranches over the next four months, with the resulting cash to be held in treasury bills. Meanwhile, a search would be held to choose the next investment manager.

The timing of the conversion of equities into T-bills was well timed by NCC. Beginning in September, the North American, and indeed global markets, suffered a huge downturn, which resulted in a worldwide recession. This economic slump was largely precipitated by an extensive devaluation of heavily leveraged real estate in the US, resulting in widespread defaults on loans and mortgages and a crisis of liquidity in the banking sector. An even deeper crunch was avoided when the national governments of developed countries engaged in heavy deficit spending on bailouts to prevent bankruptcies of manufacturing and financial companies that were deemed "too large to fail," and then on infrastructure projects to stimulate their national economies and indeed the global one. Even those vigorous actions, however, did not prevent a large downturn in equity markets. For instance, the Toronto Stock Exchange index devalued by as much as 49 percent during this economic slump,[7] and the Dow Jones Industrials by up to 55 percent.[8] Remarkably, however, the NCC endowment funds were almost entirely outside of stock-related equities during this period, and almost none of their hard-won value was lost.

In large part, this substantial dodging-of-an-economic-bullet was due to the NCC Board heeding the prescient advice of its Finance and Investment Subcommittee to move to a different investment manager, and to move into cash and T-bills. The Board, at its annual general meeting in October 2008, again acted on that subcommittee's advice and kept the endowment monies in treasury bills rather than immediately reinvesting them in equities under a new manager. In fact, the latter did not begin until January 2009, by which time the markets had begun to recover. The fact that the Conservancy had managed to conserve almost all of its endowment capital during the global recession of 2008–9 was regarded by its directors and employees as a wonderful success of money management.

At a meeting of the Executive Committee in September 2008, the directors gave approval for NCC to establish a line of credit with a major Canadian bank. Terms were negotiated based on two facilities: (1) a $2-million revolving loan, to finance up to 50 percent of the cost of acquiring particular conservation properties, which in NCC's context represented a supplemental resource to the Boswell Fund (the outstanding amount of this loan fluctuates as it is tapped to acquire properties and then repaid by fundraising), and (2) a specific term loan of $20 million to finance up to 50 percent of the costs of acquiring the Darkwoods property plus its initial stewardship activities.

The implementation of these facilities for external loans represented a saltation in the development and maturation of NCC as a large and reliable conservation organization. It signified the fact that NCC staff and directors had great confidence in the fundraising capacity of the organization. In the past, Canadian banks had been wary of lending money to charities, based partly on a concern about their reputational risk should they have to foreclose. However, the Conservancy had built a strong track record as a prudent business-minded entity that pays off its debts and that consistently works in a responsible manner, and so the loan facilities moved forward.

At the annual meeting of the Board in October 2008, the directors formally approved a policy to ensure that all securement projects provide a contribution to the Stewardship Endowment Fund (SEF). The policy required that both fee-simple and easement securements, whether purchased or donated, have a payment to the SEF equivalent to 15 percent of the appraised value of the property. The contribution to the SEF had to be made at the time of closing of the deal, and if cash had not yet been raised to make the payment it would have to be borrowed, either as a loan from the internal Boswell Fund or from an external lender. The motion included the possibility of exceptions to the 15-percent rule, which could apply to extremely large projects for which a realistic calculation of stewardship costs might rationalize a lower rate of contribution, but such allowances were expected to be rare. In actual fact, since 2007, the Conservancy had already been implementing a staff-initiated requirement for a capitalization of the SEF based on a levy of 15 percent of the appraised value of each property being acquired. However, the formal motion of the Board served to firmly legitimize that policy.

Not surprisingly, the wide-scale implications of the ongoing economic recession were the major topic of discussion at the next meeting of the Executive Committee, in December 2008. The global economy was becoming increasingly constrained by shortages of cash and credit, and governments were engaged in heavy deficit spending. For charities, the socio-economic circumstances brought risks of smaller donations from individuals, corporations, and governments. John Lounds and his executive team had been working on several business scenarios for NCC, and in the meantime had implemented several management tactics: (1) cash was being conserved to the degree possible, (2) short-term measures had been implemented to slow expenditures and signal prudence, (3) means were being explored to improve business efficiencies and strategic reductions, and growth opportunities were being examined, and (4) retaining the core resources of NCC, particularly its staff, was being emphasized, as was continuing to support the capacities for fundraising and conservation actions that were vital to the mission of the organization. Nevertheless, NCC was in a relatively good position business-wise, compared with almost all other charities in Canada. This was partly because the Conservancy had adequate cash reserves held in deferred accounts and endowment funds.

The next gathering of the Board was the winter meeting in February 2009, and the recession was again a major topic of discussion. Lounds recounted that NCC was faring relatively well, in spite of the prevailing economic climate. The Natural Areas Conservation Program partnership with the Government of Canda was an important stabilizing factor. Moreover, NCC had reduced its overall national spending by 18 percent in comparison with the previous year, largely by slowing down the pace of project implementation and planning studies, and it had instituted a hiring freeze. Lounds also noted that the Finance and Investment Subcommittee had recommended that NCC begin to reinvest endowment funds into the equities market. That had begun at a rate of 5 percent of the capital per month and would continue until the target percentage of 60 percent was reached. (The rest, according to the general policy on investments, was to be held in bonds and other relatively secure instruments.)

Also at that meeting, Michael Bradstreet, vice-president of conservation, reported that the key project to develop and implement an advanced land information system (LIS) had begun. The new LIS would amalgamate data into a single online database from the several previous systems used in the NCC regions and would have the capability to track information in much greater detail. NCC employees would be able to quickly and efficiently access information relevant to their full range of needs, from planning, securement, stewardship, and land administration, to information related to metes and bounds and other boundary data, biodiversity attributes, and financials.[9] The LIS would also allow staff to assess changes on properties, prepare reports and proposals, plan their workflow and log activity, and undertake planning studies much more easily than was previously the case. The new LIS was fully implemented in mid-2011.

Also in early 2009, NCC began to develop a new thirty-minute DRTV show called *A Force for Nature* to coincide with the national fundraising campaign. This show replaced the previous *Fighting for Canada* that had been airing since 2005. The new DRTV show highlights project areas where NCC is active by telling compelling stories about the properties and NCC staff, volunteers, and donors who are engaged in achieving these successes of conservation. The program is hosted by Denise Donlon, a television host and media executive, and is supported by celebrity spokespersons Rachel Blanchard, Jason Priestley, Ryan Reynolds, and William Shatner.

At an executive meeting in May 2009, the directors approved a new Conservation Buyer Transaction Policy. This directive is applicable to cases in which NCC has acquired a property with good natural values, but where NCC has decided that the land might be responsibly sold to another like-minded owner, with a suitable conservation agreement. The new owner would have to abide by the terms of the agreement, which depending on the property might include a prohibition on subdivision of the land, on the conversion of native grassland to tame pasture, on excessive stocking of livestock, on timber harvesting, on expansion of building footprints, or on other actions that might damage the natural values. Because a conservation easement has monetary value that can be appraised, its presence means that an encumbered property might be acquired for less than what it would be without the encumberance. Although NCC rarely sells conserved lands in this way, it is a good option for some isolated properties whose natural values would not be threatened by certain economic uses, such as grazing cattle at a suitable density. Meanwhile, the sale of such a property could provide funds that the Conservancy could use to purchase higher-priority lands. The reason for developing this new policy was to ensure that the natural values of any conserved properties that NCC might sell remain durably protected, while also securing the organization's reputation against potential criticism, providing high ethical standards in its policies, safeguarding the prior investment in the land, and exposing the property to potential conservation buyers through the open market.

In September 2009 NCC launched the program for other qualified organizations (OQOs) under the terms of the federal Natural Areas Conservation Program. This part of the program provided funding to provincial and local land trusts to help fund securement proposals that occur within a natural area having an approved NACP. The proposals were evaluated by a board of three volunteers working at arm's length from NCC: Robert Alain from the EJLB Foundation, Sandy Houston from the George Cedric Metcalf Charitable Foundation, and Linda Nowlan from World Wildlife Fund (Canada). At the close of the program a total of $11.4 million had been awarded to thirty-five projects from seventeen OQOs, with a projected 3,328 hectares (8,225 acres) being conserved by those projects.

At a meeting of the Executive Committee in September 2009, and again at the annual meeting in October, John Lounds made a presentation on the progress of NCC's project to monetize carbon credits using a portion of the ecological productivity associated with the recently acquired Darkwoods landscape in southeastern British Columbia.[10] He noted that this project had the potential to raise millions of dollars annually, which would provide support for ongoing management of the Darkwoods project, and help to retire its internal debt of a not-fully paid stewardship endowment. Two documents were provided to give the directors further background on the theory and practice of ecological carbon credits and their implementation by conservation organizations. One was a recently published literature review that had been prepared for NCC by Bill Freedman, a director and at the time chair of the Board,[11] and the other was a document by NCC scientist John Riley.[12] Lounds was given permission to finalize this innovative carbon-credit project. Further details of its implementation will be provided later in this chapter.

In October 2009, NCC entered into a collaborative initiative with Earth Rangers and other partners to develop a new program for kids called Bring Back the Wild. Earth Rangers is a non-profit organization dedicated to educating and inspiring children to become good environmental citizens.[13] Its focus is on communicating an uplifting science-based message about the importance of protecting biodiversity and making sustainable lifestyle choices. To do this, Earth Rangers annually exposes hundreds of thousands of children to interactive live-animal shows performed in their schools, at the Royal Ontario Museum in Toronto, and at community events. The stars of the live shows are charismatic critters, such as Cosmo (a ring-tailed lemur, *Lemur catta*), Koho (a bald eagle, *Haliaeetus leucocephalus*), Maverick (an American kestrel, *Falco sparverius*), Phantom (a black pine snake, *Pituophis melanoleucus*), and Timber (an American marten, *Martes americana*). The organization also engages kids via its online community of more than sixty-thousand children who have registered to be Earth Rangers and through a national outreach campaign on the youth-focused YTV cable channel. The intent of the program is to foster a generation of environmental stewards who will take positive actions to help protect endangered species and their natural habitats.

The key intersection of Earth Rangers with NCC is the Bring Back the Wild campaign, in which kids raise funds to help protect animals and their habitat. The partnership with Earth Rangers has been a great way for NCC to become more involved in educational programs for youth without having to develop an independent program.

The annual meeting of October 2010 was largely spent in workshop-style discussions related to the development of the next strategic plan for NCC that would cover the period 2012–17. To bring everyone up to a suitable level of contextual background, John Lounds presented an outline of five discussion papers prepared by NCC staff that covered the following topics: (1) progress made against the existing five-year strategic plan; (2) alternative strategies for capturing revenue; (3) impact on the organization of the completion of the Natural Areas Conservation Program; (4) a Conservancy philosophy on allowing corporate donors to share the NCC brand and marks, and on accepting donations from corporations; and (5) projects in the boreal region of Canada. Lounds further reminded everyone that all conservation actions by NCC were dependent on, and limited by, the ability of the organization to generate revenues.

One of the major outcomes of the strategic-planning workshops was a conclusion that NCC should work to broaden its reach by assuming a more influential leadership role within the community of direct-action conservation organizations. Notwithstanding that NCC has been effective in its mission of conservation planning and acquiring and stewarding properties, the sustainable protection of biodiversity requires that much larger tracts of habitat be conserved than has so far been accomplished. Moreover, a comprehensive solution requires much more than the creation of networks of protected areas. It is also necessary to implement conservation measures on "working" landscapes that are more directly serving the human economy, and NCC could also play a role in moving society forward on that important track of ecological sustainability. In many cases, governments and companies need objective advice based on conservation science about the ways that working lands can be managed on a more sustainable basis, and NCC has the capacity to help in that respect. The workshop participants identified a number of additional sectors in which a heavier engagement by NCC would likely prove worthwhile:

- In the boreal region there is not much private land to acquire, but there is a need for conservation planning and there are opportunities to retire privately held rights.
- Major biodiversity loss has been occurring in less-developed countries of low latitudes, where effective conservation action can be implemented by investments from wealthier nations, such as Canada. Within that context, the best ways for NCC to work internationally would be to focus on projects involving ecosystems and countries that provide critical habitat for migratory species that breed in Canada.

- Finally, NCC could broaden its conservation reach by making its meth-odologies and results from natural-area conservation planning broadly available to assist governments, other land trusts, and landowners find conservation solutions for problems with which they are dealing.

The strategic-planning workshops also supported the idea of NCC becoming more involved in new market-based offset products related to the enhancement or maintenance of environmental "services." In effect, these involve the quantification and sale of certified ecological offsets that help to compensate for unavoidable adverse environmental impacts caused by cer-tain economic activities. In effect, the damage is counterbalanced by offset-ting environmental gains, with the goal of achieving a net outcome that is less damaging or even beneficial. One such offset that is already being actively marketed is the sale of ecological carbon credits from NCC properties (see below), and another is that of biodiversity credits.

Biodiversity credits might involve stewardship actions that improve habitat conditions on NCC properties, such as the creation of new wet-lands to provide habitat for waterfowl or for certain species-at-risk. Certified biodiversity credits associated with that management might then be sold to private interests that, as a course of their business operations, may have dam-aged comparable habitats elsewhere. The monetization of "wetland credits" as an environmental mitigation is already a widespread practice in the United States, and there are also opportunities to engage in the practice in Canada.[14] It would even be possible to design projects that simultaneously provide both carbon credits and biodiversity credits.[15] While meeting attendees showed general support for these ideas, there was also a broadly held view that, should NCC become engaged in the sale of biodiversity credits, the overall result would have to be considerably larger than a simple "no net loss" bene-fit (which is the usual criterion in the US). One proposal was for any NCC projects to result in an enhancement of the targeted habitat by a ratio of at least three to one. It might even be possible for NCC to eventually accumulate "banks" of mitigation credits for sale to customers that are carefully selected on the basis of having already undertaken significant actions to implement sustainable solutions to their problems of environmental sustainability.

At the executive meeting of December 2010, the directors learned that eighty-five events for conservation volunteers (CVs) had been held during 2010, involving approximately twelve hundred people and seven thousand hours of volunteer time. This was an encouraging result, in view of the CV program being in its infancy. Most of the events involved people engaged in work helpful to the stewardship of protected areas, such as surveys of biodiversity, removing invasive plants, maintaining trails, or removing litter. Some events involved guided family excursions on NCC properties. These various CV activities enable supporters to build their empathy for the natural world, and for the NCC mission, through engagement that goes beyond the donation of money. The CV sector will undoubtedly become a much more prominent aspect of the NCC program in the coming years.

In June 2011, the Conservancy announced the completion of the validation and verification phases of its inaugural Darkwoods Forest Carbon Pilot Project (DFCPP).[16] The resulting sale of carbon credits involved seven hundred thousand tonnes of offsets known as Voluntary Carbon Units (VCUs) and raised about $5 million for NCC.[17] The buyers of these carbon credits were the Pacific Carbon Trust and Ecosystem Restoration Associates (ERA). The Conservancy is using the money generated from the sale primarily to help fund its management activities on the Darkwoods property, and to pay for its stewardship endowment. This groundbreaking initiative was led by NCC staff Katie Blake, Tom Swann, and Rob Wilson. At the time of the announcement of the DFCPP, John Lounds said, "We are always looking for unique strategies to fund the protection of Canada's natural heritage. . . . By harnessing the power of the carbon market, the Darkwoods Forest Carbon Pilot Project represents an innovative new avenue for helping to fund great conservation projects."[18] Robert Falls of ERA stated, "Darkwoods represents a major step forward for British Columbia and Canada in recognizing the important role our forests play in climate mitigation, while demonstrating that forests have multiple economic values, of which carbon is one."[19]

In the DFCPP, the forest productivity on the immense tract generates ecological carbon credits, which are associated with the fixation of atmospheric carbon dioxide (CO_2) into accumulating amounts of tree biomass. In effect, when NCC sells these credits into the carbon market, they serve as an offset against emissions of CO_2 and other greenhouse gases from other economic activities, such as driving vehicles or generating electricity by fossil fuel combustion. The carbon credits at Darkwoods arise as a result of NCC conducting improved forest management activities on the tract, thereby avoiding the intensive harvesting and development that may have occurred had the Conservancy not purchased the property. As a consequence, more carbon is stored on the landscape than would otherwise have occurred, and so a smaller net amount is present in the atmosphere. That carbon-storage benefit is additional to what would have occurred under the previous ownership or to what would have ensued if the property had been sold to another purchaser that would have undertaken intensive timber harvesting or property development. Because of this additionality, the enhanced carbon storage gives rise to legitimate carbon credits issued under leading internationally recognized carbon standards for the voluntary carbon offset market (see below).

To undertake the pilot project, NCC and its advisors calculated the amount of carbon stocks in biomass on the Darkwoods landscape. Although a timber harvest continues on the property, it is on a much smaller scale than previously and will be subjected to further reductions in scale. For example, in 2011 the timber harvest was 19 percent of the average during 2004–8 before NCC acquired the property. The increased carbon storage from the conservation-focused management under NCC will be monitored on a yearly basis, after the sequestration has occurred. The methodology used has been approved by the Verified Carbon Standard (VCS), an association that ensures that projects validated and verified under its auspices meet strict, internationally recognized standards.[20] The fieldwork and modelling for the DFCPP took about three years to complete and were designed to ensure that high-quality carbon credits are available, in that they are verified by a credible process and are compliant with one of the most recognized international standards (i.e., the VCS). As such, this project by NCC and its partners represents a leading-edge gold-standard methodology for the qualification of carbon credits and subsequent monetization of this kind of ecosystem service. This initial project will likely be followed by additional such developments by the Conservancy and comparable organizations.

As of late 2011, only about 5 percent of the estimated carbon credits to be generated on the Darkwoods landscape over the term of the project had been sold under the pilot program, with a large holdback established under the VCS process to act as a reserve that provides a buffer against any potential losses.

The Conservation Program, 2006–11

In 2007, the Conservancy purchased Boughton Island, located in Summerside Harbour on Prince Edward Island.[21] This 240-hectare (598-acre) island is the third-largest off PEI and the biggest that is uninhabited. Its major habitats include white-sand beaches, salt marsh, freshwater ponds, and coastal spruce forest. The island supports the largest breeding colony of great blue heron (*Ardea herodias*) in the province as well as nesting by common tern (*Sterna hirundo*) and the endangered piping plover (*Charadrius melodus*). The island was acquired for a project cost of about $2 million, but the deal itself was rather complicated. A direct purchase of the island property would have resulted in a substantial tax liability for its US vendor, so instead of an asset purchase the deal was structured as a share purchase to acquire the entirety of an offshore company, Panmure Corporation, whose only asset was Boughton Island. Immediately upon its purchase, NCC dissolved Panmure but of course retained ownership of the island. A small additional complication was the fact that the transaction involved NCC (PEI) Inc.

The funding for the acquisition of Boughton Island was provided by the Chisholm-Thomson family, with additional support from the Government of PEI, Environment Canada, the R. Howard Webster Foundation, and the US Fish and Wildlife Service through the NAWCA program. However, to close out the project there was also a public campaign that received a great deal of public attention, to the extent that small donations even came from outside of Canada, including one from Indonesia. An additional benefit of this project was the engagement of Laurie Thomson with the work of NCC. She came onto the Board in 2006 and served as its chair from 2010 to 2011.

In April 2008, the Conservancy announced its spectacular Darkwoods acquisition in the South Selkirks region of southeastern British Columbia, which at 55,000 hectares (136,000 acres) was the largest private conservation project ever undertaken in Canada.[22] The property was secured from a German forestry company known as Pluto Darkwoods Corp., whose timber harvesting was relatively sustainable so that the landscape was in reasonably good natural condition. The extensive tract is large enough to support grizzly bear (*Ursus arctos*) and other large mammals, including a small population of mountain caribou (*Rangifer tarandus caribou*), which are critically endangered in this southernmost part of their range (an aerial survey in the winter of 2010 found forty-three caribou in the South Selkirk Mountains, of which thirty-five were on the Darkwoods tract, six on lands between Darkwoods and the US border, and two in Idaho). In total, the tract provides habitat for at least twenty-nine species designated as at risk in British Columbia. Moreover, the Darkwoods property connects several large blocks of Crown land that are also in good natural condition and are administered as wildlife-management zones. In aggregate, this represents an extremely large conserved area of more than 100,000 hectares (250,000 acres).

This impressively large project involved a split-receipt donation for all the land holdings of Pluto Darkwoods.[23] Once an offer to purchase the tract was accepted by the vendor, NCC engaged in an energetic fundraising campaign, and explored various options to raise funding including the potential sale of forest carbon credits to help fund the required $12 million stewardship endowment. In spite of private support, the major funding came from the federal Natural Areas Conservation Program. External bridge financing loans of $20 million were needed to cover the securement, stewardship, and other costs. The Board approved the loans on condition that they be retired within three years. The sale of ecological carbon credits from the Darkwoods landscape provided a boost to meeting that deadline; however, at the time of writing, $8 million was still needed to complete the Darkwoods project.

In April 2008, NCC entered into an agreement for a donated conservation easement for the Canyon Ranch in the Porcupine Hills region of Alberta. The easement covered an area of 5,178 hectares (12,786 acres) and had an appraised value of about $10.7 million. Like other such easements in a grazing landscape, this one specifies that certain management actions cannot be undertaken: subdivision of the property, construction of additional roads or buildings, conversion of native grassland, draining or other significant alteration of surface water, and deliberate introduction of non-native species, other than those used in traditional agriculture. At the time, this was the largest property that NCC had ever secured in Alberta, in terms of area and value. A biodiversity assessment of the ranch found it to be remarkably diverse in habitats and species, with 138 plant communities being found, 462 species of plants, and 82 species of animals, including 59 bird species.[24] Moreover, seven of the plant communities are considered rare in Alberta, and one was found that had not previously been observed in the province. Also, there are at least eleven rare species of plants, one being new to Alberta, and seventeen at-risk animals are present. The ranch also provides habitat for large-scale movements of large carnivores and ungulates, including cougar and grizzly bear.

In September 2008, the BC Region completed its largest-ever grassland-focused project when it entered into a deal involving the Frolek Ranch, located near Kamloops.[25] This combined land purchase and conservation covenant covered 3,170 hectares (7,828 acres) and protected one of the largest intact native grasslands in the Thompson-Nicola Valley. Almost one-third of the project area (948 hectares; 2,342 acres) was purchased by NCC and has been leased back to the ranch on a long-term basis, while the other portion (2,221 hectares; 5,486 acres) is protected by conservation covenant. Some of the rare and at-risk species that occur in the varied grassland, forested, and wetland habitats on the tract are the American badger (*Taxidea taxus*), burrowing owl (*Athene cunicularia*), long-billed curlew (*Numenius americanus*), sharp-tailed grouse (*Tympanuchus phasianellus*), Great Basin spadefoot toad (*Spea intermontana*), and Okanogan fameflower (*Talinum sediforme*).

This project had a cash and donation value of $12.3 million. The key funding partners were the Government of Canada, which provided more than $6 million through the Natural Areas Conservation Program, and the Tula Foundation of Quadra Island, BC, which donated $1.7 million toward the stewardship endowment. Both the lease and covenant keep the property as a working ranch run by the Frolek Cattle Company, owned by the Frolek family, which has ranched the area for four generations. However, the terms of the agreements prohibit subdivision, while binding the property into large blocks of land suitable for both a working ranch and a large conserved area, and specifying other management actions that will conserve the native grassland and its dependent species. At an event that launched this project, Darren Dempsey, a great-grandson of George and Teresa Frolek, who started the ranch in 1906, said, "Our family did not want to see our heritage sold to developers who would urbanize and forever alter these grasslands. We chose to partner with NCC to ensure the environmental values of the land would be protected."[26]

In 2009, NCC signed an agreement with Bob Seaman, president of OH Ranch, for the donation of a conservation easement for that property in southern Alberta.[27] The agreement covered about 4,050 hectares (10,000 acres) and is among the largest ever in Canada. This project was a culmination of the vision of Daryl (Doc) Seaman, Bob's father, who wanted to see his extensive property maintained as a working ranch in good natural condition but was worried that his dream might not be met because of rapid growth of the urbanized landscape of nearby Calgary. Doc Seaman had negotiated and agreed to the provisions of the conservation easement, but raising the necessary funds for the project costs and stewardship endowment had delayed the final signing of the accord. Although Doc passed away just before the closing of the deal, he had the comfort of knowing that his conservation vision would be realized.

The OH Ranch provides habitat for a number of animals that are suffering declines of range and abundance, such as the northern pygmy owl (*Glaucidium gnoma*), sharp-tailed grouse (*Tympanuchus phasianellus*), and bull trout (*Salvelinus confluentus*). Stands of limber pine (*Pinus flexilis*) occur on several ridges, and individuals of a regional population of grizzly bear pass through it. In addition, the Government of Alberta expanded the conserved area by setting aside about twenty-four hundred hectares (six thousand acres) of Crown-leased lands on the ranch as heritage rangeland. At the time of the announcement of the OH Ranch project, Bob Demulder, the regional vice-president for NCC in Alberta, said, "OH Ranch is a unique conservation project, providing habitat for a number of different species. . . . It serves as a great example of how conservation should happen—with a number of committed partners, including government, NGOs and private landowners, all working together to conserve significant land and water for the species that depend on them."[28]

Also in 2009, the Conservancy acquired eight islands known as the Wilson Group in northwestern Lake Superior, near Rossport, Ontario. The archipelago has a total area of about nineteen hundred hectares (forty-seven hundred acres). Some of the key natural features are sandy beaches and intact coastal forest, which are rare on the shoreline of Lake Superior. Coastal cliffs in the area are used for nesting by the rare peregrine falcon (*Falco peregrinus anatum*), and these exposed habitats also support relict populations of arctic plants. Because the islands are of binational importance, The Nature Conservancy (US) was a key partner in this land acquisition, as were the Government of Canada and the Ontario Ministry of Natural Resources. In terms of dollar value, this $7-million project was, at the time, the largest private conservation acquisition ever completed in Ontario. The islands are within the Lake Superior National Marine Conservation Area, created in 2007.

In 2009, the Quebec region of NCC created the largest private conserved area east of the Rocky Mountains, when it announced its 6,505-hectare (16,062-acre) Green Mountains Nature Reserve (GMNR).[29] This assembly is binational in character in the sense that the Green Mountains range extends into adjacent Vermont, where related conservation actions are also ongoing. The greater objective is to develop extensively connected protected areas that are able to sustain large-scale ecological dynamics as well as the habitat needs of big mobile animals. The NCC assembly in Quebec involves fifteen properties totalling almost fifteen hundred hectares (thirty-seven hundred acres), which were secured over a three-year period at a cost of close to $7.4 million. Moreover, these projects are cumulative on areas that NCC has been assembling in the Green Mountains natural area for more than a decade, which amount to more than 8,595 hectares (21,221 acres) acquired at a total project cost of about $25 million. All the projects have involved collaborative funding, with the Government of Canada and the Province of Quebec being important contributors, along with many private donors. The latter includes a US organization, the Open Space Institute, whose Transborder Land Protection Fund offers grants and loans for projects that conserve habitats in the Northern Appalachian/Acadian ecoregion shared by the eastern states and the adjacent areas of Canada.[30] Financial support through this fund is guided by an ecoregional conservation plan known as Two Countries, One Forest (Deux Pays, Une Forêt), in which the Quebec and Atlantic regions of NCC are core participants.[31]

The extensive forested tract of the Green Mountains Nature Reserve provides critical habitat for at least 105 provincial species-at-risk (some are also nationally listed), including the spring salamander (*Gyrinophilus porphyriticus*), Bicknell's thrush (*Catharus bicknelli*), Green Mountain maidenhair fern (*Adiantum viridimontanum*), and American ginseng (*Panax quinquifolius*). The GMNR and adjacent greater protected areas of the Green Mountains are also vital to the survival of big animals with large home ranges, such as black bear (*Ursus americanus*), moose (*Alces alces*), bobcat (*Lynx rufus*), and the rare eastern cougar (*Puma concolor*). In addition, the GMNR has wilderness areas to which the public has limited access through several hiking trails that NCC has established with local partners. At the public announcement of this ongoing assembly, Nathalie Zinger, NCC's regional vice-president for Quebec, said, "This great natural corridor makes sense with conservation efforts being made on both sides of the Canada-U.S. border. Several partners, such as Appalachian Corridor, have demonstrated an extraordinary commitment to the preservation of this natural heritage. The success of this cross-border initiative will continue to depend on it."[32]

In 2010, the BC region of NCC acquired Chase Woods, 41 hectares (101 acres) of intact old-growth and mature coastal forest in the eastern Cowichan Valley of southern Vancouver Island.[33] This iconic forest has become exceedingly rare because of timber harvesting, suburban development, and damage caused by invasive species. However, the Chase Forest has escaped the worst of those stressors and continues to support centuries-old trees of Pacific yew

(*Taxus brevifolia*), Douglas-fir (*Pseudotsuga menziesii*), Garry oak (*Quercus garryana*), lodgepole pine (*Pinus contorta*), and Pacific madrone (*Arbutus menziesii*). The site also contains a globally imperilled forest community dominated by Garry oak. Among the rare plants occurring on the property are the white-top aster (*Sericocarpus rigidus*), farewell-to-spring (*Clarkia amoena*), and California-tea (*Rupertia physodes*). This project had a budget of about $1.7 million, of which $1.5 million was used for the purchase, associated costs, and short-term stewardship, and $200,000 was put toward a stewardship endowment. The key supporters were the Government of Canada through the Natural Area Conservation Program, the BC Trust for Public Lands, and the Cowichan Community Land Trust.[34]

In 2011, the Atlantic region of NCC acquired the Grassy Place, located at the headwaters of Robinson's River in a remote valley of the Long Range Mountains of southwestern Newfoundland. This 1,575-hectare (3,890-acre) property is well known as a productive oasis of wetlands and lowland forest, and it had long been a target for conservation. It has extensive fluvial marshes dominated by tall, waving stands of blue-joint grass (*Calamagrostis canadensis*), large patches of which are a rare habitat in Newfoundland.[35] The productive wetlands support large numbers of breeding and migrating waterfowl, as well as abundant woodland caribou (*Rangifer tarandus caribou*) and the at-risk Newfoundland marten (*Martes americana atrata*) and rusty blackbird (*Euphagus carolinus*). The management plan being prepared by NCC will allow traditional uses of the Grassy Place, but no timber harvesting or road building will occur. This project had a cost of about $792,000, including a stewardship endowment of $92,000. The key sources of funds were the federal Natural Area Conservation Program, the NAWCA program, and about sixty individual and corporate donations.

Another exciting acquisition in 2011 was a purchase from the Long Point Region Conservation Authority of a 344-hectare (875-acre) tract in Southern Ontario that consists of a famous tract of southern forest known as Backus Woods, plus two adjacent properties, made possible through generous support from The W. Garfield Weston Foundation.[36] NCC already owned several properties contiguous to that tract, parts of which are being restored from farmland to a forested condition. The area owned by the Conservancy is now 728 hectares (1,799 acres), but this is adjacent to the 1,214-hectare (3,000-acre) St. Williams Conservation Reserve of the Ontario Ministry of Natural Resources, so the aggregate protected area is about

1,900 hectares (4,700 acres). The Conservancy is still hoping to acquire additional properties adjacent to its new Backus Woods protected area, which is the largest and best-quality stand of older hardwood forest to have survived in the Carolinian ecozone of Southern Ontario. The tract supports many rare species, including twenty-three plants and animals that are listed by COSEWIC as being at risk and many others that are provincially rare.[37]

Also in 2011 NCC brought together a conservation partnership to help ensure that 160,000 hectares (400,000 acres) of spectacular wilderness in British Columbia's Flathead Valley would not be developed for coal, oil, gas, or mineral resources. NCC, working through the Natural Areas Conservation Program, joined with The Nature Conervancy (US) to provide support to the province of British Columbia. The province in turn was able to implement provisions of a Memorandum of Understanding it had signed earlier with the state of Montana to extinguish exploration and mining in the valley. The Flathead is a biologically rich area, home to 70 mammal species, including a remarkable 16 carnivores, 270 species of birds, 25 of fish, and 1,200 vascular plants.[38] The Flathead River itself is natural and undammed and was declared a Wild and Scenic River in the US in 1975. For these reasons the potential for mining in the area posed a threat and had long been an issue between Canada and the US, as well as for British Columbia and Montana.

The Flathead is adjacent to some large protected areas, including Waterton Lakes National Park in Alberta, Akamina-Kishinena Provincial Park in British Columbia, and Glacier National Park in Montana. Limited protected status was conferred to the Flathead Valley in October 2011 when the provincial government passed legislation that reserved the area from any mining of fossil fuels or minerals, while allowing licensed timber harvesting, hunting, trapping, and non-consumptive outdoor recreation to continue.[39] This designation will help to maintain natural values in that vast wilderness, including habitat for wide-ranging species and large carnivores.

13

The Nature Conservancy of Canada at Fifty

In 2012, the Nature Conservancy of Canada marked the achievement of its first half-century of working in the private sector to conserve natural areas on behalf of the biodiversity of Canada. Since its inception in 1962, NCC had been involved in conserving more than 1 million hectares (2.6 million acres) of ecologically important land, working throughout Canada from coast to coast to coast.

In 2013, the organization will also take pride in the successful completion of the largest fundraising campaign in its history. This campaign, A Force for Nature, set a goal to raise at least $500 million to secure more than two hundred thousand hectares (five hundred thousand acres) of ecologically important habitat across Canada, while also building NCC's capabilities in science, stewardship, and fundraising.

Despite their deeply felt satisfaction in the accomplishments of NCC, and an optimistic enthusiasm for the future, staff and volunteers of the Conservancy understand that much must yet be done to sustain the natural heritage of Canada. This is a perennial conundrum of biological conservation—the rapid growth of the human population and increase of its economy are resulting in increasingly precarious circumstances for many elements of biodiversity. This clear and present danger legitimizes a need for more aggressive growth in direct conservation actions, including those undertaken in the private sector by land trusts such as the Conservancy.

Nevertheless, the Nature Conservancy of Canada has had some pretty impressive accomplishments during its first half-century. Moreover, its accelerating pace of operations bode well for additional important contributions toward sustaining the natural values of Canada. In this chapter we will examine the present state of affairs and organizational structure of the

Conservancy. The intent is to provide both a historical snapshot of a dynamic organization, as well as an understanding of the benefits of its strategic and highly adaptive way of operating.

The Organization

In fiscal year 2011 (FY2011), NCC attained unprecedented levels of support for its program of direct-action conservation. The annual business of the Conservancy was approaching a consistent value of about $100 million (this was the average revenue between 2007 and 2011, although the range was $54 million to $160 million because of the disproportionate influence of large projects in certain years).[1] In that sense, NCC was raising more equity in Canada than any other not-for-profit conservation organization. Moreover, NCC was holding about $478 million of property assets, and its endowment funds totalled an impressive $63 million (at the end of fiscal FY2011).[2]

Much of the recent scale of work by the Conservancy was made possible because of the participation of the Government of Canada and other partners in the Natural Areas Conservation Program. That program included a $225 million investment by the federal government in the work of NCC and other qualified organizations. By the end of FY 2011 NCC and its partners had secured about 337,000 hectares (835,000 acres) of ecologically important land.

NCC's total revenue in FY2011 was about $98 million. This included $73 million of donated cash and grants, $15 million of donated conservation lands and easements, $3.3 million raised from property sales for conservation reinvestment (these are sales of property to sympathetic buyers, with a conservation easement attached to the deed), $1.4 million from grazing and timber rights, and $3.3 million of investment income (mostly associated with the endowment funds).

The total expenditures in FY2011 were $94.6 million, including $70 million for land securement, $8.3 million for stewardship, $2 million for science, and $14.3 million for program support, the latter including communications, marketing, philanthropy, and general operations.

The largest items of land securement in FY2011 were the Backus Woods in the Carolinian ecozone of Southern Ontario ($5.4 million), the Piedmont and Prévost Escarpments in southern Quebec ($4 million), three properties in the Golden Ranches in the Cooking Lake Moraine east of Edmonton, Alberta ($2.9 million), and the Marion Creek Benchlands in the Kootenay region of southeastern British Columbia ($1.3 million). The largest conservation agreements were the Turkey Point wetlands property in Carolinian Ontario ($4 million), the Chinook Ranch in the foothills west of Calgary, Alberta ($2.1 million), and the Arnold Bog woodland in southern Quebec ($1.76 million).

The Conservancy has invested heavily in growth of its endowment funds, which yield predictable cash flows in support of core science and stewardship activities. At the end of FY2011, the market value of those funds was $63.1 million, of which $57.4 million was in the Stewardship Endowment Fund and $5.7 million was in the Science Endowment Fund. The Ted Boswell Land Conservation Fund, used for revolving internal loans, had a value of $5.35 million. The stated value of conservation lands held by NCC was $478 million, including both fee-simple and conservation agreements. (Note, however, that this sum reflects the values at the time that projects closed; because the data are not adjusted for inflation they represent a substantial underestimate of the present market value of properties retained by NCC.)

There were 221 NCC employees at the end of FY2011. They were working in offices across the country, including one national and seven regional offices, plus many smaller ones at the subregional level, some of which were situated in the homes of local employees.

Governance

NCC is organized in a corporate structure appropriate to a private organization with an annual business volume approaching $100 million and holding almost $500 million of real assets. Its national Board of Directors holds fiduciary responsibility for the organization, sets policy relevant to country-wide operations, provides oversight of the management by executive employees, and ensures that business is being conducted in ways that achieve strategically defined objectives.[7] The seven regional boards function as committees of the national board and have an acknowledged moral commitment to diligent oversight of operations within their geographic domain.

The national Board of Directors may consist of as many as thirty directors. In 2011, twenty-seven directors from all regions of southern Canada sat on the Board. The Board of Directors is intended to comprise volunteers from diverse backgrounds who bring a variety of experiences, talents, and expertise to the governance of the Conservancy. Directors may be elected for a term of not more than three years and may be re-elected provided that they may not serve for more than six consecutive years without stepping down for at least one year. The national board has delegated the following committees to provide assistance and recommendations relevant to core aspects of its responsibility:

- The *Executive Committee* performs the duties of the Board of Directors between scheduled national meetings or when it is not practical or feasible for the full Board to meet.
- The *Governance and Nominating Committee* is responsible for periodic reviews of the structure, roles, responsibilities, and effectiveness of the Board and its committees and for nominating new directors with a view to optimizing the diversity and skill mix of the Board.
- The *Audit Committee* oversees NCC's financial principles, controls, and reporting, and monitors financial performance and changes in the risk profile of NCC; its members are financially literate, as defined by the Ontario Securities Commission.
- The *Investment Committee* oversees policies that govern the investment of financial assets and monitors the performance of short- and long-term funds, such as the endowments, as well as the functioning of external investment managers, and also ensures that funds are invested in accordance with any donor restrictions
- The *Conservation Committee* provides guidance and oversight of NCC's activities in conservation planning, securement, and stewardship, while also serving as an umbrella for the regional Science Advisory Committees.

The regional boards are also committees of the national board that have a responsibility to oversee operations and assist with fundraising within their domains. Each of the seven NCC regions has its own regional board and their chairpersons sit on the national board. In 2011, the Atlantic regional board representing the four eastern provinces had twenty-one regional directors, Quebec had fifteen, Ontario seventeen, Manitoba seven, Saskatchewan eight, Alberta seventeen, and British Columbia eleven.

Leading the Conservancy and reporting to the national board is its president and chief executive officer. John Lounds has served in that position since 1997, during which time he has overseen tremendous conservation results across Canada. Lounds is supported by an executive team organized into the following departments:

- *Office of the President,* which includes a corporate secretary;
- *Corporate Services,* headed by a vice-president to whom report a chief financial officer, a chief information officer, a director of human resources, legal counsel, and an office manager;
- *Regional Operations,* headed by a vice-president to whom report the regional vice-presidents and the managing director of North American Partnership Initiatives, the latter involving operations for the Friends of the Nature Conservancy of Canada and liaison with The Nature Conservancy (US);
- *Conservation Operations,* headed by a vice-president to whom report managers of conservation business and systems, conservation information, and the federal program;
- *Strategic Philanthropy,* headed by a vice-president supervising managers of planned giving, prospect research, and strategic initiatives; and
- *Communications,* headed by a chief communications officer to whom report a media relations coordinator, a webmaster, and an editor of digital and print publications.

The seven regional offices of NCC have a broadly similar structure to the national headquarters, although there are variations depending on the available funding and other considerations, including the regional cultures of business and conservation. Typically, each regional organization is headed by a regional vice-president that supervises persons responsible for communications, conservation science and planning, corporate services, finances, land securement, major gifts, and stewardship. In addition to a central office, the NCC regions may also maintain local bureaus in major towns or cities.

In total, there were 221 NCC employees (full-time and seasonal) in 2011. Of these, sixty-seven worked out of the national office in Toronto, twenty-one in the Atlantic region, twenty-six in Quebec, thirty-two in Ontario, fourteen in Manitoba, fourteen in Saskatchewan, twenty-three in Alberta, and twenty-four in British Columbia. NCC had offices in many regions of southern Canada, located (from west to east) in Victoria, Vancouver, Invermere, Waterton, Calgary, Regina, Brandon, Winnipeg, Thunder Bay, Guelph, London, Port Rowan, Walsingham, Creemore, Toronto, Uxbridge, Ottawa, Montreal, Saint-Michel-de-Bellechasse, Barachois, Fredericton, Charlottetown, Halifax, and St. John's.

Conservation Planning

The Conservancy takes its conservation science seriously and has developed an in-house capability to execute that function. This ability is necessary if progress in NCC's mission is to be properly achieved, and it also assures the many sponsors of NCC that their funding is being well spent to conserve the threatened biodiversity of Canada.

In fact, NCC has become a leading practitioner of using conservation science within the private sector in Canada, in the sense that it is undertaking country-wide work on a wide range of natural ecosystems. The overall model is to plan at an ecoregional scale and to then identify focal areas where conservation work by NCC and its partners would make the most difference to sustaining the biodiversity of Canada.[8] Having noted this, it is important to recognize that NCC is not primarily a "science" organization—rather, it uses conservation and ecological science as a tool to inform the planning, acquisition, and stewarding of its protected areas.

The first level of conservation planning occurs at the scale of ecoregions.[9] Because most of the imperilled biodiversity of Canada occurs in the southern regions of the country, that geography has been the focus of NCC's ecoregional planning.[10] The work is done with diverse partners, some of whom provide funding, while others provide data or collaborate in statistical and spatial analyses (the latter by using geographic information systems). As of 2011, the Conservancy had completed fourteen conservation blueprints, also known as ecoregional plans, each of which is a detailed assessment document.[11] The blueprints provide carefully selected biogeographic targets for conservation action, as well as roadmaps for moving forward and indicators of progress. Note that ecoregions along the US border are binational, and those crossing provincial boundaries are also trans-jurisdictional. The typical cost of completing a conservation blueprint is at least $500,000, not including the "priceless" value of in-kind contributions of data used in modelling and other studies, and the staff time of collaborating partners in governments, industry, and conservation ENGOs.[12]

Once a conservation blueprint is completed for an ecoregion, a smaller-scale level of planning is undertaken that is referred to as a natural area conservation plan (NACP).[13] This document has a more local focus and typically results in a plan for one or more assemblies of contiguous properties that, in aggregate, would conserve areas vital to biodiversity. Usually, the focal area conserves the habitat of species-at-risk or rare ecological communities, in addition to representative tracts of less-threatened natural values. An NACP has the following core elements:

- a vision statement for the conservation action;
- a science-based rationalization of why the natural area is an important place to undertake conservation actions;
- highlights of the specific properties that should be acquired;
- an explanation of the kinds of stewardship actions that are necessary in and around the protected areas;
- lists of biodiversity-at-risk; and
- potential sources of funding to support the project.

The latter is no small consideration because each NACP requires millions of dollars to implement, and NCC is an environmental charity that must raise all of those funds from a variety of partners in its work and mission. As of 2011, NCC had prepared NACPs for eighty natural areas (plus six second-generation NACPs). The progress of conservation action in areas with an approved NACP is reviewed annually by the regional board and the Conservation Committee of the national board. An updated NACP is prepared every five years.

Securement of Properties

Properties are identified for securement by NCC in several ways.[14] The primary means of prioritization is through the results of ecoregional conservation planning, which is intended to objectively identify and prioritize the key properties to be conserved in order to make the most difference to sustaining biodiversity in an ecoregion. However, the Conservancy may also move opportunistically on other natural lands as they come to market, so long as their securement would significantly move the conservation agenda forward, as understood through the results of an NACP. In addition, NCC may also acquire properties outside of an approved NACP, although this is generally restricted to sites with habitats of exceptional biodiversity value. Within these contexts, the focus of NCC is to acquire high-priority private property, while also encouraging appropriate conservation stewardship on adjacent or nearby lands owned by other private interests or by governments.

The value of a property targeted for securement is always determined by a fair-market appraisal conducted by an independent qualified appraiser. For larger properties valued at more than $2 million, two independent appraisals may be commissioned.[15] However, for a property that qualifies as an "ecogift" the ecogift appraisal panel can serve as the second appraisal.[16] Land agents of NCC always try to secure properties at a price less than indicated by the fair-market appraisal, either by negotiating or by encouraging the landowner to donate part or all of the value of the land. If a property is donated, as either a fee-simple acquisition or a conservation easement, the donor can be provided with a tax receipt based on the appraised value. The donor can also be exempt from capital-gains tax in the case of donations of land or an easement that has been certified as an ecogift.

All potential securement actions require the preparation and approval of a report known as a *Conservation Project Summary* that provides details about the property (whether real estate or easement), its ecological and biodiversity features (including relevant mapping), existing risks to their conservation, the project costs, and likely sources of funding. The project costs include that of the property itself, any short-term stewardship needs, a stewardship endowment equal to 15 percent of the appraised value of the property, expenditures for legal counsel or appraisals, and a reimbursement for expended staff time. The proposal is then subjected to a series of approvals: by the regional science advisory network, the regional board, and the national board. If a project is approved at these levels, it can then move forward, subject to the availability of funding. A *Conservation Project Summary* must also be prepared for any donation of land or an easement, and a stewardship endowment must be in place before those deals can close.

The securement of new conservation properties in NCC's fiftieth year amounted to about 13,752 hectares (33,956 acres), having a total land value of $61.54 million and involving 126 individual properties of which almost all (99 percent) occurred in priority natural areas.[17]

Stewardship

In the context of natural areas, stewardship is management that is undertaken to maintain or enhance ecological conditions. Stewardship actions might be as straightforward as annual visits to a rangeland property to ensure that the terms of a conservation easement are being respected, and as complex as the ecological restoration of a cultivated pasture into tall-grass prairie. Examples of steward-ship actions that are between those extremes include the erection of fencing at Old Man on His Back to keep bison within that protected area, the control of invasive alien weeds in various NCC properties, and the development and over-sight of forest management plans for those parts of the Darkwoods and Mount Broadwood properties where sustainable timber harvesting is allowed.

In a broader sense, the goal of stewardship by the Conservancy is to pro-tect, manage, and if necessary restore natural areas so that they can sustain the ecosystems that define them.[19] Once a property has been secured, the stewardship actions by NCC typically include the following:

- preparing a property management plan that is based on an inventory of species and habitats and determines the stewardship actions necessary to maintaining or improving the ecological conditions;
- undertaking on-the-ground management activities, which may include the erection of signage, management of invasive species, development of trails, or other actions;
- engaging local volunteers to help care for the property and to encourage neighbours to practise conservation management on their own lands;
- monitoring properties to determine whether key natural features are be-ing conserved and that easements are being respected;
- responding with an adaptive management regime to new threats or issues as they arise;
- if a property is to be transferred to or managed by another organization or an individual owner, developing a formal agreement such as a con-servation easement that details the permissible and necessary manage-ment and land uses; and
- at a few showcase sites, operating a seasonal interpretation facility to ex-plain the special features of the property to visitors.

These and other stewardship activities are designed and undertaken in accordance with a suite of principles that are based on the Conservancy's vision of biological conservation. The stewardship principles are stated as follows:

- *Nature first*: Lands and waters will be managed primarily for the con-servation of natural heritage, based on their biodiversity targets and the environmental conditions that sustain them.

- *Ecology and succession:* Natural ecological processes are encouraged and not interfered with, unless they must be managed to conserve particular at-risk species, communities, or larger ecosystems.
- *Restoration and replacement:* Sites may be managed to enhance particular biodiversity targets, and deliberate interventions may be taken to restore such features and to remediate past degradation.
- *Community-based stewardship:* To the degree possible, natural areas are best stewarded in collaboration with neighbouring human communities.

Much of the stewardship work of NCC is performed by regional staff persons who specialize in that field. In recent years, they have been aided by a coterie of interns who are hired each summer through the Shell Conservation Internship Program. In 2011, there were thirty-three interns, most of whom worked in positions related to stewardship, undertaking such tasks as biodiversity surveys for baseline documentation reports, monitoring of conservation agreements, and on-the-ground management such as controlling invasive species. The NCC stewardship program is also benefiting from growth in the Conservation Volunteers program, which involves local supporters donating their time to do site inspections, help with litter cleanup, and other tasks. These people are engaging in satisfying work that yields direct conservation benefits, in addition to the financial support that they may provide to NCC through donations.

The new Land Information System (LIS) is a powerful tool for conservation stewardship that was implemented in NCC's fiftieth year. This advanced software system allows NCC staff to track, monitor, and manage conservation data through a single online database. The new LIS provides extremely important benefits by allowing staff to undertake the full range of property-related activities more efficiently, ranging from securement, to stewardship and land administration, reporting to donors, and developing new planning studies and proposals for funding.

Fundraising and Communications

Being an environmental charity, the Conservancy is utterly dependent on the generosity of its supporters to provide funds for its conservation work. Nothing would happen without that support. Every purchase of land, any stewardship actions, the salaries of employees, the expenses of volunteers, and the costs of office space, travel, computers, and pencils requires the expenditure of donated monies. Consequently, like any other not-for-profit enterprise, NCC must engage in fundraising to bring in those donations, and it has established principles and procedures to execute that function.[20]

Of course, donating money to a charity is a matter of personal choice, so people must be encouraged to do this. It is commonly understood that the work of both charities and governments result in large benefits to society, which are shared among all citizens. However, unlike the mandatory taxes that support governmental actions, donations of money to charities, although encouraged by government through tax credits, are voluntary. The purpose of the communications function in an environmental charity is to help people understand that it is helpful and indeed necessary to support the work of the organization. In the case of NCC, people need to know that their money will work effectively to secure and steward natural habitats, so that natural heritage can be sustained. Moreover, this must be done without engaging in public advocacy or stirring controversy about environmental issues, because the Conservancy is a non-advocacy organization.

Much of the fundraising by NCC and other charities involves direct requests for major gifts from corporations, foundations, governments, and relatively wealthy people. This aspect is sometimes referred to as strategic philanthropy because it involves identifying and connecting with donors that are likely to make large gifts to the organization. It is also necessary to steward those donors to ensure they are satisfied with the conservation results of their philanthropy, so that they can be retained as a consistent source of support. The category of "major gifts" accounted for about $30 million in FY2011, or 27 percent of the total revenues.[21] That represented an increase of about 50 percent over the previous year, reflecting in part an eager corporate response to NCC's A Force for Nature campaign.

Fundraising and communications at NCC are divided into several targeted sectors, depending on the kinds of donors that are being solicited: the general public, individual donors, high net-worth individuals, foundations, the corporate sector, and governments.[22]

General Public

The general public receives broad-based messaging through the Conservancy's direct-response television show, the annual supplement and periodic advertisements in the *Globe and Mail*, adverts in other media such as television and digital media, and news reports based on press releases and community events that occur at various times throughout the country. NCC is also increasingly using social networking sites to reach out to the general public as well as to its existing donor base. At the end of FY2011, the NCC Facebook site was receiving about 162,000 viewings per month and had 4,200 "fans," while 4,400 people were following NCC on Twitter. A popular networking exercise in 2011–12 involved an orphaned baby porcupine that was found by NCC interns doing a site visit in Nova Scotia in the summer of 2011. The porcupine was taken to an animal rescue centre where "he" thrived and was named Todd. Its image was then shown (through the use of Photoshop) to be visiting NCC properties and other interesting places in Canada and around the world, mostly on the NCC website and Facebook page. As it turns out, the gender of young porcupines is difficult to discern. When Todd grew older, she was discovered to be a female, but her name was not changed because she had already developed popular recognition.

There is also a focused effort to attract individual donations during the Christmas season, which is a relatively generous time for philanthropy. For NCC, this involves a Gifts of Canadian Nature promotion in which a donation made to NCC results in a certificate issued that donors can give to another person instead of (or in addition to) a "physical gift" such as a fruitcake or a pair of socks.

These various communications media are intended to speak to interested people about the work of NCC and the importance of its mission. People who then wish to donate to NCC are told how they can do it: by mailing a cheque, by calling a toll-free telephone number to a national communications centre, by directly dialling any of the regional offices, or by accessing NCC's secure website.

Individual Donors

Individual donors who are already giving to NCC receive periodic direct-mail and email communications, such as *The Ark*, NCC's newsletter, that report on the work of the organization and also include invitations to donate again. Of course many of these donors will also have been exposed to public communications of the Conservancy, which also helps to strengthen their loyalty to the brand.

A total of forty-one thousand individual donors provided about 16 percent of the NCC cash revenues in FY2011, although that number is skewed by several particularly large gifts (see below). The importance of these individual donations is much greater than their relatively small percentage of the total revenues, because this funding is almost entirely undesignated, so it can be spent in ways most beneficial to the organization at the time. These supporters of NCC are also invited to join helpful groups such as the Conservation Volunteers program, which assists with stewardship.[23] They are also encouraged to become monthly donors through the Protector program[24] (there were about eight thousand people in this category at the end of 2011) or to upgrade to a certain level of giving such as the Leader in Conservation group.[25]

People who are consistent supporters of NCC are also routinely invited to public gatherings that the organization may be hosting in their region, such as project announcements, nature walks, and other events.

High Net-Worth Individuals

High net-worth individuals who support the Conservancy tend to do so with relatively large donations; in FY2011 three donors in this group accounted for one-quarter of the total revenues received by NCC from individuals. People in this group are identified as being potential donors through networking exercises among existing high net-worth supporters, members of the Board, and other development research. If such individuals are thought to potentially be sympathetic to the work of the Conservancy, they will receive an individualized solicitation, preferably during a personal meeting with a senior officer of NCC. They will also be routinely invited to formal NCC events that may occur in their region, such as receptions hosted by the Board of Directors. They may also be offered private tours of Conservancy projects that they might be interested in supporting.

Foundations

Foundations are several kinds of charitable entities. They may be a private foundation that has been endowed by an individual or family for the purpose of supporting particular causes, or a not-for-profit organization that donates to other organizations or otherwise funds charitable actions. Foundations typically have specified ways by which they receive applications for funding, and although they usually prefer to donate to specific projects, they may also support endowments or other useful actions. Once a foundation has given to NCC, prudent efforts are made to keep it engaged in the work of the Conservancy. In some cases this attention has resulted in decades of generous support. Foundations provided 12 percent of the cash and grant revenues of NCC in FY2011.

The Corporate Sector

The corporate sector may learn about the Conservancy through its mass-communications efforts, including the television show and adverts and inserts in the *Globe and Mail*, which are placed in the business section of that newspaper. High-level individuals in corporations are also solicited by personal networking undertaken by NCC directors, influential supporters, and employees whose job involves this sector of development activity. In addition, the national and regional NCC offices periodically arrange meetings to which high-level businesspersons are invited, such as a breakfast event or evening reception. Many attendees to such events later receive a general invitation by letter or in-person to support the Conservancy. Once a company has given to the Conservancy, efforts are made to maintain that engagement for as long as possible. In some cases a strategic partnership is developed that may include a degree of co-branding with NCC. Examples of this in 2011 included the following:

- the Canada's Next Top Critter contest, which allowed people to vote on-line for a species that would be featured in new advertising by TELUS, a telecommunications company that donated $1 for each vote received to a maximum of $100,000; the eventual winner was the northern saw-whet owl (*Aegolius acadicus*), a native raptor and the first Canadian species for TELUS; and
- a program with Toshiba that involved a philanthropic donation and a donation of computer hardware to support the new Land Information System, while also profiling NCC on their website, in advertisements, and through social media campaigns.

The corporate sector provided about 5 percent of the Conservancy's cash and grant revenues in FY2011.

Governments

Governments assist the work of NCC by contributing to particular projects that are occurring within their jurisdictional area or by providing program-matic funding that provides a more general kind of support, although most of the money is typically spent on securement. Support from governments is solicited in several ways. The most basic method is to make formal applications to designated funds (such as under the NAWCA program) or agencies (such as Environment Canada) for funds to support particular projects. However, requests for public-private partnership may involve years of discussions with government officials before a formal proposal is submitted and approved. The most spectacular example of governmental support of the Conservancy's work is the $225 million provided by the Government of Canada through the Natural Areas Conservation Program. But some provinces have also given program-level support for work within their domain.

Most gifts to the Conservancy are in the form of cash. However, gifts may also involve equity in the form of bonds, mutual funds, or stocks, which can be especially favourable to some donors because they are exempted from capital-gains taxes.[26] Of course, another kind of donation is one of real estate or a conservation easement, in which case a tax receipt can be provided for the appraised value of the property and there may also be a capital-gains exception for lands certified as an ecogift. If a donated piece of real estate does not have important ecological value, with the permission of the donor it will be treated as a so-called trade land and sold by the Conservancy, with the proceeds used for a more effective conservation purpose.

Many gifts do not arrive all at once, so they represent expectancies of various kinds. These can include a pledge to donate a certain amount over a specified number of years or a "planned giving" expectancy based on provisions written into a will or a life insurance policy.[27] These latter bequests have become an important and growing revenue stream for NCC and many other charities in Canada, and they are a great way for people to leave a legacy gift to an organization whose mission they admire. To help foster these gifts, NCC has begun a Nature Legacy Society that helps people to understand the tax and conservation benefits of planned giving. At the end of 2011, NCC had a roster of more than 800 expectancies in the Nature Legacy Society, and representing potential bequests of some $60 million. The actual bequest revenue in FY2011 was $1.1 million.

Financial System

All organizations are accountable to their supporters, whether they are active in the private sector, in government, or as a not-for-profit corporation. A key way in which accountability is demonstrated and monitored is through the efficacy of the accounting and financial systems that are in place, including their accuracy, the diligence of oversight by trustees or directors, and the transparency for public scrutiny.

Financial accounting at charities such as NCC is often complicated by the need to track the use of many donations and grants for which restrictions have been put in place by the donors. In such cases the donation is kept in a deferred fund and recognized as revenue only when used in a permissible way. The Conservancy also has other funds that are associated with specific uses, such as the Ted Boswell Land Conservation Fund, the Weston Family Science Fund, and the Stewardship Endowment Fund. Some of the funds also interact, such as transfers from one to the other. The complexity of fund accounting is revealed by a statement by Kamal Rajani, the chief financial officer of NCC: "It's like having several different organizations functioning as one."[28]

To deal with this reality, NCC has deployed an accounting system that tracks donor funds from the time of receipt to how and where the monies are spent. The tracking is done in several ways:

- by the various relevant funds;
- by the program, such as conservation planning, securement, or stewardship;
- by support functions, such as fundraising, communications, or general operations;
- by geography, such as national, provincial, any of the seven NCC operational regions, and in some cases by subregion;
- by the source of funding, such as the federal Natural Areas Conservation Program, the Nova Scotia Crown Share Land Legacy Trust, or by a particular foundation;
- by every individual project;
- by any agreements that NCC may have negotiated with another organization; or
- by program requirements that may include a commitment to matching value, such as under the NAWCA program.

Behind the main accounting system, a network of component systems help to organize NCC data. For example, employees log their activities and associate them with a particular project. These data are used in the Conservancy's time-and-billing system. The actual expenditure of funds requires approval authorities, and board and management policies are in place to provide responsible permissions for all financial transactions by NCC.

One of the key tasks of finance staff in the national and regional offices is providing NCC management with information it needs to assess whether policies are being consistently applied, whether accounting standards are followed, whether the personal or proprietary information of donors is being respected, and whether NCC is complying with the rules and regulations for charities set by the Canada Revenue Agency. In most cases this requires the issuing of periodic reports for internal and/or external use. Sets of internal controls have been established to ensure that cumulative improvements of accuracy and efficiency are achieved in financial reporting, with continuous updating and training of staff.

Because fiduciary responsibility is held by the national Board of Directors, the treasury function is managed centrally. The corporate financial reporting is completed on a quarterly and annual basis. The financial statements are developed from the granular level, and then reviewed by program/project managers. They are then rolled up to the regional level, reviewed by regional and national financial managers in a collaborative manner, and finally reviewed by executive NCC managers and the Audit Committee appointed by the national board.

National and regional budgets are developed from the ground up by those units using their own business plans, and are then reviewed by senior managers. Regional annual budgets are approved by their regional boards, and then the national board approves both those and the national budget. Thereafter, forecasts are prepared and monitored based on the actual and budgeted financial performance at various levels of the organization.

The Conservancy has considerable investment accounts, including those associated with deferred funds, the rotating Boswell Fund, and the science and stewardship endowments. Investments are made according to Board policies that set the levels of risk and the allocations to domestic versus foreign securities, T-bills, and cash. The investment performance is monitored regularly by the Investment Committee and reported quarterly to the national board.

The entire accounting and reporting system and actuals of the Conservancy are audited annually by an external auditor, which for many years has been Ernst & Young LLP.

A Formula for Success

In the summer of NCC's fiftieth year, the national financial magazine *MoneySense* once again gave the organization a rank of "A" in its charity review issue.[29] This was the highest grade attained among the national environmental organizations that were examined. The article also profiled the case of Roberta Langtry, a long-term supporter who in 2004 had left NCC an unexpected bequest of about $4.4 million.

Despite this sort of recognition of the Conservancy, and the major progress that the organization has been making in its mission of private-sector conservation, NCC still has two major challenges: (1) not all of the private properties vital to sustaining the indigenous biodiversity of Canada have yet been conserved, and (2) while a great deal of progress is being made, not all of the existing NCC properties are being stewarded to the high standards that the organization has set for itself.

The Conservancy has achieved a great measure of success over its first half-century of diligent work to conserve the biodiversity of Canada. Key indicators of that success include:

- accelerating increases in the area owned and stewarded by the Conservancy, and by partners to whom acquired lands have been passed;
- impressive growth in the numbers of supporters and in money and properties being donated; and
- a remarkable development of in-house science-based programs for conservation planning, acquisitions, and stewardship, all of which are conducted to a high standard.

The impressive growth of the work of NCC can be indicated in various ways, such as the increase of cash flows and endowments and of the cumulative land secured. A selection of those indicators is offered below.

The data on growth of annual revenues (cash plus donations of real estate and easements) are not adjusted for inflation, but they nevertheless show a substantial increase over the years (figure 1a). The seeming volatility in recent years is due to the influence of a few extremely large projects, such as the Darkwoods project in BC. The growth of property value is similarly remarkable. The amounts shown in figure 1b are the cumulative value of the property at the time of closing, so the data are also not corrected for inflation or changes in other factors affecting the value of real estate. The impressive growth of the value of long-term investments (figure 1c) is almost entirely related to the several endowment funds of NCC, especially the one used to help pay for stewardship activities. The increase of cumulative hectares conserved also shows extraordinary achievements (figure 1d). Note that these numbers are heavily influenced by several extremely large projects that retired mineral rights and allowed the establishment of national parks in the Yukon and in BC, as well as the more recent Darkwoods project.

These indicators are clear signals of admirable progress in NCC's mission of direct-action conservation. The prudent features of the operations of the Nature Conservancy of Canada are the following:

- a clear and effective statement of the vision and goals of the organization, which communicate an understanding of and empathy for what is being done and explain the intrinsic and environmental benefits that result from the work;
- an excellent reputation for reputable and ethical business practices;
- an assertive corporate ethos that includes belief in continuous and adaptive improvements of all business and conservation actions;
- the routine development of collaborative initiatives with like-minded partners, so that the cumulative results are greater than what might have been achieved had the various parties worked separately;
- persistence in the fostering of mutualistic relationships, which may eventually result in productive and long-lasting partnerships, as NCC has achieved with certain family foundations and governmental agencies;
- the establishment of endowments that provide enduring base-level support for otherwise difficult-to-fund work, such as science planning and routine stewardship operations;
- the pursuit of a conservation vision of protected landscapes that are as large and connected as financial resources will allow the organization to develop, as opposed to a more disconnected "islands of green" model of smaller reserves that are less likely to provide for the needs of species or ecological processes that must be sustained at a larger scale;
- a resolute focus on direct conservation actions, while leaving the arena of public advocacy and political controversy to other environmental charities (notwithstanding the great benefits achieved by NCC and certain partners to improve the taxation climate in Canada with

Figure 1

Indicators of Growth of the Revenues and Conserved Area of the Nature Conservancy of Canada[30]

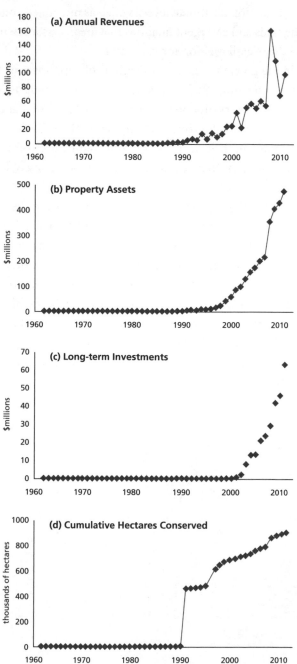

respect to donations of securities and ecologically important lands to conservation charities);

- the assembly of mutually supportive teams of employees and volunteers operating at all organizational levels, which as integrated collectives supply all the skills and emergent qualities that are necessary to moving projects and the overall mission forward; and

- a belief in the inherently good motivations of supporters of the work of the organization—this includes donors who are hoping to realize their own vision of conservation for properties they have loved and stewarded, as well as the many volunteers and employees of NCC who are seeking a greater meaning in their own lives by contributing to good and necessary conservation projects that help to sustain the biodiversity of Canada.

Clearly, much helpful progress has been made during the past decades toward the conservation of the natural heritage of Canada. This expansion has been achieved by government agencies as well as by the private sector, including by land trusts such as the Nature Conservancy of Canada. Nevertheless, an enduring solution to biodiversity conservation, either in Canada or on a global scale, has not yet been realized. If anything, ecological sustainability requires considerably more energetic efforts than have so far occurred. The further growth of conservation efforts must begin now. In the next chapter we will see how NCC is planning to achieve its portion of that necessary progress.

14

Further Down the Road

Having examined the remarkable growth and changes of the Nature Conservancy of Canada during the initial five decades of its existence, we might then ask, "What is down the road?" Although the future cannot be accurately told, there are some ways of estimating what it might look like. One obvious approach is to extrapolate recent trends, based on a scan of the likely environmental, social, political, and economic contexts within which conservation organizations such as NCC will be operating. The following is my personal view of likely environmental and conservation outcomes over the next several decades.

A scan of the environmental context reveals that the near future will include a further intensification of the Anthropocene, a recently coined term that refers to a human-dominated and substantially anthropogenic biosphere. Its characteristics include a human population that in 2012 exceeded seven billion and was still growing, with a doubling time of about fifty years. Most of these people are living in poorer countries, and in the more stable of those the social and economic priorities include policies to lift citizens to a higher standard of living, which can occur only through intensified economic growth. There is also a heavy emphasis on continued growth of the economy in presently wealthy countries, such as Canada. Much of this growth is being achieved by increasing the harvesting of both non-renewable and renewable natural resources, by intensifying agricultural and forestry practices, and by further urbanization of the populace.

These environmental changes will result in further escalations of stress on natural ecosystems, which will worsen the biodiversity crisis. The greatest damages are occurring in less-developed countries where tropical forests and other natural ecosystems of remarkable biodiversity are being widely converted into land uses for agriculture, industry, and urbanization. These sorts of conversions are also occurring in developed countries and is causing severe damage to biodiversity there, although its intensity is considerably less than in the tropics. Ecological degradation is also being caused world-wide by invasive species and the overharvesting of bio-resources. These stressors are all important in Canada. Moreover, Canada is linked to eco-logical damage occurring in other countries through international trade and commerce, migratory species, and global environmental problems such as climate change.

A scan of the social, political, and economic context suggests that the fund-raising environment for not-for-profits such as NCC will be uncertain into the near future. Global markets are being agitated by recession or its potential in developed countries and by an imperative for rapid growth in emerging economies. Canada may be largely affected through influences on exported commodities and perhaps a further downsizing of the manufacturing sector.

It is likely that there will be growth in international and domestic markets for certified environmental "credits" associated with carbon storage and bio-diversity, but the degree is unpredictable because of uncertainty about gov-ernmental responses to the threat of anthropogenic climate change. In North America, the Canadian strategy to reduce net emissions of greenhouse gases will likely mirror whatever approach is implemented in the United States. The sale of carbon and biodiversity credits will likely represent a growth oppor-tunity for NCC, and the organization must be prepared to move further into those marketplaces as opportunities arise.

In the governmental realm, administrations at all levels in Canada and globally are seeking ways by which their fiscal deficits can be reduced. Their tactics will certainly include reduced spending on a wide spectrum of pro-grams. Nevertheless, Canada has signed international agreements concerning the conservation of biodiversity, and obligations laid out in those treaties will require further mitigative actions that will include the designation of addi-tional protected areas.

Canada will have a majority Conservative government until at least 2015. The present government has stated a desire to develop a National Conservation Plan. Although the specifics of that plan are not yet public knowledge, there will undoubtedly be components relevant to protecting natural habitats, likely with a role for private-sector organizations such as NCC. I believe that provincial and territorial governments will pay increas-ing attention to conserving natural habitats within their jurisdictions and I expect that the next five years will see programmatic funding for land trusts from all of those governments. In fact, it is my view that governments will increasingly rely on the private sector to undertake conservation work all across Canada, with much of that work being done by land trusts in collaboration with governmental agencies.

In the larger realm of society, Canadians have widely expressed the desire for their country to be a beacon of enlightened progress on a range of environmental fronts. If this attitude also permeates the philanthropy of Canadians, then it would result in greater support for the work of direct-action conservation organizations such as NCC. The continuing aging of the baby boomers, a demographic bulge of persons forty-eight to sixty-six years of age in 2010, should also bode well for philanthropy as this socially conscious and relatively wealthy cohort becomes increasingly interested in legacy gifts. Improved marketing to this and other sectors will require more personalized engagement of donors to attract initial gifts and then sustain them.

However, on account of widespread disquiet over financial scandals and related public controversies during the past decade or so, it is likely that there will be greater public scrutiny of the activities of charities and a need for open reporting of their financial affairs. Within this larger social, political, and economic context, I believe it is likely that the period of 2012 to 2017 will see impressive growth of NCC's capacity for conservation planning, property acquisitions, and stewardship actions, as well as increased success in the fundraising necessary to achieve those conservation results.

As a well-organized and mature organization, the Conservancy has regularly engaged in strategic-planning exercises. The most recent one of these, to cover the five-year period of 2012 to 2017, is also a guide to the future of the organization.[1] Its development has involved key staff persons developing a framework for a five-year plan, and then engaging in workshops with other employees, including those in the NCC regions, as well as the directors and other volunteers. In the end a consensus was achieved as to the key elements of the plan, and I believe it to be a reasonable estimate of what NCC could accomplish in the next five years.

The mission of NCC will not change in the near future. It will continue to protect ecologically important areas for their intrinsic value and for the benefit of future generations. While doing so, NCC will continue to provide leadership, innovation, and creativity in the conservation of the natural heritage of Canada. Its ongoing conservation planning will help to further the understanding of threats to the natural ecoscapes of Canada, and to ensure that NCC's conservation programs address those issues in an effective manner. The organization will work to achieve durable conservation out-comes that cannot be easily undone in the future.

The conservation planning will continue to focus on ecoregional plans (conservation blueprints) and natural area conservation plans (NACPs) to pro-vide a backbone for program design and delivery. However, the scale at which the identified goals are achieved will depend on whether sufficient resour-ces can be raised to allow key habitats to be conserved, management plans developed, and adaptive stewardship actions applied. Even while partnerships have always been an important aspect of the work of NCC, it is anticipated that the proactive engagement and stewarding of collaborators will result in even greater progress. The partners will include donors and supporters who invest their time and financial resources, as well as landowners, governmental agencies, and other conservation ENGOs and land stakeholders.[2]

During its first half-century NCC emerged as a strong leader in the con-servation movement in Canada. As a result, the Conservancy is now regarded as a key player in conservation planning, in securing funding and other resour-ces, and in delivering and monitoring the effectiveness of programs. NCC will work to further energize this vital role as a credible and trusted "broker" among varied interests in industry, government, the larger conservation com-munity, and society at large. In part, this will involve NCC building a broad partnership that works toward the synthesis of a comprehensive agenda for the conservation of biodiversity in Canada.

Strategic Vision

The Conservancy has developed a strategic vision for where it expects to be at the end of 2017. Its key elements are mentioned in the following sections.[3]

Business Model

The period 2012 to 2017 will see NCC have thriving regional and local offices in all provinces. The organization will work to continue to be a leader in the transparent reporting of finances, the nurturing of donor relationships, and in the sharing of conservation information. A business objective is to raise sufficient funds to cover all expenses on an annual basis and to create by 2017 an operating reserve equivalent to six months of expenses. The plan is for the stewardship endowment fund to be built to the degree that it is able to pay for at least 50 percent of the annual costs of this aspect of NCC operations by 2017, including the salary of at least one stewardship officer in each region.

Human resource policies are planned to be measurably in line with other leading organizations in the environmental not-for-profit sector, including the pay scales. Regardless of their specialized expertise and job expectations, all NCC employees will understand that they play a vital role in the fundraising process and are ambassadors and service representatives for the Conservancy. The same is expected of directors sitting on the national and regional boards and other volunteers. NCC cultivates a team-based approach to its work, which allows the organization to "do more with less." NCC plans to to be an employer of choice in the environmental not-for-profit sector and to maintain or improve the present level of staff satisfaction.

Next Level of Business

During the next five years, to 2017, NCC will work to substantially grow unprompted recognition of the organization and trust in its conservation work among the Canadian public, the conservation community, business and industrial sectors, and governments. Its goal is a predictable annual revenue flow of at least $110–130 million (including the value of donated property).

Although there will be an improved diversification of funding sources, the main revenue streams will likely continue to be major donors in governments, corporations, and individuals. A key to meeting the funding targets will be a re-engagement of the Government of Canada in a follow-up to the successful Natural Areas Conservation Program, and also of provincial governments at their own scales. It is expected that the base of individual donors will grow by at least 25 percent, to more than 60,000 Canadians, and the number of supporters will increase fivefold, to 250,000 people[4]

The program of planned giving is being built, and unrestricted bequests should become a vital means of capitalizing the endowment funds and providing operating reserves for the Conservancy. At least 85 percent of the gross revenue will be invested in the conservation programs, and no more than 15 percent on support functions related to fundraising, communications, and administration. Biodiversity and carbon credits associated with NCC projects will likely become an increasing source of funding.

Conservation Planning

The existing portfolio of ecoregional plans and NACPs will form the backbone from which NCC's land-securement projects will be prioritized during the period of 2012 to 2017. Annual reports will be produced on the progress of all NACPs and they will be comprehensively updated on a five-year rotation. A limited number of new ecoregional plans and NACPs will be developed to fill important gaps in the existing portfolio. NCC will be proactive in sharing its science and planning capabilities with like-minded partners in the conservation community.

Direct Conservation Action

NCC plans to secure at least two hundred thousand hectares (five hundred thousand acres) of ecologically important habitat during 2012–17, and will assist in an additional 40,500 hectares (100,000 acres) that is protected by partners. At least 90 percent of this work (in terms of value) is anticipated to be undertaken at places within an approved NACP. Habitat for at least one-fourth of nationally designated species-at-risk will be targeted for NCC lands. NCC will do this work across Canada, through effective partnerships with other conservation organizations, and will also engage industry and governments to implement conservation measures on their "working" landbase. Notwithstanding the additional securement, NCC plans to move to allocate more of its financial resources to the stewardship of properties already owned than has previously been the case. Overall, it is anticipated that annual expenditures on stewardship will double from about $8 million in 2011 to $16 million in 2017.

Non-traditional Regions for NCC Action in Canada

Certain large ecoregions of Canada, particularly in the northern boreal and tundra biomes, have limited opportunities for private sector conservation action because almost all real estate is owned by federal, provincial, territorial, or Aboriginal governments. Nevertheless, NCC can assist conservation actions in those regions by helping with ecoregional planning and by retiring privately held rights of land use, such as those associated with mineral resources. The Conservancy will maintain a watching brief in those regions and will partner with like-minded conservation organizations on appropriate projects in which NCC's unique skills would be of material assistance.

International Work

Given that tropical ecosystems in less developed countries are being rapidly altered, the Conservancy may engage in collaborative international projects during the next five years, likely involving the conservation of critical habitat for migratory species that breed in Canada. A key to such work will be the identification of a governmental or non-governmental organization that would be a trusted partner in the long-term stewardship of conserved properties.

Influence and Outreach

At the local level of areas where NCC is actively working, the organization will work to continue to be a credible and reliable source of insight and information about conservation and of practical ways to conserve biodiversity. NCC anticipates engaging a larger number of volunteers in its projects and will further encourage hands-on conservation on other private lands.

15

An Enduring Solution

It is common knowledge today that natural heritage values are being extensively lost, both in Canada and throughout the world. This unfortunate fact
is reflected by extinctions of species and the endangerment of various kinds
of ecological communities in all biotic realms. In response to this damage to
biodiversity, an international consensus has emerged that it is worthwhile
and important to do what is necessary to conserve species and natural ecosystems. This must be done to conserve their intrinsic value, because of their
vital importance in maintaining ecological functions, and for the goods and
services that are provided to the human economy. Consequently, many international actions are being undertaken to conserve global biodiversity, some
of the most important of which are under the Convention on Biological
Diversity, a United Nations treaty to which Canada is signatory.

There is also a broadly held view across Canadian society that our own
natural heritage must be conserved—our native species, their distinctive
communities, and the natural landscapes and seascapes that define wilderness at larger scales. A sustainable conservation of biodiversity requires that a
comprehensive system of protected areas be implemented. At the same time,
areas "working" more directly to serve the human economy must also remain
hospitable to many native species and their necessary habitat.

The Nature Conservancy of Canada has a special role to play within this
context of societal-level measures to conserve the biodiversity of Canada. As
reflected in the mission statement, it is to work within the private sector to
"lead, innovate and use creativity in the conservation of Canada's natural heritage. We will secure important natural areas through their purchase, donation
or other mechanisms, and then manage these properties for the long term."[1]

Several times in this book it was noted that there is still much more for the
Conservancy and its partners to accomplish. Although important progress
has been made by NCC and other land trusts during the past half-century,
and also by governments and many corporations, many important private

and public lands have not yet been conserved. Moreover, natural heritage continues to suffer from ongoing degradation as local and more extensive habitats are converted into land uses for agriculture or urbanization, or damaged by pollution, timber harvesting, and other anthropogenic stressors.

Nevertheless, it is vital that people who hold empathy for the natural world remain optimistic about its prospects: in the region where they live, in Canada, and in the world more generally. To lose hope would be a terrible outcome, because then much of the surviving biodiversity would certainly be doomed. Instead of a despondent attitude we need one of courage and confidence in the conservation actions that can fix much of the ecological damage that has already been caused, while avoiding other harms that have not yet happened. Such a constructive outlook would inevitably translate into more financial and political support for the conservation mission. Indeed, such a positive outlook and constructive actions are the only way that natural values can and will be conserved.

Indeed, such a hopeful outcome is possible and viable, and there are effective ways to make it happen. One of the solutions requires enthusiastic use of ecologically friendly management of the "working" landscapes and seascapes that provide the human economy with food and other natural resources. Another is the completion of a comprehensive network of protected areas, which is a responsibility of governments, direct-action environmental charities, and all of society.

Within this context of ecological sustainability, the main constraint on the helpful actions of the Nature Conservancy of Canada and other land trusts is insufficient financial support for their mission. Fortunately, that limiting circumstance can easily be fixed if a larger community of donors would generously support private-sector conservation initiatives. Each of us can choose to make that happen, and when we do, the world will be a better place for all of its inhabitants.

Glossary

Advocacy: the public profiling of a controversial issue.

Anthropogenic: an influence caused by a human action.

Bargain Sale: *see* Split-Receipt Transaction.

Biodiversity (Biological Diversity): the richness of biological variation, at all levels of biological organization.

CA: *see* Conservation Agreement.

Carbon Credits: carbon stored in ecosystem biomass that is considered an offset against emissions of greenhouse gases from the burning of fossil fuels or other sources. One carbon credit represents an offset equivalent to the reduced emission of one tonne of carbon dioxide, or its radiative equivalent in other greenhouse gases.

CBD: Convention on Biological Diversity (1993).

CDC: *see* Conservation Data Centre.

CLTA: Canadian Land Trust Alliance.

Conservation: (1) sustainable use of a renewable natural resource, or (2) stewardship of the habitat of native species and other natural values in ways that allow them to be sustained.

Conservation Agreement: a binding agreement that binds the lands, has a value that can be appraised, and controls the kinds of activities that can be undertaken on a property. May be referred to as a conservation easement, a conservation covenant, or a conservation servitude, although the rules are not identical among these types and across jurisdictions.

Conservation Authority: an arm's-length quasi-governmental organization, organized on a large-watershed basis in Ontario, with responsibility to keep lowlands in natural cover primarily to help prevent flooding but also to conserve natural values.

Conservation Blueprint (or Ecoregional Plan): a document that records the portfolio of sites that, if conserved, will ensure the long-term survival of native species and community types of an ecoregion.

Conservation Data Centre: an organization that collects data on the distribution and abundance of species-at-risk and of communities and other kinds of biophysical habitat types.

Conservation Easement: *see* Conservation Agreement

Conservation Ecology: the application of ecological knowledge to the steward-ship of biodiversity and protected areas.

Conservation Planning: planning that seeks to identify the most important places that should be set aside, within the context of a comprehensive system of protected areas.

Convention on Wetlands of International Importance (or Ramsar Convention): an intergovernmental treaty that provides a framework for international co-operation and national action toward the conservation of wetlands and their resources.

COSEWIC: Committee on the Status of Endangered Wildlife in Canada, an arms-length organization that designates species-at-risk in Canada.

Critical Habitat: (1) a specific kind of habitat that is essential to the conservation of a species-at-risk, or (2) a specific habitat feature that is required by a species, such as the presence of cavities for cavity-nesting birds.

Ecological Gift: a donation of land under the federal Ecological Gifts Program established in 1995 as a mechanism by which people owning ecologically sensitive land can donate that property, or an interest in it such as a conservation easement, to a qualified recipient such as a land trust or a conservation-oriented governmental agency, in exchange for a tax receipt.

Ecological Integrity: an indicator related to environmental quality, but with a focus on changes in wild populations and natural ecosystems, rather than on humans and their economy. Sometimes viewed as being analogous to ecosystem health.

Ecological Reserve: a kind of protected area, usually with strict regulation of use and sometimes allowing access only for scientific research.

Ecoregion (or Ecological Region): an extensive region of general ecological similarity. Terrestrial ecoregions are classified according to their physiography, climate, and biological characteristics, and marine ones by their physiography, oceanography, and biological attributes.

Ecoregional Plan: *see* Conservation Blueprint.

EI: *see* Ecological Integrity.

Endangered: a species that is at imminent risk of extinction or extirpation in all or an important portion of its range.

Endemic: a taxon (species, subspecies, or other biological group) with a local distribution and that occurs nowhere else.

ENGO: environmental non-governmental organization.

Environmental Services (Ecological Services): vital functions such as productivity, nutrient cycling, carbon storage, flows of clean water, pollination, and others that provide essential support for life and ecosystems and also the human economy.

Extinct: a species (or taxon) that no longer exists anywhere in the world.

Extirpated: a species (or taxon) that formerly occurred in some region but now survives only elsewhere; a local extinction.

Fee-Simple Purchase: a land purchase pursuant to which a purchaser acquires the full suite of ownership rights in land.

FNCC: Friends of the Nature Conservancy of Canada.

FON: Federation of Ontario Naturalists; now Ontario Nature.

Gap Analysis: an analysis that identifies tracts that have already been designated as protected for conservation, as well as key areas that have not yet received that kind of status.

IBA: Important Bird Area.

IBP: International Biological Program.

Indigenous (or Native): refers to biodiversity that is native to some designated region and not introduced from elsewhere.

Intrinsic Value (or Inherent Value): a worth that applies to anything that has unique and irreplaceable qualities; it exists and has value "for its own sake."

Land Information System: a computerized system that gathers and stores information about conservation properties, while allowing authorized users to query the system for the purposes of planning and to respond to inquiries from donors and other partners.

Land Trust: an environmental charity whose mission is to acquire and steward private property for the purpose of conserving its natural values.

LIS: *see* Land Information System.

Modern Biodiversity Crisis: a mass extinction that is happening today and is being caused by anthropogenic influences, especially the destruction of natural habitats.

NACP: natural area conservation plan (*see* Natural Area Conservation Plan).

Native: *see* Indigenous.

Natural: (1) a term used in reference to the predominantly non-human world, or (2) a reference to habitats or ecosystems that have developed unaided by humans and that are dominated by native species.

Natural Area Conservation Plan: a conservation-planning model that is based on ecoregional planning but executed at a smaller scale of focal assemblies of properties.

Natural Heritage: the legacy of species, ecological communities, and landscapes and seascapes that are indigenous to some region.

NAWCA: North American Wetlands Conservation Act.

NAWMP: North American Wildlife Management Plan.

NCC: The Nature Conservancy of Canada.

NGO: non-governmental organization.

Niche: the ecological role of a species in a community, described by its life history, community ecology, feeding relationships, and environmental factors that limit its distribution, growth, and reproduction.

Not-for-Profit Corporation: A no-share capital corporation, which can refer to most land trusts.

ONHL: Ontario Natural Heritage League.

PMP: *see* Property Management Plan.

Property Management Plan: a plan for a particular conservation property that is based on an inventory of species and habitats and that determines the stewardship actions necessary for maintaining or improving its ecological conditions.

Protected Area: a tract of natural habitat that has been set aside from intensive economic use, such as a park, nature reserve, ecological reserve, or wilderness area.

Ramsar Convention: *see* Convention on Wetlands of International Importance.

Special Concern: a species (or taxon) that is at risk of becoming threatened because of small or declining numbers or occurrence in a limited range (formerly referred to under COSEWIC as Vulnerable).

Special Management Area: a protected area that is intended to support particular species or communities, usually of economic importance, and to achieve conservation through the protection and management of habitats. Hunting, forestry, and some other extractive industries may be permitted. *See also* Protected Area.

Split-Receipt Transaction: a land purchase for a price that is substantially less than the appraised value of the land and that usually results in a charitable tax receipt for the difference between the appraised value and the purchase price.

Stewardship: all management activities that are needed to maintain protected areas, with particular attention to biodiversity and other ecological values.

System Plan: a conservation plan that indicates areas that support the highest priority biodiversity values in order to ensure that all indigenous elements are conserved in an ecological region, including in areas that are "working" to serve the human economy in agriculture, forestry, or in other ways.

Threatened: a species (or taxon) that is likely to become endangered unless factors affecting its risk are mitigated.

TNC: The Nature Conservancy, an organization headquartered in the United States.

Trade Land: real estate that is donated with the express intention of it being sold and the proceeds used to support the core work of a land trust.

Undesignated Funds: monies that had not been donated for use in a particular land acquisition or another specified purpose and so can be used in ways that are most beneficial to the organization at a particular time.

VCS: Verified Carbon Standard for greenhouse-gas trading.

Weed: a plant that is unwanted by people in some management-related context.

WHC: Wildlife Habitat Canada.

WHSRN: Western Hemisphere Shorebird Reserve Network.

Wilderness: wild and uninhabited tracts that are little used by people, especially not for resource extraction and other intensive activities.

Wilderness Area: a protected area that is managed to preserve its natural condition, with low levels of non-intensive, non-extractive visitation being permitted.

Wild Life: any kinds of wild organisms.

Wildlife: a term that commonly refers to species of animals that are hunted.

WWF: World Wildlife Fund.

Y2Y: the Yellowstone to Yukon Conservation Initiative.

———•◆•———

Members of the National Board of Directors of the Nature Conservancy of Canada[1]

Trustees/Directors	Term	Chair
Martin Abell, Toronto, ON	2007–2011	
Pierre Alvarez, Calgary, AB	2011–2012	
Shelley Ambrose, Toronto, ON	2008–2012	
F.S. Auger, Toronto, ON	1966–1967	
A. Charles Baillie, Toronto, ON	2007–2011	
Tim Banks, Charlottetown, PE	2004–2009	
Bill Barkley, Victoria, BC	2004–2006	
Jim Baroffio, Calgary, AB	1991–1994	
Kim Bassey, Winnipeg, MB	2011–2012	
Louise Beaubien Lepage, Montreal, QC	1980–1990	
Tom Beck, Calgary, AB	1983–1991	
Dorothy Beckel, Ottawa, ON	1081–1985	
Wilfred G. Bigelow, Toronto, ON	1978–1989	1985–1986
Ted Boswell, Ottawa, ON	1994–2004	1999–2000
James Bowland, Toronto, ON	2011–2012	
Sheldon Bowles, Winnipeg, MB	1999–2006	
Angus Bruneau, St. John's, NL	1997–2004	
Joseph H. Bryant, Calgary, AB	1999–2000	
Daniel A. Burns, Vancouver, BC	2008–2010	
Edward F.G. Busse, Regina, SK	2004–2009	
Glen Campbell, Toronto, ON	2004–2005	
Richard Cannings, Penticton, BC	2012	
Robert S. Carswell, Montreal, QC	1981–2008	1995–1996
Paul M. Catling, Ottawa, ON	2004–2009	
Bill Caulfeild-Browne, Tobermory, ON	2004–2012	
R. Gordon Chaplin, Cambridge, ON	1981–1992	1989–1990

Trustees/Directors	Term	Chair
Paul J.G. Kidd, Windsor, ON	1979–1982	
Harold (Hal) Kvisle, Calgary, AB	2008–2012	2012
Elva Kyle, Regina, SK	1989–2002	1997–1998
Lise Lachapelle, Montreal, QC	2002–2006	
James G. Laidlaw, Toronto, ON	1986–1992	
Darlene Lavender-Mannix, Calgary, AB	1994–1995	
George H. Ledingham, Regina, SK	1963–1975	
Leonard Lee, Ottawa, ON	2001–2007	
Gilles Lemieux, Montreal, QC	1974–1977	
F. Aird Lewis, Toronto, ON	1962–1980	1962–1969
Dwain M. Lingenfelter, Calgary, AB	2002–2005	
John A. Livingston, Toronto, ON	1962–1975	
Denis Losier, Moncton, NB	1994–1995	
J. Stuart MacKay, Toronto, ON	1983–1985	
John P.S. Mackenzie, Toronto, ON	1966–1984	1974–1976
Kevin McBurney, Vancouver, BC	2012	
Ann McCaig, Calgary, AB	2003–2005	
Kathryn McCain, Toronto, ON	2005–2010	
Peggy McKercher, Riverside Estates, SK	1994–1997	
Donald McLean, Delta, BC	2000–2005	
Donald G. McNeil, Bedford, NS	2009–2012	
Eliza Mitchell, Tatlayoko Lake, BC	2011–2012	
Garfield R. Mitchell, Toronto, ON	2006–2011	
George M. Mitchell, Halifax, NS	1983–1991	
	1997–2000	
Mary Mogford, Toronto, ON	1993–1998	
George H. Montgomery, Westmount, QC	1963–1965	
J. Sherrold Moore, Calgary, AB	1994–2005	
John Morgan, Montreal, QC	2006–2012	
Michael W. O'Brien, North York, ON	1994–2005	2001–2003
Jim Pantelidis, Toronto, ON	2002–2005	
Jean Paré, Montreal, QC	2004–2010	
Michael J. Paterson, Winnipeg, MB	2006–2012	
Freeman Patterson, Shampers Bluff, NB	1988–1993	
Alain Perez, Montreal, QC	2001–2004	
Ann Petley-Jones, Halifax, NS	2009–2012	
Adele Poynter, St. John's, NL	2005–2010	
Nathalie Pratte, Montreal, QC	2008–2012	
Michael Rae, Toronto, ON	1997–2000	

APPENDIX 2

---·•·---

Chief Executive Officers of the Nature Conservancy of Canada

Job Title	Term
F. Aird Lewis (executive director)	1969–1981
Charles Sauriol (executive director)	1981–1983
Lloyd Mayeda (executive director)	1983–1985
Gerry T. Glazier (executive director)	1986–1989
John Eisenhauer (executive director)	1989–1997
John Lounds (president and executive director)	1997–2012

Notes

—————•◆•—————

Chapter 2 The Nature Conservancy of Canada

1. The Nature Conservancy of Canada, "Mission and Values," http://www.natureconservancy.ca/en/who-we-are/mission-values/ (accessed September 2012).
2. Ibid.
3. Ibid.
4. Ecological integrity (EI) is an indicator related to environmental quality, but with a focus on changes in wild populations and natural ecosystems, rather than on humans and their economy. EI is a complex indicator that is characterized by the relative dominance of native species, self-organized communities, and landscapes and seascapes that are characteristic for the natural environmental regimes that are present. EI is monitored as a way of determining the importance of system-level ecological damage caused by anthropogenic stressors. EI is a highly relevant indicator of the condition of protected areas, and it is also applicable to assessing places or regions where the human economy is dominant in land-use decisions. B. Freedman, J. Hutchings, D. Gwynne, J. Smol, R. Suffling, R. Turkington, and R. Walker. *Ecology: A Canadian Context* (Toronto: Nelson Canada, 2010).

Chapter 3 The Natural World

1. Wikipedia, "Star," http://en.wikipedia.org/wiki/Star (accessed August 2011).
2. Freedman, *Ecology*.
3. Edward O. Wilson, *Biophilia* (Cambridge: Harvard University Press, 1984).
4. Of course, people also harbour a degree of fear of the natural world, which poses hazards to life and security. Interestingly, some influential commentators on Canadian culture, such as Northrop Frye and Margaret Atwood, have noted that this bipolar attitude about the natural world is a frequent theme in our literature. Even while our attitudes range from the highs of love and respect in the good times, to the lows of fear and loathing during difficulties, we are undeniably intimately tied to the natural world and are utterly dependent on it for sustenance. Kate Turner and Bill Freedman, "Nature as a Theme in Canadian Literature," *Environmental Reviews* 13 (2005): 169–97.
5. Freedman, *Ecology*.
6. Ibid.
7. Ibid.
8. Bill Freedman, *Environmental Science: A Canadian Perspective*, 5th ed. (Toronto: Pearson Education Canada, 2010).
9. Gross domestic product (GDP) is the estimated value of all goods and services produced in an economy in a particular year.
10. Natural Resources Canada, "Canada's Forests: Statistical Data," http://canadaforests.nrcan.gc.ca/statsprofile/economicimpact/ca (accessed August 2012).
11. Aldo Leopold, *A Sand County Almanac* (New York: Oxford University Press, 1949).
12. Freedman, *Ecology*.

Chapter 4 Threats to the Natural World

1. Freedman, *Ecology*.
2. Ibid.
3. Ibid.
4. COSEWIC, "COSEWIC: Committee on the Status of Endangered Wildlife in Canada," http://www.cosewic.gc.ca (accessed August 2011).
5. COSEWIC, "Summary of COSEWIC Assessment Results as of May 2012," http://www.cosewic.gc.ca/rpts/Full_List_Species.html (accessed October 2012).
6. These data are from personal communications with various NCC staff and other ecologists, plus information in Freedman, *Ecology*.

Chapter 5 Conservation

1. Freedman, *Ecology*.
2. G. Pinchot, *The Fight for Conservation* (New York: Doubleday, Page and Company, 1910), chapter 4.
3. W. Stegner, "The Best Idea We Ever Had," *Wilderness* 46, Spring (1983): 4–13.
4. 1 square kilometre = 100 hectares = 247 acres
5. Wikipedia, "Banff National Park," http://en.wikipedia.org/wiki/Banff_National_Park#cite_note-0 (accessed March 2011).
6. Environment Canada, *Canadian Biodiversity Strategy: Canada's Response to the Convention on Biological Diversity* (Hull, QC: Biodiversity Convention Office, Environment Canada, 1995).
7. Environment Canada, *Canada's 4th National Report to the United Nations Convention on Biological Diversity* (Hull, QC: Biodiversity Convention Office, Environment Canada, 2004).
8. Bill Freedman, "The Biodiversity Crisis" in *Environmental Science. A Canadian Perspective* (Toronto: Pearson Education Canada, 2010), 514–37; Monte Hummell, ed., "Canadian Wilderness Charter" in *Endangered Spaces: The Future for Canada's Wilderness* (Toronto: Key Porter Books, 1989), 275.
9. See chapter 2, endnote 4.

Chapter 6 Land Trusts and Conservation

1. The Trustees of Reservations, "Trustees History," http://www.thetrustees.org (accessed August 2011).
2. A conservation agreement, is registered against title to land that sets out rights and restrictions relating to the use of the land. This form of property has an appraisable economic value. Land-use restrictions can be included in the agreement to protect the natural values of the land. Typical restrictions might preclude subdivision of the property, its conversion into residential use, the harvesting of timber, or the conversion of native habitat into use for cultivated agriculture or tame pasture. The term *easement* is used in the enabling legislation in Alberta, Manitoba, New Brunswick, Nova Scotia, Ontario, Prince Edward Island, Saskatchewan, and the US. The term *covenant* is used in the enabling legislation in British Columbia, and *servitude* is used in Quebec.

    For the first thirty years or so of NCC's existence, the only practical way that it and other land trusts could protect land was to own it. It was also possible to negotiate restrictive covenants with landowners, but at the time they did not necessarily provide for long-term conservation. Another possibility was to enter into a long-term lease under which a landowner kept title but leased the property to a land trust, or vice versa in which a land trust leased back to the original owner, usually for use as a natural (unbroken) grassland pasture. The difficulty with these arrangements was that, according to laws of the time, an agreement between a land trust and a landowner under which the latter promised to conserve the land, pay taxes, and so on would not bind a future landowner. Because the landowner's promises did not run with the title to the land, the land trust ran the risk that future owners would not agree to be bound by the conservation agreement.

However, this changed for the better of conservation in Canada in the 1980s and 1990s. One province after another passed legislation that sanctioned conservation agreements under which a land trust could enter into an agreement with a landowner that would bind future owners to the same terms and conditions. This new legal context helped land trusts considerably. For example, many ranchers objected to losing ownership of their lands but might be happy to enter into a conservation agreement whereby they would continue to use the property as before, even if they lost the rights to subdivide, build new structures, or convert native grassland into tame pasture.

A simple way of describing such a conservation agreement is that the owner transfers or cedes development rights to the land trust. In economic terms this typically meant that the market value of the property was diminished. However, that could be offset by the land trust providing the owner with a tax receipt for a charitable donation in the amount of the difference in the value of the property before and after the agreement. If the owner sold the conservation agreement rather than donating it, the land trust could secure that "property" by paying the difference of value rather than a much higher price for outright ownership of the real estate.

Conservation agreements are often highly detailed and complex arrangements. They must comply with the statutory provisions of the province where the land is situated, but those statutes vary among jurisdictions, which increases the legal costs. Appropriate conservation agreements also require considerable negotiating and drafting skills. Once a conservation agreement is signed, the land trust has a perennial obligation to make sure the terms of the agreement are obeyed. In spite of all this, conservation agreements have become a valuable tool in the arsenal of land trusts.

See also The Nature Conservancy of Canada, "What Is a Conservation Agreement?" http://www.natureconservancy.ca/site/PageServer?pagename=ncc_help_giftsofland_easements (accessed August 2011); The Nature Conservancy of Canada, *Managing Conservation Agreement Risks*, 2011, Internal NCC briefing note; Wikipedia, "Conservation Easements," http://en.wikipedia.org/wiki/Conservation_easement (accessed August 2011).

3.   Trade lands are real estate that is donated with the express intention of it being sold, with the proceeds being used to support the core work of the land trust.

4.   Richard Brewer, *Conservancy: The Land Trust Movement in America* (Hanover, NH: University Press of New England, 2003).

5.   The Nature Conservancy, *2010 Annual Report*, 2011, http://www.nature.org/aboutus/ouraccountability/annualreport/index.htm?s_intc=footer (accessed September 2012).

6.   The Nature Conservancy of Canada, "Annual Reports, 2008–2011," http://www.natureconservancy.ca/en/who-we-are/annual-reports/ (accessed September 2012).

7.   Wikipedia, "Nature Conservancy Council," http://en.wikipedia.org/wiki/Nature_Conservancy_Council (accessed August 2011).

8.   Canadian Land Trust Alliance, "Promote. Protect. Preserve," http://www.clta.ca (accessed August 2011).

9. Land Trust Alliance, "Together, Conserving the Places You Love," http://www. landtrustalliance.org (accessed August 2011).

10. See chapter 6, endnote 2, and its listed documents.

Chapter 7 The Beginning of the Nature Conservancy of Canada, 1962–71

1. Conservation authorities are organizations in Southern Ontario that were authorized in 1946 under the provincial Conservation Authorities Act. This was done in response to concerns being expressed by agricultural, naturalist, hunting, and fishing groups who were concerned about the degradation of renewable bioresources as a result of land development and other practices associated with urbanization and agricultural and forestry practices. Because a particularly important concern was extensive soil erosion and flooding, the conservation authorities were organized according to watersheds. The conservation authorities used programmatic funding from the provincial government and monies raised in other ways to acquire properties as conservation lands and to manage them as integrated watersheds, while also encouraging public use for recreation. Today, thirty-six conservation authorities make up a network called Conservation Ontario. Conservation Ontario, "Natural Champions," http://conservation-ontario.on.ca/index.html (accessed August 2011).

2. Toronto and Region Conservation, "Hurricane Hazel," http://www.hurricanehazel.ca (accessed November 2011).

3. Estimated based on inflation between 1954 and 2011, using the Bank of Canada inflation calculator at http://www.bankofcanada.ca/rates/related/inflation-calculator/ (accessed November 2011).

4. Ontario Nature, "History/Milestones," http://www.ontarionature.org/discover/history. php (accessed November 2011).

5. Bruce Falls, "We've Been Thinking . . . about the Nature Conservancy in Britain," *Bulletin of the Federation of Ontario Naturalists* 77 (1957): 4–6.

6. William W.H. Gunn, "The Nature Conservancy of Canada," *The Ontario Naturalist* 1, no.3 (1963): 13–18.

7. Likely this interest was mostly on accumulated monies raised but not spent for the Rattray project, and so kept in a capital account rather than being brought into the income statement. In 1966, the prime interest rate averaged 5.2 percent. Bank of Canada, "Historical Bank Rates," CANSIM V122530, http://www.bankofcanada.ca/wp-content/uploads/2010/09/annual_page1_page2_page3.pdf (accessed May 2011).

8. Bird Protection Quebec, "Sanctuaries," http://www.pqspb.org/bpq/ (accessed November 2011).

9. Robert Carswell and Lance Laviolette, both of Montreal, email messages to author, December 14, 2011.

10. Hamilton Naturalists Club, "Spooky Hollow Nature Sanctuary," http://www. hamiltonnature.org/HLT/spookyHollow.htm (accessed August 2011).

11. Ontario Nature, "History," http://www.ontarionature.org/discover/history.php (accessed August 2011).

12. J. Elliott, "Rattray Marsh Conservation Area, Mississauga," *Field Botanists of Ontario Newsletter* 22, no.1 (2010): 1–2; R. Hussey and J. Goulin, *Rattray Marsh: Then and Now* (Ajax, ON: Rattray Marsh Protection Association, 1990); Information was also obtained from the minutes of various meetings of the NCC Board of Trustees during the period when the Rattray Marsh project was active.

13. The Nature Conservancy of Canada, *Report of Activities: 1967*, 1967, Internal NCC Report (Toronto).
14. John J. Williams, manager of conservation lands, Otonabee Region Conservation Authority, email message to author, January 2011.
15. Charles Sauriol, *Green Footsteps: Recollections of a Grassroots Conservationist* (Toronto: Hemlock Press, 1991).
16. Ibid.
17. Ibid.
18. Dennis Garratt, conservation manager, Nova Scotia Nature Trust, email message to author, June 2011.
19. Scott Macmillan, *MacKinnon's Brook Suite*, 2002, Ground Swell Records, Warner Music Canada. For a music video of this work, see http://www.douglasporter.ca/html/edit/editBROOK.htm (accessed September 2012).
20. The Nature Conservancy of Canada, *Minesing Wetlands Natural Area Conservation Plan* (Toronto: NCC, 2011).
21. The Convention on Wetlands of International Importance, often referred to as the Ramsar Convention after the name of the city in Iran where the treaty was negotiated, is an intergovernmental treaty that provides a framework for international co-operation and national action toward the conservation of wetlands and their resources. The mission of the Ramsar Convention is "the conservation and wise use of all wetlands through local and national actions and international cooperation, as a contribution towards achieving sustainable development throughout the world." The secretariat of the Convention is located in Gland, Switzerland. A wetland designated under the convention is recognized as being important at an international scale in terms of its ecology and intersection with the human economy. The Ramsar Convention on Wetlands, "The Ramsar Convention and Its Mission," http://www.ramsar.org (accessed September 2012).

Chapter 8 A Freshening Breeze, 1972–80

1. The Nature Conservancy of Canada, *Annual Report 1972* (Toronto: NCC, 1973).
2. Data from the respective annual reports for TNC and NCC for the years 2009 and 2010.
3. World Resources Institute, "EarthTrends Database," http://earthtrends.wri.org (accessed 2011).
4. G. LaRoi, T.A. Babb, and C.E. Perley, *Canadian National Directory of IBP Areas*, 2nd ed., The Conservation of Terrestrial Biological Communities Subcommittee of the Canadian Committee for the International Biological Program (CCIBP/CT) and the Associate Committee on Ecological Reserves, National Research Council of Canada (NRCC/ACER) (Edmonton: University of Alberta Press, 1976). There are also provincial and regional IBP reports dealing with sites believed to be important to conservation.
5. The legal term *mortmain* refers to the perpetual and inalienable ownership of real estate by a corporation or other legal entity. Laws prohibiting mortmain were first enacted in England in the Middle Ages, a time when religious orders were recognized as a legal "person" separate from their office holders of authority, such as an abbot or bishop. Because the church would never die, land could be held in perpetuity by a religious organization, a circumstance that led to the accumulation of large amounts of non-taxable wealth in the form of real estate, even agricultural estates. This contrasted with the secular feudal practice of the time, in which nobility would hold land

granted by a king in exchange for service, often in war, or other levies, such as taxes. However, upon the death of such a landholder, the property would revert to the king. The mortmain system was favourable to the churches of the time, but irksome to the kings. The first constraints on the system were included in the Magna Carta of 1215, followed by more specific laws, the first of which was enacted by Edward I in 1279. In effect, the mortmain laws required that permission be received from the Crown before land could be perpetually vested in a corporation. Today, however, statutes prohibiting mortmain have been abolished in almost all countries, including Canada, where the last relevant law was the Mortmain and Charitable Uses Act of Ontario, which was repealed in 1982. The provisions of that act which governed the holding of land by land trusts and other charities were transferred to the Charities Accounting Act. Those provisions do not unduly constrain the landholding enterprise of land trusts, such as NCC, for the purposes of advancing the conservation of biodiversity in Canada. Mary Louise Dixon, "Repeal of the Mortmain and Charitable Uses Act and Amendment of the Charities Accounting Act in Ontario," *The Philanthropist* 3, no.3 (1983): 32–34; Wikipedia, "Mortmain," http://en.wikipedia.org/wiki/Mortmain (accessed May 2011).

6. An Important Bird Area (IBA) is recognized as providing habitat that is globally important for the conservation of bird populations. An IBA may occur on public or private property, and it does not necessarily have protected status. There are about ten thousand IBAs worldwide, including 597 in Canada. IBA Canada, "Important Bird Areas in Canada," http://www.ibacanada.com (accessed October 2012).

7. The Western Hemisphere Shorebird Reserve Network (WHSRN) is aimed at protecting critical habitats of shorebirds in the Americas, including areas used for nesting, for migration, and during the non-breeding season. Six WHSRN sites have been designated in Canada, but there are at least forty-seven additional potential ones. A site ratified at the hemispheric level would host greater than five hundred thousand shorebirds annually, or 30 percent of the flyway population of a particular species, based on peak abundance. Garry Donaldson and others, *Canadian Shorebird Conservation Plan* (Hull, QC: Canadian Wildlife Service, 2000); http://www.birdlife.org/action/science/sites/neotrops/andes/background/12_CanadianShorebirdConservPlan.pdf.

8. Western Hemisphere Shorebird Reserve Network, "Fraser River Estuary," http://www.whsrn.org/site-profile/fraser-river-estuary (accessed August 2011).

9. John Riley, *NCC Acquisitions through the Ivey Foundation's Escarpment Fund, 1972 to 1983*. J. Riley sent this document in note form based on files at NCC and the Ivey Foundation, email message to author, June 2011.

10. Ojibway Nature Centre, "Overview of Ojibway Prairie Complex," http://www.ojibway.ca/complex.htm (accessed August 2011).

11. James Duncan, associate vice-president of conservation, NCC Ontario Region, email message to author, June 2011.

12. Développement durable, Environnement Faune et Parcs, "Ecological Reserve Tantaré," http://www.mddep.gouv.qc.ca/biodiversite/reserves/tantare/res_03.htm (accessed August 2011).

13. Parks Canada, "Gulf Islands National Park Reserve of Canada," http://www.pc.gc.ca/pn-np/bc/gulf/index.aspx (accessed May 2011).

14. The Nature Conservancy of Canada, *Backus Woods Property Management Plan*, 2011, Internal stewardship document (NCC Southwestern Ontario Subregion).

15. The Nature Conservancy of Canada, "875 Acres of Carolinian Canada Habitat Protected Thanks to The W. Garfield Weston Foundation Gift to The Nature Conservancy of Canada," news release, February 15, 2011.

16. Robin Fraser, long-term NCC solicitor and director, email message to author, 2011.
17. Parks Canada, "Main Duck and Yorkshire Islands," http://www.pc.gc.ca/pn-np/on/lawren/natcul/natcul1/a.aspx#main (accessed August 2011).
18. Canadian Wildlife Service, "National Wildlife Areas in Ontario: Long Point," http://www.on.ec.gc.ca/wildlife/nwa/eng/longpoint/longpoint_htm-e.html (accessed May 2011).
19. Michael Bradstreet, vice-president of conservation and a long-term researcher at the Long Point Bird Observatory and local resident, email message to author, March 2011.
20. Michael Bradstreet, NCC vice-president of conservation, personal message to author, March 2012.
21. Oak Hammock Marsh Interpretive Centre, "Wetlands, Wildlife and Nature at Oak Hammock Marsh Interpretive Centre," http://www.oakhammockmarsh.ca/nature/index.html (accessed August 2011).
22. National Capital Commission, "Mer Bleue Conservation Area," http://www.canadascapital.gc.ca/bins/ncc_web_content_page.asp?cid=16297-16299-9735-113846-9743&lang=1&bhcp=1 (accessed August 2011).
23. The Nature Conservancy of Canada, "Oak Ridges Moraine," http://www.natureconservancy.ca/site/News2?page=NewsArticle&id=5660&news_iv_ctrl=0&abbr=on_ncc_ (accessed August 2011); Wikipedia, "Oak Ridges Moraine," http://en.wikipedia.org/wiki/Oak_Ridges_Moraine (accessed August 2011).
24. The Nature Conservancy of Canada, "Happy Valley Forest," http://www.natureconservancy.ca/site/PageServer?pagename=on_ncc_work_projects_happyvalleyforest1 (accessed May 2011).
25. T. Kraus, *Recovery Strategy for the Small Whorled Pogonia* (Isotria medeoloides) *in Ontario* (Peterborough, ON: Ontario Recovery Strategy Series, Ontario Ministry of Natural Resources, 2011): http://www.mnr.gov.on.ca/stdprodconsume/groups/lr/@mnr/@species/documents/document/stdprod_075585.pdf.
26. COSEWIC, "Two Ontario Species Lost? Stay Informed," news release, December 1, 2008: http://www.cosewic.gc.ca/eng/sct7/sct7_3_17_e.cfm.
27. Ontario Parks, "Misery Bay," http://www.ontarioparks.com/english/mise.html (accessed August 2011).
28. James Duncan, associate vice-president of conservation, NCC Ontario Region, email message to author, June 2011.
29. Louise Gratton, NCC Quebec Region, email message to author, July 2011.

Chapter 9 Steady Progress, 1981–89

1. The Nature Conservancy of Canada, *Annual Report 1981* (Toronto: NCC, 1982).
2. Bank of Canada, "Historical Bank Rates," CANSIM V122530, http://www.bankofcanada.ca/wp-content/uploads/2010/09/annual_page1_page2_page3.pdf (accessed May 2011).
3. The term *ecoregional* refers to a spatial and temporal framework that is bounded by ecological patterns and realities, rather than geopolitical ones. As such, an ecoregional conservation plan (or natural-area conservation plan) is undertaken on the basis of the boundaries of distribution of distinctive ecological communities and wide-ranging species, and so it may not correspond much with the borders of provinces, states, or countries.
4. Wildlife Habitat Canada, "2011 WHC," http://www.whc.org (accessed May 2011).
5. Kamal Rajani, chief financial officer, email message to author, June 2011.
6. The North American Waterfowl Management Plan (NAWMP) is an international action plan to conserve migratory birds throughout North America. Its vision is to

recover waterfowl populations to their 1970s abundances by conserving their necessary habitats. Canada and the United States signed the NAWMP in 1986, and Mexico joined in 1994. The NAWMP is a partnership of governments at various levels: federal, provincial/state/territorial, and municipal, as well as NGOs, private companies, and individuals. Projects undertaken under the plan are international in scope but are implemented at regional levels and are intended to contribute to the protection and improvement of habitat and wildlife across North America. In Canada, the NAWMP is involved in four regional joint ventures: Pacific Coast, Canada Intermountain, Prairie Habitat, and Eastern Habitat. Much of the US-sourced funding for direct-action NAWMP objectives (i.e., those that achieve on-the-ground results, such as habitat protection or improvement) has been provided through the North American Wetlands Conservation Act (NAWCA), which was enacted by Congress in 1989. The act requires that any funding from the US federal government, typically through the Fish and Wildlife Service, must be matched at least one to one by donations from non-federal US sources, such as from private companies, foundations, or individual donors. Between 1986 and 2009, the four joint ventures in Canada had secured a total of 2.1 million hectares (5.2 million acres), 93 percent of which were in the Prairie Habitat region. Expenditures over that period to secure habitat in Canada totalled $1.62 billion ($Can), of which 49 percent was provided by US sources (48 percent federal and 52 percent non-federal) and 51 percent by Canadian sources (40 percent federal, 31 percent provincial/territorial, and 29 percent non-governmental).

See North American Waterfowl Management Plan, Home page, http://www.nawmp.ca/eng/index_e.html (accessed May 2011); North American Waterfowl Management Plan, "Canadian Habitat Matters: 2009 Annual Report," http://www.nawmp.ca/pdf/HabMat2009AnnualReport_E.pdf (accessed May 2011); North American Wetlands Conservation Council (Canada), Home page, http://www.wetlandscanada.org/nawca.html (accessed May 2011); Kamal Rajani, chief financial officer, provided NCC data related to NAWCA, email message to author, June 2011.

7. Kamal Rajani, chief financial officer, email message to author, June 2011.

8. Carolinian Canada, "Greening the Future of Southwestern Ontario," http://www.carolinian.org/ (accessed June 2011).

9. Ibid.

10. Estimated based on inflation between 1985 and 2011, using the Bank of Canada inflation calculator at http://www.bankofcanada.ca/rates/related/inflation-calculator/ (accessed November 2011).

11. James Duncan, associate vice-president of conservation, Ontario Region, email message to author, August 2011.

12. The Nature Conservancy of Canada, *Annual Report 1985* (Toronto: NCC, 1986).

13. NatureServe Canada, "A Network Connecting Science with Conservation," http://www.natureserve-canada.ca/ (accessed June 2011).

14. Ibid.

15. NatureServe, "NatureServe. A Network Connecting Science with Conservation," http://www.natureserve.org/ (accessed August 2011).

16. A report relevant to Ontario was produced by the Ontario CDC: Kevin Kavanagh and Sheila McKay-Kuja, *A Classification of the Natural Communities Occurring in Ontario, With Special Reference to the Great Lakes Shores* (Peterborough, ON: Ontario Natural Heritage Centre, 1992).

17. P.M. Catling and V.R. Brownell, "A Review of Alvars of the Great Lakes Region: Distribution, Floristic Composition, Biogeography and Protection," *Canadian Field-Naturalist* 109 (1995): 143–71; C. Reschke and others, *Conserving Great Lakes Alvars: Final Technical Report of the International Alvar Conservation Initiative* (Chicago: The Nature Conservancy, 1999).

18. David N. Ewert and others, *Biological Ranking Criteria for Conservation of Islands in the Laurentian Great Lakes* (Arlington, VA: The Nature Conservancy, 2004); Karen E. Vigmostad and others, *Great Lakes Islands: Biodiversity Elements and Threats*. Report to the Great Lakes National Program Office of the Environmental Protection Agency, 2007; Bonnie L. Henson, Daniel T. Kraus, Michael J. McMurtry, and David N. Ewert, *Islands of Life: A Biodiversity and Conservation Atlas of the Great Lakes Islands* (Toronto: Nature Conservancy of Canada, 2010).

19. The Nature Conservancy and the Nature Conservancy of Canada, *Binational Conservation Blueprint for the Great Lakes*, TNC Great Lakes Program, Chicago, and TNC Ontario Region, Port Rowan, ON. View several blueprints at http://nhic.mnr. gov.on.ca/projects/conservation_blueprint/blueprint_main.cfm.

20. As in other cases of donations to NCC that are noted as being anonymous, NCC followed all provisions of relevant federal and provincial legislation, but the donor has not given permission for his or her identity to be public knowledge.

21. Ontario Parks, "Manitou Islands," http://www.ontarioparks.com/english/mani.html (accessed August 2011).

22. Brier Island Lodge, "Welcome to Brier Island," http://www.brierisland.org/index. html (accessed August 2011).

23. Parks Canada, "Gwaii Haanas National Park Reserve and Haida Heritage Site," http:// www.pc.gc.ca/eng/pn-np/bc/gwaiihaanas/index.aspx. (accessed June 2011).

24. Great Canadian Parks, "Gwaii Haanas National Park," http://www.greatcanadianparks. com/bcolumbia/gwaiinp/page8.htm (accessed June 2011).

25. Rachel F. Holt, *Special Elements of Biodiversity in British Columbia*. Prepared for the Biodiversity BC Technical Subcommittee for the Report on the Status of Biodiversity in BC: http://www.biodiversitybc.org/assets/Default/BBC%20Special%20Elements.pdf (accessed June 2011).

26. Parks Canada, "Gwaii Haanas National Marine Conservation Area Reserve and Haida Heritage Site," http://www.pc.gc.ca/progs/amnc-nmca/cnamnc-cnnmca/gwaiihaanas/ index_e.asp (accessed June 2011).

27. The Nature Conservancy of Canada, "Sandy Point, Newfoundland & Labrador: Where Land, Sea and Sky Meet," http://www.natureconservancy.ca/site/ PageServer?pagename=at_ncc_work_projects_sandypoint1 (accessed August 2011).

28. Ottawa Field-Naturalists Club, "The Alfred Bog," http://www.ofnc.ca/conservation/ alfredbog/index.php (accessed August 2011); Frank Pope, "The Alfred Bog," http:// www.ofnc.ca/conservation/alfredbog/ (accessed May 2011).

29. National Capital Commission, "The Amazing Mer Bleu," http://www.canadascapital. gc.ca/bins/ncc_web_content_page.asp?cid=16297-16299-9735-113846-9743&lang= 1&bhcp=1 (accessed August 2011).

30. Ron Reed, "Alfred Bog: The Price of Preservation," *Seasons* 29, no.3 (1988): 20–25.

31. Atlantic Coastal Plain Flora Conservation/Recovery Team, "Nova Scotia's Coastal Plain Flora," http://www.speciesatrisk.ca/coastalplainflora/ (accessed December 2011).

32. Ann and Sandy Cross Conservation Area, "Cross Conservation Area," http://www. crossconservation.org/main/page.php?page_id=50 (accessed August 2011).

33. Parks Canada, "Gulf Islands National Park Reserve of Canada," http://www.pc.gc.ca/eng/pn-np/bc/gulf/index.aspx (accessed August 2011).
34. The Nature Trust of New Brunswick, "George M. Stirrett Preserve," http://www.naturetrust.nb.ca/en/preserve-george-stirrett (accessed August 2011).
35. Environment Yukon, "Coal River Springs Territorial Park," http://www.env.gov.yk.ca/parksconservation/CoalRiverSprings.php (accessed August 2011).
36. Environment Yukon, "Coal River," (accessed June 2011).

Chapter 10 Working from Coast to Coast to Coast, 1990–97

1. The Nature Conservancy of Canada, *Annual Report 1990* (Toronto: NCC, 1991).
2. Marc Denhez, *You Can't Give It Away: Tax Aspects of Ecologically Sensitive Lands* (Ottawa: NAWCC (Canada) and National Roundtable on the Environment and Economy, 1992): http://www.nrtee-trnee.com/eng/publications/cant-give-away/NRTEE-cant-give-away.PDF.
3. See chapter 6, endnote 2, for an explanation of conservation agreements.
4. Ecological carbon credits are associated with the fact that ecosystems store large amounts of organic carbon in their biomass, while also typically increasing that storage year over year. Because organic carbon originates as carbon dioxide absorbed from the atmosphere by photosynthesis, the ecological storage and annual uptake can be viewed as offsetting some of the emissions of that and other greenhouse gases by anthropogenic activities, such as using fossil fuels as a source of energy or converting natural ecosystems into ones used in agriculture or for urbanization. Potentially, ecological carbon credits associated with conservation projects can be tallied and sold to companies or organizations that are seeking to reduce their net emissions of greenhouse gases. Such "carbon markets" have become an increasingly prominent mechanism for society to reduce the net emissions of greenhouse gases while attempting to meet international commitments such as the Kyoto Protocol of the United Nations. In 2011, NCC made its first sale of carbon credits, associated with a large protected area in southeastern British Columbia called the Darkwoods project. This project is described in chapter 12.
5. The Nature Conservancy of Canada, "Waterton Park Front Project," http://www.natureconservancy.ca/site/PageServer?pagename=ab_ncc_work_projects_waterton1 (accessed August 2011).
6. The Nature Conservancy of Canada, "Darkwoods: Sometimes Bigger Is Better," http://www.natureconservancy.ca/site/PageServer?pagename=bc_ncc_work_projects_dw (accessed August 2011).
7. Yellowstone to Yukon Conservation Initiative, Home page, http://www.y2y.net (accessed November 2011).
8. The Nature Conservancy of Canada, *Annual Report 2000* (Toronto: NCC, 2001).
9. The fundraising ratio of about twelve to one was similar to that of the populations at the time, which was nine to two; World Resources Institute, "EarthTrends Database Population: Total Population, Both Sexes," http://earthtrends.wri.org/searchable_db/index.php?theme=4 (accessed August 2011).
10. Bird Studies Canada, "IBA Site Summary: Matchedash Bay, Waubaushene, Ontario," http://www.bsc-eoc.org/iba/site.jsp?siteID=ON035 (accessed August 2011); William G. Wilson and Edward D. Cheskey, "Matchedash Bay Important Bird Area Conservation Plan," Canadian Nature Federation, Bird Studies Canada, Federation of Ontario Naturalists: http://www.ibacanada.com/conservationplans/onmatchedashbayiba.pdf.

11. P.M. Catling and V.R. Brownell, "New and Significant Vascular Plant Records for Manitoba," *Canadian Field Naturalist* 101, no.3 (1987): 437–39.
12. P.M. Catling and J.D. Lafontaine, "First Documented Record of *Oarisma powesheik* (Lepidoptera: Hesperiidae) in Canada," *Great Lakes Entomologist* 19 (1986): 63–66.
13. The Nature Conservancy of Canada, "Manitoba Tall Grass Prairie Preserve," http://www.natureconservancy.ca/site/PageServer?pagename=mb_ncc_work_projects_tallgrass1 (accessed July 2011); Nature North, "Manitoba's Tall Grass Prairie Preserve," http://www.naturenorth.com/summer/wildlife/wildF.html (accessed August 2011); Wikipedia, "Manitoba Tall Grass Prairie Preserve," http://en.wikipedia.org/wiki/Manitoba_Tall_Grass_Prairie_Preserve (accessed July 2011).
14. Ibid.
15. A forb is a perennial herbaceous plant that is not grasslike, meaning it is a dicotyledonous or broadleafed plant.
16. Ojibway Nature Centre, "Overview of Ojibway Prairie Complex," http://www.ojibway.ca/complex.htm (accessed August 2011).
17. Gene Fortney, NCC Manitoba Region, email message to author, July 2011.
18. Parks Canada, "Grasslands National Park," http://www.pc.gc.ca/pn-np/sk/grasslands/index.aspx (accessed August 2011).
19. Parks Canada, "The Swift Fox—A Long Road Home," http://www.pc.gc.ca/pn-np/sk/grasslands/edu/edu1/c.aspx (accessed August 2011); Parks Canada, "Black-footed Ferret Update," http://www.pc.gc.ca/pn-np/sk/grasslands/edu/edu4.aspx (accessed August 2011).
20. Bird Studies Canada, "IBA Site Summary: Dorchester Cape and Grand Anse, Bay of Fundy, New Brunswick," http://www.bsc-eoc.org/iba/site.jsp?siteID=NB038 (accessed June 2011); Bird Studies Canada, "IBA Site Summary: Shepody Bay West, Bay of Fundy, New Brunswick," http://www.bsc-eoc.org/iba/site.jsp?siteID=NB009 (accessed June 2011).
21. See chapter 7, endnote 21.
22. The Western Hemisphere Shorebird Reserve Network (WHSRN) is a conservation initiative that was launched in 1986 with the aim of protecting critical habitats throughout the Americas in order to sustain healthy populations of shorebirds. Collaborators in the WHSRN include governments and conservation NGOs. The WHSRN Hemispheric Council is a body responsible for the entire network and its strategic planning, while national councils design and implement actions within their domains. WHSRN and its site partners have conserved more than 12.6 million hectares (31 million acres) of shorebird habitat. Western Hemisphere Shorebird Reserve Network, "About WHSRN," http://www.whsrn.org (accessed November 2011).
23. Parks Canada, "Vuntut National Park of Canada," http://www.pc.gc.ca/pn-np/yt/vuntut/index.aspx (accessed July 2011).
24. British Columbia Parks, "Brackendale Eagles," http://www.env.gov.bc.ca/bcparks/explore/parkpgs/brackendale_eagles/ (accessed July 2011).
25. The Nature Conservancy of Canada, *The Book of Eagles* (Vancouver: NCC and *Beautiful British Columbia Magazine*, 1997).
26. Tame pasture is grassland that has been seeded to alien species of forage plants. The ecological integrity of tame pasture is much degraded compared with that of native grasslands dominated by indigenous forage species. Both kinds of grassland can be used for grazing livestock, but some ranchers prefer tame pasture because of the perception of a higher productivity of forage plants. Over the longer term, however, native grasslands are more resilient to changes in environmental conditions, and of

course they support enormously higher levels of indigenous biodiversity, including many species-at-risk. The conversion of native grasslands to tame pasture is one of the most threatening agricultural practices to the native biodiversity of the prairie region of Canada.

27. The Nature Conservancy of Canada, "Old Man on His Back Prairie and Heritage Conservation Area," http://www.natureconservancy.ca/site/PageServer?pagename= sk_ncc_work_projects_omb1 (accessed July 2011).
28. Sharon Butala, *Old Man on His Back* (Toronto: HarperCollins Canada, 2002).
29. Ibid.
30. Jordan Ignatiuk, director of land conservation, NCC Saskatchewan Region, email message to author, March 9, 2012.
31. BC Parks, "Gowlland Tod Provincial Park," http://www.env.gov.bc.ca/bcparks/ explore/parkpgs/gowlland_tod/ (accessed August 2011).
32. Newfoundland and Labrador Department of Environment and Conservation, "King George IV Ecological Reserve," http://www.env.gov.nl.ca/env/parks/wer/r_kge/index. html (accessed July 2011).
33. Parks Canada, "Gwaii Haanas National Marine Conservation Area Reserve and Haida Heritage Site," http://www.pc.gc.ca/progs/amnc-nmca/cnamnc-cnnmca/gwaiihaanas/ index_e.asp (accessed June 2011).
34. Parks Canada, "Gwaii Haanas National Park Reserve and Haida Heritage Site," http:// www.pc.gc.ca/eng/pn-np/bc/gwaiihaanas/index.aspx (accessed June 2011).
35. Wendt Henton, "Gift Means Marine Museum for Canada," *Globe and Mail*, March 20, 1997; James McCarten, "Oil Giants Give up Charlottes Rights," *Calgary Herald*, March 20, 1997.
36. In other circumstances, water rights may also be associated with the flow of rivers used for hydroelectricity and the contents of reservoirs used for irrigation or for municipal water supply.

Chapter 11 A Campaign for Conservation, 1998–2005

1. The Nature Conservancy of Canada, *Annual Report 1998* (Toronto: NCC, 1998).
2. Marc-André Pigeon, *Tax Rules Governing Charities and Non-profit Organizations* (Ottawa: Library of Parliament, 2003): http://dsp-psd.pwgsc.gc.ca/Collection-R/ LoPBdP/PRB-e/PRB0304-e.pdf.
3. Tom J. Beechey and others, "Ontario Parks Legacy 2000: Program, Planning, and Science Dimensions" in *1999 Annual Meeting of the Parks Research Forum of Ontario* (Guelph, Ontario, April 1999), 481–89: http://casiopa.mediamouse.ca/wp-content/ uploads/2010/05/PRFO-1999-Proceedings-p481-489-Beechey-Guthrie-Duncan-Turner-Sargant-and-Powell.pdf (accessed July 2011).
4. A conservation blueprint, also referred to as an ecoregional plan, is a document that records the portfolio of sites that, if conserved, will ensure the long-term survival of native species and community types of an ecoregion. A conservation blueprint is developed by the assessment of data that represent key attributes of the biodiversity of an ecoregion, including its native species, ecological communities, environmental conditions, and functional qualities. When NCC develops a conservation blueprint, it relies heavily on spatial data about biodiversity housed in relevant conservation data centres. (In 2011, Canada had seven such centres.) NCC may also obtain relevant information from additional partners, such as governmental agencies, other conservation NGOs, and forestry companies. The key data for identifying priority sites for

conservation are related to the locations of species-at-risk, of other rare or endemic species, of endangered community types (such as tall-grass prairie or rare kinds of forest), and the functional connectivity of habitats and populations within and across ecoregions. Other vital information is used to establish the natural condition and variations of landscapes, such as the distribution of communities and their defining species, as well as spatial changes in such key environmental factors as climatic factors, soil types, and moisture regimes. These sorts of information are then used to map the broader ecological conditions as well as the locations of elements of biodiversity and their specific target areas that are most in need of conservation. Some of those areas may already be conserved in protected areas, but a gap analysis reveals others that are not, and these become the targets for conservation action by NCC and other organizations. See C.R. Groves, *Drafting a Conservation Blueprint: A Practitioner's Guide to Planning for Biodiversity* (Washington, DC: The Nature Conservancy and Island Press, 2003); The Nature Conservancy of Canada, "Conservation Blueprints," http://www.natureconservancy.ca/site/PageServer?pagename=ncc_work_science_blueprints (accessed July 2011).

5.   As in other cases of donations to NCC that are noted as being anonymous, NCC followed all provisions of relevant federal and provincial legislation, but the donor has not given permission for its identity to be public knowledge.

6.   Yellowstone to Yukon Conservation Initiative, Home page, http://www.y2y.net (accessed November 2011).

7.   The Nature Conservancy of Canada, "Shell Conservation Internship Program," http://www.conservationinterns.ca (accessed August 2011).

8.   Ibid.

9.   The Nature Conservancy of Canada, "Miss Roberta Langtry," http://www.natureconservancy.ca/site/News2?page=NewsArticle&id=5401&news_iv_ctrl=0&abbr=on_ncc_ (accessed July 2011).

10.   The Nature Conservancy of Canada, *Annual Report 2005* (Toronto: NCC, 2006).

11.   The Nature Conservancy of Canada, "The Carden Alvar," http://www.natureconservancy.ca/site/PageServer?pagename=on_ncc_work_projects_cardenalvar1 (accessed July 2011).

12.   The Ecological Gifts Program was established by the Government of Canada in 1995 as a mechanism by which people owning ecologically sensitive land could donate that property, or an interest in it such as a conservation easement, to a qualified recipient such as a land trust or a conservation-oriented governmental agency under terms favourable to the donor under the Income Tax Act of Canada and the Taxation Act in Quebec. The Ecological Gifts Program is administered by Environment Canada in co-operation with dozens of partners, including other federal departments, provincial and municipal governments, and environmental non-government organizations, such as NCC. As of April 2011, the program had been involved in 892 ecological gifts valued at over $569 million, protecting more than 140,000 hectares (346,000 acres) of natural habitat. Environment Canada, "Ecological Gifts Program," http://www.ec.gc.ca/pde-egp/default.asp?lang=En&n=FCD2A728-1 (accessed July 2011).

13.   Catling and Brownell, "A Review of Alvars"; Reschke and others, *Conserving Great Lakes.*

14.   A life estate (or life interest) is a concept in common law that allows for continued ownership of land or land-use rights through the duration of the life of one or more designated persons. A life estate can be passed to other persons, and can be sold, but even if that happens it will expire with the lives of the originally designated persons. In the Elkington case, the life estate allowed for continued occupation of the home on the property until the passing of Mr. Elkington.

15. The Nature Conservancy of Canada, "Cowichan Garry Oak Preserve," http://www. natureconservancy.ca/site/PageServer?pagename=bc_ncc_CGOP (accessed July 2011).

16. Garry Oak Ecosystem Recovery Team, "Cowichan Garry Oak Preserve," http://www. goert.ca/news/2007/03/cowichan-garry-oak-preserve/ (accessed July 2011).

17. The Nature Conservancy of Canada, "Campbell River: A Gift of Stewardship," http:// www.natureconservancy.ca/site/News2?page=NewsArticle&id=9817&news_iv_ctrl= 0&abbr=bc_ncc_ (accessed July 2011).

18. P.F.J. Eagles and T.J. Beechey, eds., *Critical Unprotected Natural Areas in the Carolinian Life Zone of Canada*. Identification Subcommittee, Carolinian Canada, Nature Conservancy of Canada, Ontario Heritage Foundation, and World Wildlife Fund (Canada), 1985; Natural Heritage Information Centre, "Middle Island," http://www. carolinian.org/CarolinianSites_MiddleIsland.htm (accessed July 2011); Y. Robert Tymstra, "Middle Island's Hidden Treasures," *Seasons*, 32, no.3 (1992): 16–21. http:// www.middlebass2.org/MiddleIslandsHiddenTreasures.shtml (accessed July 2011); Tammy Dobbie, *Middle Island Conservation Plan* (Point Pelee National Park, 2008); Parks Canada, *Middle Island Conservation* (Point Pelee National Park, July 2010): http://www.pc.gc.ca/pn-np/on/pelee/plan.aspx (accessed July 2011).

19. James Duncan, email message to author, July 5, 2011.

20. C. Boutin, T. Dobbie, D. Carpenter, and C.E. Hebert, "Effects of Double-Crested Cormorants (*Phalacrocorax auritus* Less.) on Island Landscape, Vegetation and Seedbank," *Restoration Ecology* 19, no.6 (2011): abstract; Dobbie, *Middle Island Conservation Plan*; Tammy Dobbie and Rachel Thorndyke, *Report on Research and Monitoring for Year 3 (2010) of the Middle Island Conservation Plan* (Leamington, ON: Parks Canada, Point Pelee National Park, 2011); Parks Canada, *Middle Island Conservation*.

21. Larry Simpson, *Big Skies and Big Vision*. Remarks presented at an NCC function in Calgary in May 2012.

22. Larry Simpson, NCC Alberta Region, email message to author, March 2012.

23. Ibid.

24. As of 2012, The W. Garfield Weston Foundation and members of the extended Weston family had provided NCC with more than $95 million to support the acquisition and stewardship of ecologically important habitats across Canada. John Lounds, NCC president, email message to author, February 2012.

25. The Nature Conservancy of Canada, "Clear Creek Forest," http://www. natureconservancy.ca/site/PageServer?pagename=on_ncc_work_projects_clearcreek1 (accessed July 2011).

26. Graham Buck, "Pit and Mound Restoration: When a Tree Falls in Clear Creek Forest," in *Parks Research Forum of Ontario (PFRO) 2003 Proceedings*, 385–99: http://casiopa. mediamouse.ca/wp-content/uploads/2010/05/PRFO-2003-Proceedings-p385-389-Buck.pdf (accessed July 2011).

27. Ontario Parks, *Clear Creek Forest: Terms of Reference*, http://www.ontarioparks.com/ english/planning_pdf/clea_ToR.pdf (accessed July 2011).

28. Catling and Brownell, "A Review of Alvars"; V.R. Brownell and J. Riley, *The Alvars of Ontario: Significant Alvar Natural Areas in the Ontario Great Lakes Region* (Toronto: Federation of Ontario Naturalists, 2000).

29. Ontario Ministry of Natural Resources, *Establishing Strawberry Island and Queen Elizabeth The Queen Mother M'Nidoo M'Nissing as Recommended Provincial Parks, and a Recommended Addition to Misery Bay Provincial Nature Reserve*. Environmental

Registry, Government of Ontario: http://www.ebr.gov.on.ca/ERS-WEB-External/
displaynoticecontent.do?noticeId=MTEyNjk5&statusId=MTY5MDIw&language=
en (accessed July 2011).

30. The Nature Conservancy of Canada, "Bayers Island," http://www.natureconservancy.
ca/site/PageServer?pagename=at_ncc_Bayers_Island (accessed July 2011).

31. The Nova Scotia Crown Share Land Legacy Trust (NSCSLLT) is an innovative not-
for-profit organization, established at arm's length by the Government of Nova
Scotia with the aim of providing matching funds to support the work of qualified
land trusts, especially NCC and the Nova Scotia Nature Trust. The NSCSLLT was
established in 2008 and was capitalized with about $23.4 million from monies given
to Nova Scotia by the Government of Canada as a share of revenues from the production of offshore fossil fuels. Nova Scotia Crown Share Land Legacy Trust, Home page,
http://nscsllt.biology.dal.ca (accessed July 2011).

32. The Nature Conservancy of Canada, "The Musquash Estuary," http://www.
natureconservancy.ca/site/PageServer?pagename=at_ncc_work_projects_musquash1
(accessed July 2011).

33. The Nature Conservancy of Canada, "Tatlayoko Lake Valley," http://www.
natureconservancy.ca/site/PageServer?pagename=bc_ncc_work_projects_tatlayoko1
(accessed July 2011).

34. The Nature Conservancy of Canada, "Happy Valley Forest," http://www.
natureconservancy.ca/site/PageServer?pagename=on_ncc_work_projects_
happyvalleyforest1 (accessed July 2011); Wikipedia, "Happy Valley, King, Ontario,"
http://en.wikipedia.org/wiki/Happy_Valley,_King,_Ontario (accessed July 2011).

35. Quotation from the NCC 2005 DRTV program *Fighting for Canada.*

36. City of Montreal, "Natural Habitats: Lachine Rapids," http://ville.montreal.qc.ca/
portal/page?_pageid=5697,32927640&_dad=portal&_schema=PORTAL (accessed
November 2011).

37. Calvin Dunkley, hotel employee, email messages to author, July 17 and July 20, 2011.

38. DiCienzo family, "Marcy's Woods: A Private Nature Reserve Committed to
Environmental Preservation," http://www.marcyswoods.ca (accessed July 2011).

39. Linda Stephenson, NCC Atlantic vice-president, email message to author, February
2012.

40. The Nature Conservancy of Canada, "A Fish Tale: NCC Helps Protect Quebec's
Unique Copper Redhorse," http://www.natureconservancy.ca/site/News2?page=
NewsArticle&id=10335&news_iv_ctrl=0&abbr=qc_ncc_ (accessed July 2011);
N. Vachon, *COSEWIC Assessment and Update Status Report on the Copper Redhorse*
Moxostoma hubbsi *in Canada* (Ottawa: Committee on the Status of Endangered
Wildlife in Canada, 2004): www.sararegistry.gc.ca/status/status_e.cfm (accessed
July 2011).

41. Fisheries and Oceans Canada, "Patrol Project in Quebec Aids Copper Redhorse
Recovery," *InfoOceans: The Quebec Region Newsletter*, 13, no.5 (2010): http://www.qc.
dfo-mpo.gc.ca/infoceans/201010/article4-eng.asp (accessed July 2011).

42. Michael Bradstreet, NCC vice-president of conservation, provided data about the
Norfolk project in several email messages to author, March 2012.

43. The Nature Conservancy of Canada, "The Sutton Mountain Range," http://www.
natureconservancy.ca/site/PageServer?pagename=qc_ncc_work_projects_sutton
(accessed July 2011).

Chapter 12 A Force for Nature, 2006–11

1. The Nature Conservancy of Canada, *Conservation Impact: The Nature Conservancy of Canada Annual Report 2006* (Toronto: NCC, 2007).
2. Kamal Rajani, chief financial officer, email message to author, December 2011.
3. These "conservation sales" involve selling a property to a conservation-minded buyer, with an appropriate conservation easement binding the title to the property. Often this involves the sale of property with natural grassland whose stewardship needs can be met by grazing cattle at an appropriate density. The value of the easement can be appraised and its presence means that the buyer can acquire the land at a relatively low cost. Meanwhile the land trust can reinvest the proceeds of the sale in other aspects of its work, including the acquisition of other properties.
4. Canadian Museum of Civilization, "Astrolabe—Attributed to Champlain," http://www.civilization.ca/cmc/exhibitions/tresors/treasure/222eng.shtml (accessed July 2011).
5. The Nature Conservancy of Canada, "NCC Applauds New Initiative to Conserve 500,000 Acres of Ecologically Significant Lands across Canada," news release, http://www.natureconservancy.ca/site/News2?abbr=ncc_media_&page=NewsArticle&id=7021&news_iv_ctrl=1021 (accessed July 2011).
6. Ibid.
7. "S&P/TSX Composite," *Globe and Mail*, July 2011: http://www.theglobeandmail.com/globe-investor/markets/indexes/chart/?q=tsx-I (accessed July 2011). According to these data, the S&P/TSX reached a peak of 15,073 in June 2008, falling afterwards to lows of about 7,700 at several times between September 2008 and February 2009, for an overall decline of about 49 percent.
8. "Dow Jones Industrials," *Globe and Mail*, July 2011: http://www.theglobeandmail.com/globe-investor/markets/indexes/chart/?q=DJIA-I (accessed July 2011). According to these data, the DJIA reached a peak of 14,065 in October 2007, falling to lows of about 6,300 in early 2009, for an overall decline of about 55 percent.
9. Metes and bounds is a system or method that may be used to define tracts of land or real estate. The system is typically used to describe larger properties for which more accurate systems are not necessary and might be prohibitively expensive, such as a tract of forest, a farm, or a political boundary such as that of a city or township. The system typically uses local features of the geography to define the boundaries of a property, such as prominent physical characteristics (e.g., a point of land bordering a waterbody) and sometimes botanical ones (e.g., a large tree of a particular species; however, the use of such "witness trees" is an archaic practice), along with directions and distances. The boundaries of a property are described in a running prose, working from a defined beginning point to other key positions (including their direction and distance) and eventually back to the origin. The description may include spatial references to adjacent properties, and perhaps note their owners. If there are no suitable natural markers, then key points on the boundary may be designated with wooden or metal stakes. Within this system, the word *mete* refers to a straight run along a boundary, specified by its orientation and the distance between two markers. The term *bounds* refers to a more general description of a property, such as a boundary that runs along a particular roadway, that is beside a lake or that is adjoined by a building. Wikipedia, "Metes and Bounds," http://en.wikipedia.org/wiki/Metes_and_bounds (accessed July 2011).
10. See chapter 10, endnote 4, for an explanation of carbon credits.

11. Bill Freedman, Graham Stinson, and Paresh Lacoul, "Carbon Credits and the Conservation of Natural Areas," *Environmental Reviews* 17 (2009): 1–19. http://article. pubs.nrc-cnrc.gc.ca/RPAS/rpv?hm=HInit&calyLang=eng&journal=er&volume= 17&afpf=a08-007.pdf.

12. John Riley, "The Emerging Market for Carbon Offsets" (discussion paper, NCC Ecosystem Services, The Nature Conservancy of Canada, Toronto, 2009).

13. Earth Rangers, "Earth Rangers: Partnering with Children to Bring Back the Wild," http://www.earthrangers.org (accessed December 2011).

14. Bruce McKenney, *Environmental Offset Policies, Principles, and Methods: A Review of Selected Legislative Frameworks*, Biodiversity Neutral Initiative, http://www. forest-trends.org/documents/files/doc_541.pdf (accessed September 2012); Leonard Shabman and Paul Scodari, "Past, Present, and Future of Wetlands Credit Sales" (discussion paper 04-48, Resources for the Future, Washington, DC, 2004): http:// ageconsearch.umn.edu/bitstream/10858/1/dp040048.pdf.

15. Nick Davidson, ed., "Achieving Carbon Offsets through Mangroves and Other Wetlands" (Expert Workshop meeting report, Danone Group, IUCN, Ramsar Convention Secretariat, Gland, Switzerland, 2010): http://www.ramsar.org/pdf/ DFN_report_Final.pdf.

16. The Nature Conservancy of Canada, "Darkwoods Forest Carbon Pilot Project," http://www.natureconservancy.ca/site/PageServer?pagename=bc_ncc_projects_dw_ carbon (accessed August 2011); The Nature Conservancy of Canada, "Using the Trees to Save the Forest: The Nature Conservancy of Canada Launches North America's Largest Forest Carbon Credit Project," news release, http://www.natureconservancy. ca/site/News2?page=NewsArticle&id=14768 (accessed August 2011).

17. One carbon credit represents an offset equivalent to the reduced emission of one tonne (one thousand kilograms) of carbon dioxide, or its radiative equivalent in other greenhouse gases. For example, the gas methane is about twenty-four times as potent a greenhouse gas as is carbon dioxide, so 1,000 kilograms of CO_2-emission credits are comparable to 41.7 kilograms of those of CH_4.

18. NCC, "Using the Trees."

19. Ibid.

20. Verified Carbon Standard, "A Global Benchmark for Carbon," http://www.v-c-s.org (accessed August 2011).

21. The Nature Conservancy of Canada, "Boughton Island, Prince Edward Island," http:// www.natureconservancy.ca/site/PageServer?pagename=at_ncc_work_projects_ boughton1 (accessed July 2011).

22. NCC, "Darkwoods: Sometimes Bigger."

23. The exact financial amounts and terms of this project are subject to a confidentiality agreement and cannot be disclosed.

24. The Nature Conservancy of Canada, *Conservation Project Summary—Canyon Ranch* (Calgary: NCC, 2008).

25. The Nature Conservancy of Canada, "Conserving British Columbia's Heritage Grasslands," http://www.natureconservancy.ca/site/News2?abbr=bc_ncc_&page= NewsArticle&id=10515 (accessed August 2011).

26. Ibid.

27. The Nature Conservancy of Canada, "Making History on the OH Ranch," http:// www.natureconservancy.ca/site/News2?abbr=ab_ncc_&page=NewsArticle&id= 10405&security=1401&news_iv_ctrl=1062 (accessed August 2011).

28. Ibid.

29. The Nature Conservancy of Canada, "The Protection of the Transboundary Corridor in the Green Mountains," http://www.natureconservancy.ca/site/News2?page= NewsArticle&id=13690&news_iv_ctrl=0&abbr=ncc_media_ (accessed August 2011).

30. Open Space Institute, "The Open Space Institute," http://www.osiny.org/site/ PageServer (accessed August 2011).

31. Two Countries, One Forest, "Reinventing Conservation for the 21st Century," http://www.2c1forest.org (accessed August 2011).

32. NCC, "The Protection."

33. The Nature Conservancy of Canada, "Chase Woods, Cowichan Valley," http://www.natureconservancy.ca/site/PageServer?pagename=bc_ncc_chase (accessed August 2011).

34. The BC Trust for Public Lands was created in 2004 by the Government of British Columbia. The Trust received a one-time endowment of $8 million to support the conservation of biodiversity by land trusts in the province. The trust provides funds for conservation planning as well as for the acquisition of ecologically important properties. A Conservation Lands Forum was created to coordinate priority setting, identify conservation opportunities, and facilitate partnerships to accomplish those goals. The forum consists of a partnership of governmental and conservation organizations working in BC, the latter including the Nature Conservancy of Canada, the Nature Trust of BC, the Land Conservancy of BC, and Ducks Unlimited Canada. Government of British Columbia, "$8 Million to Create BC Trust for Public Lands," news release, October, 6, 2004, http://www2.news.gov.bc.ca/nrm_news_ releases/2004SRM0036-000815.htm.

35. A fluvial marsh is a relatively productive wetland that is situated in shallow water along a stream or river. Like other marshes, this community is dominated by taller grasslike plants, such as cattail (*Typha*), bulrush (*Bolboschoenus* or *Scirpus*), bluejoint (*Calamagrostis*), or reed (*Phragmites australis*).

36. The Nature Conservancy of Canada, "875 Acres."

37. The Nature Conservancy of Canada, *Backus Woods Property Management Plan*, 2011, Internal stewardship document (NCC Southwestern Ontario Subregion).

38. The Nature Conservancy of Canada, "Conservation Groups Join to Help BC Protect the Flathead River Valley," http://www.natureconservancy.ca/site/News2?abbr=bc_ ncc_&page=NewsArticle&id=14279&news_iv_ctrl=1021 (accessed August 2011); The Nature Conservancy of Canada, "Flathead River Announcement Backgrounder," http://www.natureconservancy.ca/site/DocServer/Backgrounder_Flathead_Feb_ 2011_V3.pdf?docID=6030 (accessed August 2011).

39. Government of British Columbia, "Legislation Introduced to Protect Flathead Watershed," http://www.newsroom.gov.bc.ca/2011/10/legislation-introduced-to-protect-flathead-watershed.html (accessed December 2012).

Chapter 13 The Nature Conservancy of Canada at Fifty

1. The Nature Conservancy of Canada, *The Nature Conservancy of Canada Annual Reports 2007–11* (Toronto: NCC, 2008–12).

2. The Nature Conservancy of Canada, *The Nature Conservancy of Canada Annual Report 2011* (Toronto: NCC, 2012).

3. Ibid.

4. Ibid.

5. Ibid.

6. Ibid.

7. The Nature Conservancy of Canada, *Board of Directors (National) Manual* (Toronto: NCC, 2010).

8. As a reminder, the term *ecoregional* refers to a spatial and temporal framework that is bounded by ecological patterns and realities, rather than geopolitical ones. As such, an ecoregional conservation plan (or natural area conservation plan) is undertaken on the basis of the boundaries of distribution of distinctive ecological communities and wide-ranging species, and so it may not have much correspondence with the borders of provinces, states, or countries. See also the next endnote.

9. An ecoregion (or ecological region) is an extensive defined area within which the environmental conditions, landforms, biota, and ecological dynamics have a general and characteristic similarity. Terrestrial ecoregions are classified according to their physiography, climate, and biodiversity characteristics, and marine ones by physiography, oceanography, and biodiversity attributes. An ecoregion covers a relatively large area and supports characteristic and geographically distinct assemblages of natural communities and species. The World Wildlife Fund has designated 867 terrestrial and 450 freshwater ecoregions in the world, whose boundaries approximate the original extent of natural formations prior to major recent anthropogenic disruptions or changes. Freedman, *Ecology*; Wikipedia, "Ecoregion," http://en.wikipedia.org/wiki/Ecoregion (accessed August 2011).

10. To see a map of the ecoregions for which NCC has prepared conservation blueprints, go to the Nature Conservancy of Canada, "Canada's Ecoregions," http://science.natureconservancy.ca/initiatives/ecoregmap_w.php (accessed September 2011).

11. The Nature Conservancy of Canada, "Conservation Blueprints," http://www.natureconservancy.ca/site/PageServer?pagename=ncc_work_science_blueprints (accessed September 2011).

12. Michael Bradstreet, NCC vice-president of conservation, provided estimate in email to author, May 2012.

13. The Nature Conservancy of Canada, *Approval Process Related to Natural Area Conservation Plans and Securement Activities* (Board Policy No. B–8-2008), http://science.natureconservancy.ca/oqo/B_Approval_Process_Related_to_NACPs_and_Securement_Activities.pdf.

14. The Nature Conservancy of Canada, *Securement Manual* (Toronto: NCC, 2006).

15. The Nature Conservancy of Canada, *Appraisals* (Management Policy No. M-5-2010) (Toronto: NCC, 2010).

16. In 1995, the Government of Canada created the Ecological Gifts (Ecogift) Program under the Income Tax Act to provide a way for Canadians with ecologically sensitive land to protect nature and leave a legacy for future generations. The Ecogift Program is administered by Environment Canada. If a donation of a property or easement is certified as an ecogift, then tax advantages can be claimed by the donor to offset capital gains. Depending on the province in which the property or easement is located, either the provincial government or a conservation organization or land trust facilitating the donation will certify the land as being ecologically sensitive. Once certified, a panel of accredited appraisers will review and approve the appraised value (fair market value) of the land on behalf of the minister of environment. The minister will issue a final statement of fair market value, which will be reflected in a charitable tax receipt. Any modification to the terms and conditions of an ecogift must be approved ahead of time by Environment Canada. As of 2011, 902 ecological gifts valued at over $571 million had been donated across Canada, protecting more than 140,500 hectares (347,000 acres) of natural

habitat. The Nature Conservancy of Canada, "The Ecogift Program," http://www.natureconservancy.ca/site/PageServer?pagename=ncc_help_giftsofland_ecogift (accessed August 2011); Environment Canada, "Ecological Gifts Program," http://www.ec.gc.ca/pde-egp/default.asp?lang=En&n=FCD2A728-1 (accessed August 2011).

17. NCC, *Annual Report 2011*.
18. Ibid.
19. The Nature Conservancy of Canada, *Stewardship Manual* (Toronto: NCC, 2004).
20. The Nature Conservancy of Canada, *Fundraising and Accountability* (Board Policy No. B-1-2010) (Toronto: NCC, 2010).
21. The Nature Conservancy of Canada, *President's Report*, September 3, 2011.
22. The Nature Conservancy of Canada, *Fundraising Manual (Draft)* (Toronto: NCC, 2011).
23. The Nature Conservancy of Canada, "Conservation Volunteers," http://www.natureconservancy.ca/site/PageServer?pagename=vfn_home (accessed September 2011).
24. The Nature Conservancy of Canada, "Give Monthly," http://www.natureconservancy.ca/site/PageServer?pagename=ncc_help_protectors (accessed September 2011).
25. The Nature Conservancy of Canada, "Become a Leader in Conservation," http://www.natureconservancy.ca/site/PageServer?pagename=ncc_help_lic (accessed September 2011).
26. The Nature Conservancy of Canada, "Nature Conservancy of Canada Applauds Charitable Giving Incentives in Federal Budget," http://www.natureconservancy.ca/site/News2?page=NewsArticle&id=5084 (accessed September 2011).
27. The Nature Conservancy of Canada, "Make a Planned Gift. Leave a Legacy to Protect Canada's Natural Heritage," http://www.natureconservancy.ca/site/PageServer?pagename=ncc_help_legacy (accessed September 2011).
28. Kamal Rajani, NCC chief financial officer, email message to author, February 2011.
29. Sarah Efron, "The Charity 100: Make Your Donations Go Further," *MoneySense* Summer 2011: 44–55. Note that the high ranking of NCC was again repeated in 2012.
30. The data are based on a compendium developed from annual reports of NCC.

Chapter 14 Further Down the Road

1. The Nature Conservancy of Canada, *Strategic Plan: 2012–2017*, internal planning document (Toronto).
2. A "donor" is a person who has provided NCC with funds within the past two years. A "supporter" is anyone who has proactively engaged with NCC in the past two years, including donors, volunteers, and persons who have asked to receive communications from NCC, including by having a "my NCC" account on the NCC website. At the end of FY2012, the donor base was about forty-seven thousand people.
3. NCC, *Strategic Plan, 2012*.
4. Ibid.

Chapter 15 An Enduring Solution

1. NCC, "Mission and Values," 2012.

Appendix 1 Members of the National Board of Directors of the Nature Conservancy of Canada

1. Only persons serving at least two years are shown.

Index

———◆◆———

employees: enhancement, 73; executive director as, 70; hiring, 118; initial, 43; needs at NCC, 59; organization, 32; regional staff, 93; retaining, 69; role, 207; science work, 97, 124, 160; Toronto, 52, 93, 96; as trustees, 43, 59, 74; in 2011, 184, 186
endangered species in Canada, 21
endowment funds of NCC: establishment, 44; FY2011, 183; management, 165; market value, 184; for NCC funding, 72, 74; recession of 2008–9, 166; for science, 119, 130; for stewardship, 119, 130, 136, 155
environment, 36, 37, 203–4
environmental services, 172
equities, 182
equities market, 168
Executive Committee, 70, 79, 185
executive departments of NCC, 186
executive director, 69, 70
Executive Director's Report, 108
executive positions of NCC, 32
Expectations of National and Regional Board Members, 127, 133
external loans, 166
extinctions: in Canada, 20–21; man-made, 15, 17–23; natural, 15–17; remedies to, 15, 19
extirpated species in Canada, 21

Facebook site, 193
Falls, J. Bruce, 38, 39
Falls, Robert, 173
Federation of Ontario Naturalists (FON), 38–39, 46
fee-simple purchases, 33
15 percent levy, 55, 72, 136, 167
Fighting for Canada, 133–34, 168
Finance and Investment Committee, 165
Finance and Investment Subcommittee, 130, 166, 168
Finance Committee, 54, 130
financial ranking of NCC, 99
financial reporting, 44, 131, 198
financial situation of NCC, 44, 182, 183–84
financial support for NCC, 211
financial system, 98, 196–98
financing and funding: bridge financing, 104, 123, 134, 135, 157; early years, 42–43; in first Annual Report, 52–53; future of, 207; and government, 61, 63–64, 103, 137, 161–63, 176–77, 179, 195–96; land trusts, 30, 34–35; lines of credit, 134–35, 157, 166; matching funds, 48–49, 76; operational funding, 72; revolving funds, 104; undesignated funds, 43; from the US, 76; wetlands survey, 85

fish and fishing, 23, 27
Fitz-Randolph, Mabel, 147
Fitz-Randolph property (NB), 147
Flaherty, James, 121–22
Flathead Valley (BC), 181
Flathead Watershed, 155–56
Flathead Watershed Area Conservation Act, 155–56
Flat Island (Newfoundland), 88
Foothills Pipelines (Yukon) Ltd., 91
forestry, 13, 27
Fortney, Gene, 99, 110
Forward Planning Report, 58–59
foundations, fundraising, 194–95
founders of NCC, 39
Fowle, David, 38, 39, 42, 71
Francis, George, 71, 78, 101
Fraser, Robin, 42, 57, 79, 101, 104, 122, 123
Freedman, Bill, 96, 100, 104, 107, 170
French name of NCC, 57
Friends of the Nature Conservancy of Canada (FNCC), 97, 163–64
Frolek family, 177
Frolek Ranch (BC), 176–77
Fromm, Erich, 10
funding. *See* financing and funding
fundraising: beer sales, 161; business participation, 154–55; by children, 70; future of, 204, 205, 207; goals, 80; high net-worth individuals, 125, 194; importance, 192; improvements, 76–77; individuals, 193–94; major gifts, 192; models and expansion, 98–99; national drive, 84; target sectors, 192–96; and TNC, 81; trustees' donations, 56; in 2011, 191–96. *See also specific campaigns*
Furbish's lousewort (*Pedicularis furbishiae*), 91

Garnett, Jan, 101–2
Garry oak (*Quercus garryana*), 22, 138–39
General Fund, 98
general public, fundraising, 192–93
general-purpose fund, 74
George Stirrett Nature Preserve, 91
Georgian Bay (Ontario), 97, 109
Georgian Bay Land Trust (GBLT), 97
gifts. *See* donations
Gifts from Canadians, 128–29
Gifts of Canadian Nature, 193
Gifts to Canadians, 128
Glazier, Gerry, 81, 85
Globe and Mail, 128, 129, 143, 195
Governance and Nominating Committee, 185
governance of NCC, 70, 133, 135–36, 184–86

Index